CIMINO

THE DEER HUNTER, HEAVEN'S GATE,
AND THE PRICE OF A VISION

CHARLES ELTON

ABRAMS PRESS, NEW YORK

If you don't get it right, what's the point?

—MICHAEL CIMINO, EASTMAN KODAK PRINT AD, 1980

ABRAMS The Art of Books
195 Broadway, New York, NY 10007
abramsbooks.com

CONTENTS

PROLOGUE

I DROVE UP to Michael Cimino's house a mile off one of the roads that cross Alto Cedro Drive high above Los Angeles, on a hot August day in 2018. Off the beaten track in the Hollywood Hills, the streets seemed ghostly and unnaturally empty of people. While two, three, four cars sat in the driveways I passed, flashy convertibles and hulking SUVs, I got the strange feeling that there was no one inside the houses. One thing was certain: Cimino was not going to be at home; he had died in June 2016.

I parked a little way from the house. It was certainly *alto*—my ears had popped on the way up there—but the *cedro* were few and far between. I got out of the car and walked down to the gates. Although many of the other homes were obscured by hedges of trees, I could at least see the rough shape of them. Cimino's was different: it was set on a bluff invisible from the road because of the sharply curved drive. I knew the house was a single story and L-shaped because I had viewed it from above on Google Earth the night before. Some of the neighboring ones were similarly shaped, and I imagined that if they were pushed toward one another, they would fit together like the blocks in a game of Tetris.

Of all Hollywood directors, Cimino is one of the most fascinating, mysterious, and enigmatic figures, both reviled and praised, his controversial behavior well-documented but often misunderstood. I had thought a lot about him and his house, and it had acquired a particular resonance for me. Maybe because Cimino seemed to have invented himself, to have been almost a fictional character—indeed *was* a character in a crazy French novel published in 2017, in which the hero pursues Cimino through New York—I thought of truly fictional characters whose houses revealed the secrets of their owners, maybe *Citizen Kane*'s Xanadu, Norma Desmond's crumbling mausoleum on Sunset Boulevard, or *Rebecca*'s gothic mansion: *Last night I dreamed I went to Manderley again. It seemed to me I stood by the iron gate leading to the drive, and for a while I could not enter, for the way was barred to me.*

Standing there did seem dreamlike. There was an iron gate, and the way was, indeed, barred to me—there was a thick chain and padlock. I was there for many reasons, but the main one was that I had heard something extraordinary: the house had been locked up after Cimino died two years before, and nothing had been touched since, like Miss Havisham's wedding feast.

Cimino had bought this home in 1972, when he came to live in Los Angeles. He had felt ambivalent about the move, leaving behind a

The house in the Hills (Author's collection)

successful career in advertising and the city in which he had spent most of his life. Instrumental in persuading him to go was the most compelling and enigmatic figure in the Cimino diaspora—a woman named Joann Carelli. Her precise role in the fifty years of their life together has always been a source of conjecture, but many people regarded her as a kind of Sunset Boulevard Mrs. Danvers, loyal and aggressively protective, disliked by many people in Hollywood.

Maybe, by some improbable form of osmosis, just being near the house would illuminate some of the ambiguities in Cimino's life for me, a bewildering mixture of truths and untruths, some circulated by others, but many by him. However, one thing was undeniably true: he became one of the most reviled figures ever in the industry. Scandals tend to fade over time, but thirty-eight years after the disaster of his movie *Heaven's Gate*, it is still a Hollywood myth. I have found nobody there—even people who were born after the movie opened in 1980—without a view on it.

After the modest success of the first movie he directed, the Clint Eastwood vehicle *Thunderbolt and Lightfoot*, and the monumental success of *The Deer Hunter* in 1978, Cimino was given the Hollywood version of droit du seigneur: he could make more or less what he wanted, and what he wanted was *Heaven's Gate*, an ambitious Western that he wrote and directed.

At that time, the average budget for a film was around $9 million, although many were cheaper—*Rocky* cost just over $1 million in 1976. Cimino's movie was originally budgeted at $11.5 million and ended up at an unprecedented $40 million. That would not have been so hard to bear for the studio that financed it, United Artists, if it had been a success or even, at worst, a prestigious succès d'estime with great reviews. It was neither. Not only were the reviews unanimously vicious, but nobody went to see it. After a week, UA did something no studio had ever done before: they withdrew it, putting a $40 million movie on the shelf. Two years later, United Artists went out of business, and everyone believed that it was Cimino's movie that had bankrupted them.

There have been many crimes in Hollywood over the years, from David Begelman, a multimillionaire studio chief, stealing $10,000 from an actor to *Cleopatra*'s producer Walter Wanger shooting his wife's lover in the groin. What was different about Cimino's "crime" was that it was not actually illegal, but that made no difference: in the court of Hollywood opinion, he had been found guilty, and there would be no parole for good behavior.

For him, the punishment was much worse: banishment from the career that had promised so much and from his work as a director who had total control over his movies. Cimino retreated to his refuge in the hills—a Hollywood version of house arrest. If he had worn an ankle bracelet, the words "Heaven's Gate" would have been engraved on it.

While it was true that almost every critic hated the film at the time, within twenty-five years of its release, many critics, particularly in Europe, came to regard *Heaven's Gate* as a masterpiece, one of the greatest Westerns ever made. For Cimino, of course, the truth was that the film had been a masterpiece from the beginning, but he had always had an ambivalent relationship with the truth. This was, after all, a man who had said, "I am not who I am, and I am who I am not," a statement designed to be either obfuscating or illuminating, depending on your view of Cimino.

Of all the things Cimino was, there were many things he was not. He was not born in either 1952 or 1941, as he told people. He was not inspired to make *The Deer Hunter* because of his stint as a Green Beret, because he never actually was one. He said he was the screenwriter of the movie, but another writer was credited. He talked of a much-loved daughter, but he was not actually her father. In the last twenty years of his life, he vehemently denied that he had had any plastic surgery done, but he became so unrecognizable that nobody believed him.

What is extraordinary is how implausible some of his stories about himself were. Sometimes they would contradict one another, but he obviously relished the contradictions. His tales seemed like a series of shameless bluffs that he was daring people to disprove. What was not a bluff was Cimino's belief, later to be shared by others, that he was a great director. However, in the last twenty years of his life, he did not direct a single movie. Instead, inside the house, he worked constantly. He said he had written at least fifty scripts, although few people know exactly what they were.

At the Locarno Film Festival in 2015, the year before he died, he made a haunting statement about his writing. During a Q&A session, someone asked him a question: "I believe you have a room in your house that is stacked to the ceiling with stuff that you've written, and I wondered what still keeps you writing."

"God knows!'" Cimino said. "Only the Lord knows, not I. That room, at one time, was very neat. Everything was in piles, very organized, but as you know, in the wonderful state of California, we have things called earthquakes, and after years of many earthquakes, this very neat room of files, piles of screenplays, is now a mountain, a confused mess, so it's very difficult for me to find anything." He paused, and then said quietly, "I keep the room locked because I can't bear to look at it."

The house, both a refuge and a prison after his last film in 1996, was central to his working life. Most of his friends had never been there. One of the few who had told me a story that was sad and touching. Cimino hired the English choreographer Eleanor Fazan to plan a technically complex sequence for the opening sequence of *Heaven's Gate*—an elaborate graduation ceremony at Harvard in 1870, during which more than one hundred people waltz to "The Blue Danube" around a giant oak tree. She was flown out to Los Angeles to work with him and teach the actors how to dance.

One day they were working at the house—spotless and like a beautifully designed hotel, she told me—and when they had finished, Cimino asked her if she would like a glass of champagne. She followed him into the kitchen, where—this being Beverly Hills—there was a fridge the size of a room. He opened the door, and she saw that it was empty except for two things: a half bottle of champagne and a single sandwich with one bite taken out of it.

I thought of these things as I stood outside the gates of Cimino's house. I did not care whether there was anything in the fridge. I was haunted by that other room, the room that had been neat with stacks of scripts and files before the earthquakes made them tumble in disarray, the room that Cimino kept locked because he could not bear to look at it.

PART I

1939–1976

CHAPTER 1

THE TARNISHED COAST

SOMETIMES AFTER SCHOOL, if Michael was not practicing with the wrestling team, he, Mike Strasberg, Murray Fudim—both of whom walked to school with him every day—and other friends like Arthur French, Charles Kauffmann, and Richard Gazda, would all go to the Italian ice-cream parlor on Post Street and hang out with the gang from Westbury High School.

Mike Strasberg told me this. I had posted a notice on the school website asking anyone from the Class of '56 who knew Cimino to get in touch. Strasberg was the only one who did. It turned out that he had been in middle school with Cimino as well. Retired to Arizona, still sharp and funny at eighty, he is one of the few from that class who is still alive. Although he has not had much contact with his school friends for many years, Strasberg said he would be happy to track down some of them. He found three, a loose group of friends who casually crisscrossed one another's school and social lives, ignoring the rough boundaries of the various ethnic communities in Westbury—Italian, Jewish, and Irish—which had drifted out of the boroughs of New York City to the cheaper, leafier, and safer towns of Long Island still unspoiled and rural in the 1950s before ribbon development turned it into an unending semi-urban sprawl.

Cimino lived with his parents and brothers on Whitney Street, on the town's west side, an area called Breezy Hill that was informally defined by the number of Italian families there, each block inhabited by people from certain towns and regions. Although most of them spoke Italian in the house and English outside, Cimino's family did not. Years later, honored at the Locarno Film Festival in Switzerland, he could hardly manage more than "*Ciao, bella gente*" when he spoke to the crowd. He never talked about his Italian roots and tended to avoid questions about the date his family emigrated to the US or even where they came from. As if to distance himself from his past, he also altered the sound of his surname—his school friends still pronounce it as his family did: "*Simino*," Arthur French said to me in a bemused way, "I guess Hollywood gave him the 'Cimino'"—Chi*meeno*—but in fact, he had changed it almost as soon as he left Westbury.

To some extent, the various ethnic groups tended to hang out with their own—Italians with Italians, Jews with Jews—and many of Cimino's friends came from the same background as him: Vinnie Iannie and Bill Camutti and Thomas Lagnese. Lagnese, probably the person he was closest to, was the only one Cimino really kept up with after he left school. Lagnese, now dead, told Arthur French that Cimino had been the best man at his wedding.

"Westbury was a very quaint town," French told me. He became a policeman ("I patrolled the town I grew up in"), and he said that in those days there was a police booth, often unattended, that had a desk and a telephone in it, where notes reading "Come and see me" would be left for the officers. Everybody knew everyone else. On the quiet streets, hedges were sculpted, vegetables grown in the gardens. "There was a little dairy farm with cows. You could barter—trade tomatoes for eggs. People made wine from their grape arbors. Outside a restaurant called the Greentree Inn, there were pitching posts for horses. It was a special place to grow up," French said.

The innocence we ascribe to small-town America mostly comes from the movies. It's hard not to look back at Westbury in the 1950s as the kind of community you see in them, somewhere between *Back to the Future's* Hill Valley and *It's a Wonderful Life's* Bedford Falls. On the Universal lot in the San Fernando Valley, there was a permanent town square set that was used over and over again in movies. Dressed differently, it is recognizable in both *Back to the Future* and *To Kill a Mockingbird*. Naturally, because Westbury was a real town, it was more sprawling and less perfect than a film set, but it incorporated many of its elements. It had a town hall, but not one with an imposing clock tower above it like Marty McFly's Hill Valley; it had a diner, but not the movie kind filled with clean-cut teenagers out of a Norman Rockwell painting.

In reality, the teenagers were not always so well-behaved. Arthur French told me that Cimino gave his parents "a lot of stuff," that maybe he resented having to move from Brooklyn to the suburbs when he was ten. "He had some disciplinary problems," he said. "Michael's parents were difficult. If you went over to the house, they wouldn't talk to you." In the 1950s, mostly fueled by scaremongering movies, teenagers had become curiously threatening to the older generation. Marlon Brando's 1953 motorbike movie *The Wild One* and James Dean's *Rebel Without a Cause* in 1955 implied that disaffected teenage gangs were going to turn on the small towns they had grown up in and maraud down every quiet main street.

However, Westbury remained the quaint town that Arthur French described: Cimino and his friends appropriated only the lightest kind of gang culture into their lives, more of a fashion statement than a call to arms. "We were wearing dungarees with rolled-up collars and white buck shoes. The Italians came out wearing chartreuse pants with nine- or ten-inch cuffs and jackets with different-colored arms. They stood around with their toes pointed outward, cigarettes rolled up in the sleeves. We called them 'Greasers,'" Mike Strasberg told me. Like the kids in *West Side Story*, they had nicknames. Cimino's friend Pete Shiro was known as Moondog. Another was called Snake. Thomas Lagnese was called Flea to differentiate him from his cousin with the same name, who was known as Mosquito.

Cimino's bad-boy identity was rather superficial, though—the furthest he really went was to have a pompadour. Although he hung around with the Italian gang, Arthur French never saw him wearing their extravagant outfits, and he did not have a nickname. In fact, he was not very social. Another classmate, Barbara Grywin, remembered that "he was very quiet, very somber. Not very gregarious, not a lot of friends.

He tried to excel in everything he did." His passion was drawing. "His art was in his heart. At the drop of a hat, he could make a sketch of anything. He was very creative as an artist." He told Charles Kauffmann that he wanted to be a drafting engineer and design buildings.

He also loved wrestling. He was small—five-five or five-six—but was well-built. He had a set of weights in his basement, and his friend Richard Gazda, who was also on the wrestling team, worked out for hours with him. The basement of the house on Whitney Street was busy. He wanted to be a jazz drummer, and he asked Charles Kauffmann to help him. Kauffmann told me, "I was a drummer in the high school band. I had a set of drums, and Michael came over to my house in his car and we'd take it back to his house because they had a big basement. There was a jazz club in Westbury called the Cork N' Bib where Gene Krupa performed."

None of his friends saw much more of his home than the basement. Cimino seemed to lead a life isolated from his family. His parents were a shadowy presence in the house. Richard Gazda told me that although he hung out with Cimino a lot, he never met his brothers. Charles Kauffmann, despite often drumming with him in the basement, did not even know that Cimino had any brothers until I told him.

MICHAEL CIMINO
Mike — Columbia bound to study design engineering — better not wrestle with this fellow—member of the W.H.S. Wrestling Team — also keeps in trim by being on the Green and Gold Track Team — Wrestling, Track.

Westbury High School yearbook, 1956

To his friends, Cimino was almost as elusive as his family. "At the time I knew him, he was quite nice and friendly—not overly outgoing, but he was quite well-liked. He was pleasant," Arthur French told me, a curiously lukewarm statement to make about a childhood friend. It was as if Cimino did not want to extend himself any further than that, did not want to reveal too much to anyone. Charles Kauffmann said, "There was something about the secrecy he wanted to keep. There was something strange."

After the friends graduated in 1956, Cimino went to Michigan State University to study graphic arts. Apart from one meeting a few years later with Mike Strasberg, none of the other three friends ever saw him again. When he became well-known, they were amazed. Arthur French told me, "I was surprised, very, very surprised, that he became a famous movie director." Charles Kauffmann said, "Oh my God, when he got the Academy Award, when they announced his name, I couldn't believe it. My Lord have mercy!"

In the years after high school, they had all tried to get in touch with Cimino. Kauffmann told me, "My son was out in Hollywood making movies, and I thought if anyone could help him it would be Michael, but he didn't respond." Richard Gazda said, "I tried to get in touch via his agent, but it was a lost cause." Mike Strasberg contacted him toward the end of his life, but Cimino did not reply.

Twenty years ago, Arthur French had a small school reunion at his house, and the talk got around to Cimino, the only Oscar-winning graduate of Westbury High School and still a subject of fascination to the friends he had left behind. Surprisingly, Thomas Lagnese said he had recently spoken to Cimino, and when Charles Kauffmann asked if he could have the number, Lagnese told him that Cimino had forbidden him to give it out. Kauffmann was hurt: "I don't know why he was so secret. I was Michael's friend. I was not a stranger."

SOMETIMES CIMINO SAID he was born in 1952, sometimes in 1943. In Hollywood, it is not uncommon to alter the year of your birth, but it is not so usual to have a selection of them to hand out. In a *Vanity Fair* interview in 2002, he was asked about this: "Let's put an end to all this once and for all," he said, and pulled out what looked to be a photocopy of his passport. It showed his birthdate as February 3, 1952. The only accurate part of that is the day. The year of his birth was actually 1939.

Generally, he would not talk about his past. Sometimes he would give a reason for this: "I want to avoid autobiographical perspectives. One doesn't need to know the life of Tolstoy in order to understand his books." But there were times when he would let his guard slip, as he did in the *Vanity Fair* piece: "I don't talk about my family—it's too painful. It was like a Eugene O'Neill play. I don't want to talk about it. Every part of it hurts." That's not a casual dismissal of an intrusive question about his past—it's almost as revealing as actually talking about it. He declined to divulge how many brothers he had or what their names were, only that "My siblings were like him [Cimino's father], tall and thin." In contrast, "I was just a tiny kid." Asked about his relationship with them, he replied, "Nothing, nothing, nothing." He was vague about where he had grown up. Sometimes he said it was "mostly" in New York. He "briefly" went to Westbury High School.

His forceful refusal to talk about his childhood was so extreme that the interviewer, Steve Garbarino, asked him if maybe there had been abuse in his family. "There is worse—being ignored. I'm just disconnected from the family. . . . My family is no one's goddamned business." He was only prepared to reveal his parents' professions: his father, also Michael, was a music publisher who had a business called Cimino Publications that released sheet music like *The Bacharach and David Songbook*. He also organized marching bands at football games. His mother, Lucia—generally called Lucy—was a seamstress who made wedding gowns. He seemed to hint at some problems in the marriage: "My mother and father were completely different. They looked very different, too." In 1979, during the making of *Heaven's Gate*, his longtime secretary, Patty Nelson, told me that she was amazed to take a phone call from Lucy Cimino, who wanted to talk to her son. Nelson had worked for Cimino for five years and had presumed his mother was dead because he had never mentioned her, nor had she ever called before.

In 2001, when he was sixty-two, he had not lost his resentment. He said that after he went into movies, his father did not speak to him for a year. And his mother: "We have very bad relations. Don't go there.

After I was in the business for years, I get a call from my mother, saying, 'Well. Now I know you're famous.' I say, 'Why?' She says, 'Your name was in the *New York Times* crossword puzzle.' It only took her six years."

In an interview in the local paper, she had said rather enigmatically that on the way to being a movie director "something happened to change him." Whatever that change was, it separated him from his family forever. All his life he talked about a childhood in Westbury that was different from the one his school friends remember.

Along with the casual ethnic divides of Westbury, there was another one, and it seemed as if Cimino wanted to cross it. In the first half of the century, the north of Long Island was a magic domain for the rich and privileged that became known as the Gold Coast. There were nearly 1,200 mansions on large estates, built as summer places by old-money families like the Vanderbilts, the Dodges, and the Woolworths, as well as by people whose money came from less traditional sources, like King Zog of Albania and John Gotti, head of the Mafia's Gambino family. Jay Gatsby built his opulent house there, in West Egg, a thinly fictionalized version of Great Neck, which was twelve miles from Westbury.

The line that divided the Gold Coast from the more tarnished and heavily populated south of the island was the Jericho Turnpike, and it ran right through the middle of Westbury. North of the highway was called Old Westbury, and it was very different in feel from the other, middle-class section of the town where Cimino grew up. Even now, the "Old" part has few roads and great swathes of green where the estates used to be. "All the millionaires belonged to the Meadowbrook Country Club, where they had four polo fields," Arthur French told me. "A lot of people worked on the estates of the rich people. Westbury itself was a workingmen's town."

A profile of him in 1990 reported that "Mr. Cimino grew up in Old Westbury, Fitzgerald's Gold Coast." His father, he said, "was very tall and thin. . . . He was a bit like a Vanderbilt or a Whitney, one of those guys." Even though the details sometimes changed, his stories all emphasized one thing: his upbringing was privileged.

Much later, Cimino reported that a friend of his had said, "Michael is an aristocrat who seeks the common man." What he said about himself seemed to confirm that: "I was always hanging out with kids my parents didn't approve of. Those guys were so alive. When I was fifteen, I spent three weeks driving all over Brooklyn with a guy who was following his girlfriend. . . . He had a gun, and . . . he was going to kill her. There was such passion and intensity about their lives. When the rich kids got together, the most we did was cross against a red light."

But once, hidden in the mirage of his past and the hostility to his parents and siblings, he let slip something rather poignant, a fleeting glimpse of a lost and golden childhood before it all went wrong: "I was a child prodigy. Like Michelangelo, who could draw a perfect circle at age five. I was extremely gifted." Just as the circle was perfect, he needed everything else to be as well. He told a story of walking with his mother through Westbury dressed in his smartest clothes and wearing white buck shoes. Some mud got on them, and he simply waited for his mother to get on her hands and knees to clean off the mud and make them, too, perfect again.

THE IMDB ENTRY for the novelist, screenwriter and producer T. Rafael Cimino notes that he is "the nephew of Writer/Director Michael Cimino." Cimino, whose first name is Todd, proved to be rather elusive. When I finally tracked him down, he told me that his father, Peter, was Michael's younger brother. He said there were two other brothers, Edward and Christopher, but he had never met them. He said that Peter, who had been a medical practitioner in Key Largo, Florida, was dead.

Todd told me he had had an eclectic range of careers—deputy sheriff, lawyer, firefighter, paramedic, customs officer, and marine coordinator for *Miami Vice*—before going into the movie business and becoming a novelist. At the moment, he said, he was working on the second season of *Big Little Lies* and was in partnership with Scarlett Johansson. He was keen to emphasize that he generated his own success without his uncle's help.

He confirmed some of Cimino's stories about his childhood. "One thing I can tell you is that on many levels I think there was a lot of dysfunction in the family." Todd said his father, Peter, was also unhappy: "[He] imposed this self-exile, and Michael imposed this self-exile. Over the years, I had to question why these boys wanted to exit the family, what there was about this family that was so toxic that they just wanted to leave." He told me that neither Michael nor Peter went to either of their parents' funerals. The two brothers who stayed home were close, but Michael and Todd's father did not speak for many years.

It was unclear from Todd's story exactly how close he was to his uncle. "My association with Michael was somewhat limited," he told me. When he went to Los Angeles, did he socialize with him? "I've never seen Michael in LA." Did you ever hang out? "No, he was a social and familial porcupine."

But, according to Todd, Cimino had done one familial thing for his nephew: Todd said that in 1999, Michael was invited to the wedding of Spike Jonze and Francis Ford Coppola's daughter, Sofia, in Napa Valley. Todd told me, "He extended an invitation through my father to me and asked if I'd be interested in going. I was ready to get back into the entertainment business, so I said yes."

I asked Todd if he thought it was an odd thing for Cimino to do, to contact a brother he had not spoken to for years and ask a nephew he had never met to come to a wedding of people he didn't know. "Strangely I felt he owed it to me," he answered. "There's a lot of resentment, because I had worked so hard to get where I was." I asked him what it was like being Cimino's date, and he corrected me: "I wasn't his date. Michael didn't go."

Todd told me that his father and Cimino reestablished contact around that point. Peter had retired as a doctor and had gone into property development in northern Florida. "Being in business makes you reliant on everything you've got at your fingertips. Maybe in my father's mind he saw Michael as a resource." By 2001, Todd said the brothers had stopped talking again: "The land development didn't pan out. I loaned him money, and I'm assuming that Michael may have done so too. Then my father lost everything."

Peter moved to eastern Florida, where he died, Todd told me. "We had not talked for two years before his passing, and it wasn't until my sister called me to say that he had passed away that his name was even mentioned. Michael had nothing to do with the funeral or anything else. I had tried to reach out to him, but the number I had for him had changed, was disconnected. I sent a note to his lawyer. I never heard back."

Todd said he had not managed to tell the other two brothers, Edward and Christopher, about Peter's death either because he had no idea where they lived or how to contact them—or if they were even alive. If he could not find them, it was unlikely I would be able to either.

CHAPTER 2

COFFEE MOMENT IN MALIBU

MICHAEL CIMINO HAD wanted to be many things, but not particularly a movie director. As a child he had been a gifted artist, and he would continue painting all his life; his high school yearbook reported that he was "Columbia bound to study design engineering," but instead he went to Michigan State to study graphic art and then to Yale, where he took a postgraduate degree in fine arts. Later, in New York, he took ballet lessons and studied with Lee Strasberg at the Actors Studio. None of this was scattershot—it was simply a cumulative array of talents in which he wanted to excel.

In his last year at Michigan State, he became art director and later managing editor of the school magazine *Spartan*. Influenced by the striking typography of Paul Rand and Saul Bass, he designed an astonishingly original series of covers with bold graphics and startling images that could not have been more different from the fusty and conventional ones that the magazine had used before him. *Spartan* reported in its January 1959 issue, "While working over the minute details for the covers or hashing out the layout, Mike strives for the unique. . . . He is making plans to study at Yale and looking towards a career in publishing or architectural design as well as graphics." The yearbook noted that, "As for women, he prefers blondes. His hobby is drinking, preferably vodka."

Cimino at Michigan State, 1959
(Photograph courtesy Lucy Cimino
archive)

Positioning himself as a kind of junior Dean Martin does not conform to anyone else's recollection of him, but it was a persona that he slipped in and out of all his life.

David Freeman, who later became a successful screenwriter, was studying playwriting at the Drama School at Yale while Cimino was getting his fine art degree. He never saw him chasing women, blonde or otherwise. Freeman told me that they met because Cimino would hang around in the Drama department and pick his brains about playwriting. Cimino later said, "I used to walk by the drama school and think, 'That's where I belong,' but I didn't have the courage to make the change." Freeman remembered him being more interested in plays than movies and never saw him at the Yale Film Society. Sometimes Cimino came to parties at the apartment Freeman shared, and he remembered him being rather unassuming. "He was shy and self-absorbed, but when Mike spoke, you thought, 'He's one smart guy,'" Freeman told me. "Although he never gave you any personal information, it was fun to hear him riff, but you never believed anything he said. He seemed to be looking for a passion, something to latch on to. He was frustrated that he didn't know what to do with his intellect and energy."

After he left Yale in the summer of 1963, Cimino moved to New York, and within five years had become one of the most successful and highly paid directors of television commercials. He told different stories of how he got his start, but there are always different versions of anything that happened in Cimino's life. He said that he got a job with a small company that produced documentary and industrial films: "They taught me how to use a Moviola [a machine used to edit film]. I operated the Moviola and I swept the floors. I was hooked—I decided to become a filmmaker." He also told a more exciting version of the story: "I met some people who were doing fashion stuff—commercials and stills. And there were all these incredibly beautiful girls, and then zoom—the next thing I know, overnight, I was directing commercials. . . . And one beautiful model after another—sometimes three at a time—and I was just having a ball."

Francis Grumman, a cameraman who worked with Cimino off and on all his life, had heard a less glamourous but more ballsy version of his start in the industry: he walked in off the street, with no appointment, to the most prestigious advertising design house in New York—Ferro Mogubgub Schwartz—and talked his way into a job. He was twenty-four.

Since the end of the war, advertising had gone through an extraordinary change There had been a huge increase in population. The things that had been in short supply during the war—clothing, refrigerators, automobiles, and appliances—began to be manufactured in huge quantities to supply the increasing demand, and they all had to be promoted. Before 1950, the only advertising media had been newspapers, magazines, radio, and billboards, but now there was the relatively new medium of television. In 1950, there were three million sets, and by 1960 there were 55 million. It was the exponential growth of television that fueled the advertising industry. At the beginning of the 1960s, $12 million was spent on TV spots, and that number rose to $128 million by its end.

Just as the content of early television was not particularly sophisticated, nor were the ads and sponsorship that funded it. The major problem was the technology: there was no real way of prerecording. It would not be until the end of the 1950s that videotape became cheap and reliable enough to use. This meant that everything on TV was live and local—a simultaneous national network did not come until later, when coaxial cables joined all the television stations. The staple diet was news, cooking shows, and variety shows, all shot live. When it was time for an ad, the cameras moved to an adjoining set and shot them live as well.

The commercials were very simple: salesmen talking directly to the camera or two housewives in a kitchen extolling the virtues of coffee, the latter of which, in the almost exclusively male world of advertising, were condescendingly described as "2 C's in a K." There was very little room for style, wit, or sophistication with such a crude setup. The ads were almost entirely aspirational—"When you got it, flaunt it"—and promised better coffee, better cars, and better vacuum cleaners and extolled a vision of suburban America that could be made more perfect by buying a newer model of almost anything.

The business itself was rather conventional, no more exciting than working in insurance or any kind of business—standard rat-race stuff. Sloan Wilson's 1955 bestseller about advertising characterized its hero in the title, *The Man in the Gray Flannel Suit*, a conformist executive commuting to Madison Avenue from the suburbs every day and returning to his wife and children in the evening. He and the other admen were not consorting with—in Cimino's words—"one beautiful model after another."

It was only when Cimino entered the industry in 1963 that it was beginning to acquire the kind of excitement and glamour portrayed in the TV series *Mad Men*. There were two reasons: television began to be broadcast in color, and videotape-recording technology had dramatically improved. Now, neither the shows nor the commercials that paid for them had to be shot live, and there was an exponential rise in quality for both. Ads left the restrictive confines of the studio and became short films that could be shot in far-flung locations, and the industry began to attract a new breed of copywriters and directors.

George Lois, probably one of the most influential admen of the era, said, "That dynamic period of counterculture in the 1960s found expression on Madison Avenue through a new creative generation—a rebellious coterie who understood that visual and verbal expression were indivisible, who bridled under the old rules." For the first time, ads became witty and inventive, often cutting through the conventional and aspirational style of the 1950s. Lois's immensely successful series of ads for Volkswagen—an almost unknown car in the US at the time—were counterintuitive in a country that cherished large and flashy vehicles: in one, a tiny Beetle is lost in a huge expanse of white on the page, and the slogan simply read, "Think small." Another one said cheekily, "It makes your house look bigger."

The man who gave Cimino his first job, Pablo Ferro, was at the forefront of George Lois's new "rebellious coterie." Born in Cuba, exotic enough in the white-bread world of Madison Avenue, he was not a man in a gray flannel suit—he favored jewelry and flowing scarves. He was immensely well connected: Julian Barry, later to write the Dustin Hoffman movie *Lenny*, said, "Pablo's apartment was a beehive of creativity and '60s madness. People came and went at all hours."

The way Ferro shot commercials was both innovative and startling. Influenced by the new techniques of the French nouvelle-vague filmmakers, he experimented with kinetic quick-cutting, often using static images like drawings, engravings, and photographs and infusing them with speed, motion, and sound. The TV ad he directed for Stanley Kubrick's *Dr. Strangelove* in 1964 used an amazing 125 images in one minute.

Ferro Mogubgub Schwartz operated out of three floors of a building on Forty-Sixth and First. Cimino might have just been sweeping floors or operating a Moviola when he arrived there in the summer of 1963, but he was working with a team of the most creative and original people in advertising and design. He quickly knew that he wanted to direct. "I had this terrible urgency to learn all I could as fast as I could because there was so much to learn that if I didn't learn it fast I'd be so goddamn old, I'd never be able to make a movie," he said. He began to study films, sometimes seeing them twenty times. His desire to master every aspect of cinema was obsessive.

Sal Butta, who ran a small animation company in Manhattan, painted an intriguing picture of Cimino's desire to learn. He told me, "Pablo Ferro called and said that he had just hired Mike Cimino and he wanted to come and hang around and see how you guys work. I said fine, and he'd come up to my studio every morning with a cup of coffee and a bagel and watch us work and ask a lot of questions. He learned these animation and storyboard techniques from us and applied them to his later films. He was a great kid. I loved him. He came in his hand-tailored suits. He seemed a high-end type of guy even then."

Starting out as a graphic artist, as Cimino did, was not an unusual way of becoming a director—Pablo Ferro himself took the same route. While the early directors in commercials had been cameramen, new talent was now coming from the print medium. By November of that year, Cimino was directing a TV ad for the Steve McQueen movie *Love with the Proper Stranger*. Alan Pakula, later to direct *All the President's Men*, was the producer, and his agent wrote to him to say that "Mike Cimino has assured me that he will do everything in his power, in the short time available, to come up with something worthy of your fine film."

His ascent was swift. Within eighteen months, *Business Screen* magazine reported, "Michael Antonio Cimino, an award-winning film director and designer, has joined MPO as a director. Cimino will not only direct but will work on special assignments involving graphic design concepts and unusual approaches to live film."

MPO was Madison Pollack O'Hare. It was a new kind of setup that reflected the aggressive hunt for talent by advertising agencies looking for the best and the brightest to run their campaigns. Housed in a large building on Third Avenue, MPO was what became known as a "full-service shop"—a kind of creative factory. On its staff were directors, cameramen, set designers, makeup artists, and wardrobe supervisors. In the basement there were nine sound stages. MPO would provide the entire crew and became part of every stage of production. By the mid-1960s, it was responsible for 10 percent of all the commercials shot in New York. Francis Grumman, a cameraman there, told me, "Each director had a show reel, and the producers would show these around to the ad agencies. 'You want this guy for Colgate, you want this guy for Pepsi?' It was like a wholesale market for talent."

Just as he had when he moonlighted at Sal Butta's animation company, Cimino learned quickly. Grumman said, "I didn't know where he came from, but suddenly—boom—he was at MPO. I noticed this little guy. He would come in and whisper to other directors during their shoot. I had no idea who he was. It was always remarkable to see him. He was a little bit roly-poly, a small guy. I got a call from a producer at

MPO who said, 'Do you want to work with Michael Cimino?' He had begun to get all the big jobs for companies like Canada Dry and Kool cigarettes, so it was a feather in my cap to work with him."

Cimino had a predictably lavish version of his swift rise at the company: "Do you remember *Blow Up*? That was me. I lived that. I had the same car, a Rolls-Royce convertible." He had also bought a brownstone on Fifty-Third Street. Francis Grumman said, "He lived well and partied well. He had a lot of influential friends. Very funny—he had a great sense of humor. He was generous, but if somebody did something he didn't like, he would cut them off. I knew him pretty well, but he was always closed off. You could only get to know him so far. I won't go as far as to say secrets, but my guess is that there must have been a lot of things he didn't want people to know about."

George Parker was an English adman who was creative director of the agency Benton & Bowles. He told me that Cimino was well-known for being evasive about the truth and was already lying about his age and his height: "He was always knocking five or six years off even though he was barely thirty. He claimed he was just shy of six foot when it was obvious he wore massively built-up shoes and was probably about five foot four."

With his success, Cimino began to manage his career ruthlessly. Mike Strasberg, his friend from Westbury High School, met him in Manhattan to see a Bob Dylan concert, and he remembered Cimino asking him, "How much money is enough money?" According to Francis Grumman, "This guy's mind was already at the highest end of Hollywood operations." He set himself apart from the collegiate atmosphere of MPO. Contract negotiations were done on a fairly casual basis there, but Cimino did something that nobody else did: he would not show up himself but got a team of lawyers to sort out his contract. He also insisted on residuals, which were unheard of in the world of commercials. The agencies would send a fixed number of physical copies of the commercials to various TV stations. If it was a success, they ordered more, and Cimino would get a piece of the extra payment.

Because of the ephemeral nature of advertising, few of his commercials have survived, but the three I found show an extraordinarily confident talent. The black-and-white Pepsi commercial he shot at

Disneyland in 1965 has all the elements that have always been a staple of advertising—glamorous blondes, smiling faces, and young people loving the product—but Cimino added something uniquely his own: an almost subversive reinvention of the form. Like the crude one-shot studio ads of the 1950s, most ads remained linear—neighbor on doorstep, finger on doorbell, hostess brewing new blend of coffee, inhale aroma, shared moment of bliss.

Cimino's commercial breaks the rules. It looks like it was shot by Jean-Luc Godard on a day off from À bout de souffle with a kinetic energy and a kaleidoscopic array of effects—jump cuts, point-of-view shots, slow motion, rack zooms, vertigo-inducing camerawork. In the space of a minute, he produces an almost exhausting impression of the unbridled joy you can get from drinking Pepsi. The ad, like all of Cimino's, is beautifully lit and shot. He handpicked the best cameramen that MPO employed, people like Gordon Willis, who later shot The Godfather, and Owen Roizman, who was responsible for The French Connection in 1971. Francis Grumman said, "Most directors were doing it by the seat of their pants. Michael thought out everything first and made storyboards. Everything was in his mind before he turned on the camera. He had an extreme talent for everything—wardrobe, hair, makeup. He had such taste and was very strongly opinionated about what he wanted."

One of his most successful commercials was for United Airlines in 1967. He took a song called "Take Me Along" out of a 1959 Broadway musical flop and created an ad that was styled like a big-budget Hollywood musical. The form was breathtaking, even if the content reflected the sexist culture of the time: a variety of housewives plead musically with their husbands to take them along on their business trips while there's an implication that the men are keener to take their secretaries. The men are in gray suits, but Cimino echoes United's color branding with the women's bright pastel dresses. The intricate choreography is kinetically shot from above, Busby Berkeley–style, as well as from below, where the camera looks up at the dancers through a glass floor. The elaborate set design and the Americana imagery would become staples of Cimino's later work. In the first year of the promotion, United Airlines' revenues rose by 30 percent while the rest of the industry managed only a 20 percent hike.

Later that year, he made his most famous commercial. *Business Screen* magazine reported, "MPO were awarded the Silver Phoenix for the Eastman Kodak commercial *Yesterdays,* signifying the world's best television commercial of 1967. MPO's Michael Cimino directed." It went on to win twelve more awards and was so highly regarded that a book was written about it: *The Anatomy of a Commercial: The Story of Eastman Kodak's "Yesterdays."*

A hundred and ninety pages long, it goes into extraordinary detail and is instructive in showing how sophisticated, complicated, and important commercials had become in selling a product—in this case the new Kodak Instamatic camera. A year before shooting started, a detailed script for the two-minute ad was written by a copywriter at J. Walter Thompson, Eastman Kodak's ad agency. It is a simple, even corny, idea: a middle-aged couple are clearing their attic and find an album of their old photographs. The process of going into production involved a chain of corporate decision-making as labyrinthine as a Hollywood studio's—marketing and creative directors at Eastman Kodak, as well as a whole team of planners and account executives at J. Walter Thompson. It was going to be an expensive enterprise, its length making it an epic compared to the simpler, shorter, and cheaper run-of-the-mill ads. A two-minute slot on primetime television cost around $120,000 at the time—nearly $1 million in today's money.

The producer at JWT, Warren Aldoretta, went to MPO and saw Cimino's reel. "I was impressed by it. He brought to his commercials excitement, taste, energy, and tremendous awareness," he said. Cimino came on board with some of his surprising techniques. When he cast it, he brought actors in "not to make them says lines prepared in a script: we had them dance." He was, as usual, demanding: "Although people don't always agree with me, I have a feeling about detail which may seem irrelevant to some people. . . . Naturally, costs go up."

What seemed fairly simple was actually much more complicated. The couple looked at eight photos—but in the story, they ranged from 1934 up to the '60s, and period locations had to be found in which to take the pictures (the house exterior, an old gas station, a church). Then Cimino wanted them to be aged—deckle-edged prints were not made anymore, so they had to find a special trimmer. The actors had to be youthened and aged, with many changes of costumes and wigs. The shoot took six days—two on the intricately built attic set and four on location in Connecticut. Cimino shot eight thousand feet of film—around five hours that was eventually cut down to two minutes. The commercial aired on July 23, 1967.

Although he was much less of a hired hand than other directors, his powerful position in the industry did not extend to entirely getting his own way. He did not like the version of the old Jerome Kern song "Yesterdays" that was used. Nor did he approve of the final product shot. He took the adversarial position he maintained all his working life: "Most relationships are battles right down to the line." Francis Grumman told me that when account executives interfered on set, "Michael would just bulldoze through it. Almost from the very beginning, he was, 'If you want me to direct, I do it my way.' He was not shy about his talents. He was aggressive about how he wanted to do things."

As he became more creative and successful, the advertising agencies began to find him "difficult," and, although the ads he made were among the most prestigious in the industry, they became increasingly expensive. Charles Okun, a friend of Cimino's who was a production manager on some of the commercials and worked with him later on *Heaven's Gate*, said, "The clients of the agencies liked Cimino. His visuals were fabulous, but the amount of time it took was just astronomical. Nothing was easy with Michael."

George Parker, the creative director responsible for the Maxwell House account, worked with Cimino for two years because the results were so good, even though he was "a pain in the ass."

Parker and Cimino worked together on a commercial, to be shot in Malibu, that involved a couple walking along the beach with their dog on a misty morning before returning to their home for what Maxwell House always called "The Coffee Moment." "Mike decided that it would be a nice visual touch if their dog chased seagulls on the beach, which would then fly off through the mist into the early-morning sun," Parker noted in his memoir. This required the services of a bird wrangler, who said that the only birds that were untrainable were seagulls, but they could use crows instead, which would only be seen in silhouette. A big hole was dug in the sand, and the crows were kept there under a canvas tarpaulin. As the couple walked by, the cover would be pulled away and the birds would fly into the sun.

"We did the first take, and it was perfect. 'OK,' yelled Mike. 'That was pretty good. Let's do another.' The bird wrangler looked at Mike with a certain amount of consternation. 'What's the problem?' asked Mike. 'Well, the birds have gone.' 'Gone?' yelled Mike, stomping his tiny, high-heeled feet. 'And exactly where the fuck have the birds gone?' 'Home,' replied the wrangler. 'Well, then go home and bring the fucking birds back,' screamed Mike."

In *The Anatomy of a Television Commercial*, published in 1970, three years after *Yesterdays* first aired, the author reported that the director was now "in Hollywood, working on his first feature. Can Mr. Cimino bring the same degree of tireless concentration and detailed effort [to movies] that he perfected in the television commercial field? . . . It should not be too hard."

CHAPTER 3

THE SECRET WORLD

WHEN CIMINO WAS at the height of his commercials career, he met Joann Carelli, a dynamic and forceful agent a couple of years younger than him. Patty Nelson, Cimino's longtime secretary, remembers Carelli telling her that they had first encountered each other at a party. He offered to drive her home, and she was amazed by his car—"Who drives a Rolls-Royce in New York!" Nelson remembers her saying. She felt that Cimino was drawn to Carelli's look and style. At that time, according to one of his relatives, Cimino, despite his talk of blondes and models, had a steady girlfriend named Pat, who worked for an airline. All his family adored her, but one day she was gone and Carelli was there.

In 2002, thirty-five years after Cimino and Carelli's relationship began, an interviewer who spoke with him reported, "[Cimino] sat down and ceremoniously unwrapped a package. Inside was a lovely, old-fashioned oil portrait he had done of Ms. Carelli as a young woman, painted in a style reminiscent of Mary Cassatt. He had already picked out the frame and planned to surprise her with it on Christmas morning. 'This is the way she looked when I first met her,' he said, gazing lovingly at her image."

Soon after that first meeting, she became connected to him as—depending on which description you go with—his muse, lover, enabler, consigliere, hatchet woman, bad cop, gatekeeper, or some alchemical combination of all of them. Later, they were also twin orphans against the enduring storm of *Heaven's Gate*, which she produced. "She had this kind of power. It was really extraordinary," one of Cimino's early collaborators told me. In 1980, in one of the very few interviews Carelli ever gave, she would not be drawn out about her relationship with Cimino and only said, "A talented person chooses someone to work with because of their talent." When I asked her what the nature of their bond was, she said rather aggressively that they were simply best friends. There is, of course, nothing wrong with that description, except it's like calling a tornado a breeze.

If you join together some of Cimino's references to Joann Carelli over the fifty years of their life together, they amount to a kind of love letter that is both romantic and professional. "My girl. . . ." "She's simply the person I trust most in the world." "My secret weapon." "My closest friend, Joann." "She was indispensable." "Joann is behind every one of my films." "As always, she had a stronger intuition than me." "Joann was always there." "We were deeply in love."

Cimino was sometimes playful when he talked of her, private jokes that would have meant little to anyone else: "Giovanna is her real name, but she insists on 'Joann,' which I don't like." He dedicated his novel *Big Jane* "To Giovanna." In the movie he made of Mario Puzo's novel *The Sicilian*, released in 1987, the name of the lead character's girlfriend—Justina—was changed to Giovanna, and the actress's hair was colored and styled to resemble Carelli's. When I asked her about it, she said it was just a coincidence and that Cimino had probably changed the name because Giovanna is a more common name than Justina.

However, as always with Cimino, it was hard to work out what the reality of their bond was. They were "together"—they eventually had neighboring apartments in New York and adjoining beachfront houses in East Hampton—but all through his life he referred, in an overemphatic way, to many girlfriends, although nobody I talked to had much recollection of any of them. In 2002, he said, "I've had a lot of experience with women. I kind of have a handle on what they love, what turns them on." An interviewer noted that "his conversation is peppered with references to the 'Persian girl,' the 'Asian girl,' the 'English girl,' and even royalty. . . . [He says,] 'I've dated a hundred women, one after the other.'"

Whatever the truth, the closeness of their relationship was not in question. For people who worked with them, it seemed both unfathomable and clear at the same time. There was something that set them apart, and it was impossible to spend time in their company without feeling the power of their force field, which was both protective and aggressive. They were like twins who shared a private language. Eoghan Harris, an Irish screenwriter who worked on a project with Cimino, remembered having dinner with them. He told me, "Cimino sat silently eating for at least thirty minutes while Carelli communed—there is no other word—with him, cocking her head like an interpreter as if listening to him on invisible headphones, and then turning to me and saying, 'Michael says . . .'"

Carelli told me that she believed he was a kind of innocent savant and she had to assist him. She told me, as if Cimino was too pure for the sordid world of movies, that the crude and probably crooked financiers they had to deal with were unable to comprehend him. However, many people remember him as being quite able to cope on his own. The unimaginative producers, dim number crunchers, and studio apparatchiks he attacked for denying him the right to achieve his expensive vision often had no trouble understanding him.

People came up with bizarre reasons for their symbiotic closeness: Nicholas Woodeson, then a young British actor who was given his first part by Cimino in *Heaven's Gate*, told me that he had heard a story that Carelli and Cimino both came from Mafia families, hers more powerful than his. When pressure was put on him to join the family business, according to this story, she had used her influence to get him out of his mob obligations so he could follow his dream of being a movie director. Another crew member told me rather melodramatically that she felt Carelli must have had "something over Cimino, some secret that could have destroyed him."

However, everything that anyone said about them was pure speculation, an attempt to explain the unexplainable. Neither Cimino nor Carelli were going to explain it either: people could think what they wanted.

JOANN CARELLI DEFINES flying under the radar. She has almost never been interviewed. If you google her, she is identified as Cimino's "girlfriend and collaborator," and she is identified in a photograph—but the picture is of someone else. There is almost nothing about her online except as the producer of record of *Heaven's Gate*.

Because I knew that she and Cimino lived at United Nations Plaza in New York, I wrote to her at that address. I was not expecting a reply, and indeed, I did not get one to either that letter or the next. Then I had a stroke of luck. When I interviewed Eleanor Fazan, the choreographer who had seen the bitten sandwich in Cimino's fridge, she told me that, unlike many people who worked with Carelli, she had been fond of her. She and Cimino had even stayed in Fazan's apartment in London. They had remained in touch for a while after *Heaven's Gate*, but they had not been in contact for thirty years.

I wrote to Carelli again, giving her Fazan's phone number and email address. I said that Fazan was a friend of mine, and if Carelli wanted, she could contact her, and she would give me a good rep. To my amazement, Carelli called her. According to Fazan, they talked a little about old times and her devastation over Cimino's death. Then Fazan asked her if she was calling to check up on me. Carelli said that she'd never heard of me. She was calling, she said, because she had been going through some of Cimino's things and she had come across an old address book that had a number for Fazan, and she was just checking if it was the right one. She added that she and Cimino had agreed they would never get involved in a biography. Then she unexpectedly said that Fazan could give me her email.

I wrote again, and it felt almost surreal when the most enigmatic character in the Cimino story surfaced and actually called me. "This is Joann Carelli," she said in a guttural, unreconstructed New York accent. "I'm not going to tell you *anything*." However, we talked in a very general way for nearly an hour, and to my surprise, she agreed to meet me at a particular restaurant in Manhattan the following week. She declined to give me her phone number.

In her late seventies, she is still enormously attractive, but I could feel that force field. When we met, she told me contemptuously that there were many people like me who said they were passionate about Cimino, and she had never talked to any of them. It rather begged the question of why, then, she was sitting opposite me in a restaurant. When

I told her I was on my way to Los Angeles to do some interviews, she told me that I would simply be listening to a lot of lies.

I could tell that she felt that charm was a waste of time. She also had that rather disconcerting quality of being indifferent to whether you liked her or not, but she had a mesmerizing presence. We stayed at the restaurant until the waiters began putting the chairs on the tables, and while she did not exactly tell me "anything" either then or at the many subsequent meals we had, just getting to know her—as far as it was possible to get to know her—was illuminating. It was hard not to be impressed by her Quixotic and passionate defense of Cimino against the liars, the naysayers, the Cimino-phobes, the banished collaborators, and the vicious critics who attacked them both after *Heaven's Gate*.

At that first dinner, she was prepared to tell me a little about herself: her father had been an Italian tailor, and she grew up in Lower Manhattan. She put herself through college at Parsons School of Design, studying graphic art, then worked as an artist in advertising. A photo retoucher she knew wanted to work on bigger magazines and asked her if she would be his agent. Then one of the directors at MPO, a brilliant and anarchic third-generation Japanese American called David Nagata, who was a friend of Cimino's, asked if she would represent him. Nagata was an unusual figure in the Waspy world of Madison Avenue: he had had such a terrible time in the wartime internment camps for Japanese Americans that he jokingly celebrated Christmas on December 7, the day that Pearl Harbor was attacked. Her success with Nagata as a star client grew, and she spent time with him in London working with the top British commercials directors—Hugh Hudson, who later directed *Chariots of Fire*; Donald Cammell, who wrote and directed *Performance* in 1970; and Robert Brownjohn, who designed the iconic James Bond title sequence for *Goldfinger*.

Carelli was evasive about exactly how her relationship with Cimino moved into a higher gear after their first meeting, but she did say something curious: at the beginning, she had not detected anything particularly special about him. Although she told me that she had never actually been his agent, others told me that she soon became involved in his work. George Parker, the producer of Cimino's Maxwell House Malibu commercial, said, "Carelli was his handler. She reined him in."

Francis Grumman told me that, "She tried to protect him against the agencies. She had no fear. There must have been some decision-making in her mind that Michael was the star she wanted to follow. I think from the beginning she was attracted to his talent and his mind. Lovers? It's hard for me to say because Michael was strange about those things. He needed her. They were like brother and sister."

In an industry of compulsive glory grabbers, Joann Carelli underplayed her contribution to Cimino's working life. In every interview he gave about his crucial move to Hollywood in 1971 to try to become a movie director, he consistently said that it was Carelli who persuaded him to do it, but she denied this—he had made the decision himself, she told me. She always spoke of him deferentially, as if he was the genius and she was a submissive handmaiden. When he asked her to read scripts for him, she told me that she never expressed her opinion before he had expressed his. When looking for actors or other collaborators, she sometimes drew up a short list, but she never influenced him—he was the one who always made the final choice. I asked her why she was prepared to be so subservient, why she had devoted fifty years of her life to his. She simply told me that she had no ego—a not entirely convincing statement from such a powerful woman.

All successful actors or directors in Hollywood tend to have an entourage—agents, managers, assorted sycophants, hangers-on, yes-men. Cimino had an entourage of one. When the successful years end, the entourage tends to vanish. Carelli did not. He had nine years of triumph, followed by *Heaven's Gate,* and then nearly forty years in the wilderness, during which she never left him. I asked someone who knew them well why. "First, there was a kudos in being with a genius," he said. "Later there was another kind of kudos—that of being the only one to understand a misunderstood genius." To Mady Kaplan, an actress who worked with Cimino twice and became a friend, it was very simple: "They existed in a secret world. Joann was life-sustaining for him."

CHAPTER 4

THUNDERBOLT IN HOLLYWOOD

ALTHOUGH HE WAS still making commercials, Cimino had begun to write screenplays. "Joann Carelli . . . actually talked me into doing it," he said in an interview. He was never content with just one project, and, in order to be more prolific, he sought out collaborators to work with. Wanting a writing partner did not necessarily indicate a lack of confidence on his part. Stanley Kubrick, one of the most confident auteurs ever, had a writing collaborator on *2001: A Space Odyssey*, *The Shining*, and *Eyes Wide Shut*, as well as others. Billy Wilder never wrote a script on his own. However, both of them tended to acknowledge others' contributions more than Cimino did.

A producer recommended a young playwright, Harvard-educated Deric Washburn, who had had a one-act play produced as part of a triple-bill off-Broadway. To earn a living, Washburn worked as a carpenter. He remembered the first time he met Cimino: "He took me to lunch, and he shows up in a Rolls-Royce. Lunch means driving down to the Battery and having a hot dog in the Rolls. Then back to his garage, where he had two spaces, to keep the Rolls protected. I guess he was looking for a writer, and as I later realized, he'd already found a whole lot of writers. Now, you never know, because Mike's name was up on the script and the other writers were never on the scripts. He had stacks of scripts with his name on them."

Washburn and Cimino did not mix socially. "There was always a big distance," he told me. "You were never going to close that distance." Washburn made an effort: "I remember trying to get to know him a little better. A friend had a house in Poughkeepsie, and I invited him up for the weekend. He shows up in his Rolls-Royce, and he's not comfortable there. But he wanted something from me, I think. Mike and I got closest when we started talking about a story. Then it was amazing. It was like one person. It was like a dance. We could boil together."

By that point, Cimino had a young agent, Michael Gruskoff, who worked at Creative Management Associates in Los Angeles, a prestigious agency representing directors and actors like Robert Redford and Woody Allen. Gruskoff was impressed by the commercials and Cimino's reputation in New York and believed that he could help Cimino become a movie director. Gruskoff, now in his eighties, takes his meetings at the Nespresso showroom around the corner from Rodeo Drive. He told me that he and Cimino had become good friends. When he organized meetings for Cimino in Hollywood, he would stay with Gruskoff and his family and play with his children. Eccentrically, he would sometimes drive his Rolls from New York to California rather than fly.

Cimino's decision to try to get into the movie business coincided with an extraordinary time in its history: 1970 is usually regarded as the beginning of the "new" Hollywood, the moment when the rules changed. The most important one had been that the studios, not the filmmakers, were the muscle on the films they made. Even famous directors were really hired hands—they were essential and unimportant at the same time. It would not have occurred to anyone, particularly the studios, to call a filmmaker—with the possible exceptions of Chaplin and Hitchcock—an auteur, with all the power and vision that the word implied.

What changed in the 1970s was that the directors became the muscle, and initially, their films put a galvanizing jolt of adrenaline into the business. They seemed to have acquired almost supernatural powers: Steven Bach, the United Artists executive who later oversaw *Heaven's Gate*, said, "What a director does is a mysterious thing. When push comes to shove, their vision must be allowed to operate without the kinds of strictures you would apply to a contractor who was building your swimming pool." It's a telling metaphor that underlines both the respect and the disdain that Hollywood can have for directors.

What was different about many of the new directors was that they were young and untested. Youth—unless you were an actor or actress—never had much currency in Hollywood: it implied a worrying inexperience that could be costly. The industry liked directors to have paid their dues (with the exception of the twenty-five-year-old Orson Welles with *Citizen Kane* in 1941—but then he was the exception to everything). Robert Wise, who later directed *The Sound of Music*, spent ten years as an editor before being allowed to make B movies. Vincente Minnelli had worked as a costume and set designer before he directed *Cabin in the Sky* in 1943, when he was almost forty. When looking for three directors to helm the various segments of one of the last bloated road show movies, 1962's *How the West Was Won*, the producer, Bernard Smith, said, "We wanted old pros, not young geniuses."

To the surprise of the old guard, at the end of the 1960s, some inexpensive movies made by "young geniuses" turned out to be unbelievably successful. What they lacked in experience was compensated for by an authentic voice. Whatever the forty-eight-year-old director Laslo Benedek—whose first film was *The Kissing Bandit*, in 1948—had brought to Marlon Brando's famous teenagers-on-the-rampage movie *The Wild One* in 1953, it was not that. Now, the new mavericks were writing and directing movies about subjects they understood, and they tapped into a burgeoning and enfranchised youth culture of loud music and strident protest.

Now, what had traditionally been no-go areas for the movies became viable subjects and were treated as part of normal life—lots of sex, violence, and any kind of contempt for the establishment. The new movies felt relevant and sexy. The tag line on the poster of one of the first—Haskell Wexler's *Medium Cool* in 1969, about the riots in Chicago the previous year—summed it up: "Beyond the age of innocence . . . into the age of awareness." It was as if Troy Donohue and Sandra Dee had been allowed through the white picket fence onto the mean streets of real life.

Like troublesome teenagers, the new group of directors—Francis Ford Coppola, Peter Bogdanovich, Martin Scorsese, Brian De Palma, and Hal Ashby, among others—were known as "the movie brats." They might have bad table manners, but their exam results were excellent. They turned unlikely and antiestablishment films into gold. By taking a chance on whatever seemed smart and fresh, by hiring young directors and writers in a scattershot way and not giving them too much money, the studios felt that the magic of low-budget gold might happen again. That these projects were funded by the establishment itself was an irony that neither the filmmakers nor the studios worried about much. Another irony was that unlike most revolutionaries, who have a contempt for the old guard, some of these ones had an unexpected reverence for it. Bogdanovich loved John Ford and George Stevens, who had made *A Place in the Sun* in 1951; De Palma was obsessed with the formalist movies of Hitchcock. What they wanted was to use the techniques of the brilliant, but establishment, old directors on their own terms and in their own new way.

The tectonic shift that edged the power toward the young filmmakers had begun just before the turn of the decade. In his seminal 1998 book about Hollywood in the 1970s, *Easy Riders, Raging Bulls*, the influential critic Peter Biskind wrote that "the thirteen years between *Bonnie and Clyde* in 1967 and *Heaven's Gate* in 1980 marked the last time it was really exciting to make a movie in Hollywood." He quotes Robert Altman as saying, "The pictures you wanted to make were the ones they wanted to make."

Actually, nobody wanted to make *Bonnie and Clyde*, but the mercurial and forceful twenty-nine-year-old Warren Beatty persuaded Jack Warner to finance it. Beatty had never been in a really successful film, but he was something of a name and the movie was cheap. It could fly under the radar because Warner was overseeing more important projects, the kind of expensive, old-fashioned films he had always made, like the bloated *Camelot* in 1967, which, ironically, *Bonnie and Clyde* and others like it would decimate.

When Beatty showed the finished movie to Warner, he was horrified. It was a blend of farce and brutal killing. It portrayed two petty criminals with unsavory sexual problems who never repented of their crimes and died in a violent shootout that was filmed in excruciating slow motion. The reviews were brutal. The *New York Times* called it "a cheap piece of bald-faced slapstick that treats the hideous depredations of that sleazy, moronic pair as though they were as full of fun and frolic as the jazz-age cut-ups in *Thoroughly Modern Millie*." There was only one critic who disagreed: Pauline Kael in *The New Yorker*. The opening paragraph of her review was an extraordinary rallying cry for a new kind of cinema: "How do you make a good movie in this country without being jumped on? *Bonnie and Clyde* is the most excitingly American American movie. . . ." What she wrote changed everyone's perception of the movie. A week later, something astonishing happened: Joe Morgenstern, the *Newsweek* critic who had initially demolished the movie, printed a retraction, saying that his review had been "grossly unfair and regrettably inaccurate." The film eventually made $70 million on a budget of $2.5 million.

The cinema of the auteur director had been kick-started, but it took some time for the business to recalibrate itself. The studios were heading into alien territory without a map. The traditional American values that had always been applauded in movies were being replaced by something chillingly subversive. However, Hollywood was a quick learner: it soon realized that the subversive could be profitable.

Dennis Hopper and Peter Fonda's *Easy Rider* in 1969 was certainly subversive; it was angry, violent, and antiestablishment. It was also cheap, as most of the early director-led films were, and in Hollywood, there is not much downside to cheap. It was unthinkable that any film with a poster tag line that read "A man went looking for America. And couldn't find it anywhere" could ever reach anything more than a niche audience of radicals. On a budget of $360,000, it grossed more than $60 million and was the third highest earner of the year. It was nominated for two Oscars—a tentative recognition by the reactionary Academy of Motion Pictures Arts and Sciences that it was trying to adjust to a new world.

Of course, traditional movies still continued to be made and were profitable—*Love Story, Airport, The Poseidon Adventure*—but they did not have the prestige and radical chic of the new cinema that produced films like *The Last Picture Show, Taxi Driver,* and *M*A*S*H*. Bizarrely, the studios attempted to make these kinds of movies themselves, but the results tended to be neither as authentic nor as economical. MGM released the expensive *The Strawberry Statement* about the student riots at Columbia, and Universal shoehorned Anthony Quinn as a radical leather-trousered professor on a giant Harley Davidson into their student riot movie, the glibly titled *R.P.M.* They were all flops. Only the new breed of directors and writers seemed to know the secret blend of herbs and spices that made these films work, and they were not telling anyone else.

Ned Tanen, an ambitious executive at Universal, was handed a $5 million fund to produce a slate of cheap—under $1 million—long-shot movies, and he asked Cimino's agent, Michael Gruskoff, to run the production slate, but he opted to take an overall three-picture deal as a producer instead. (He went on to make *Young Frankenstein* with Mel Brooks and Werner Herzog's *Nosferatu the Vampyre*.) It was obvious which demographic Universal were trying to attract: "Producer Mike Gruskoff is . . . on a youth kick. The former agent has three with it pictures in the works: 'The Last Movie,' now being directed in Peru by that guru of the young, Dennis Hopper; 'Conquering Horse,' an Indian drama to be directed this summer by 27-year-old Mike Cimino [in fact, he was thirty]; and 'Running Silent,' a science fiction item to be directed by 27-year-old Douglas Trumbull," reported the *New York Times*.

Cimino had brought Gruskoff the *Conquering Horse* project, based on the 1959 novel by Frederick Manfred. Cimino had not found the project by himself. It was given to him by Thomas McGrath, one of the "whole lot" of writers that Deric Washburn suspected he kept up his sleeve. McGrath was an unlikely collaborator. Some twenty years older than Cimino, he was a poet from North Dakota who had spent time in Hollywood in the '50s, when he had been blacklisted. In an interview he said, "I used to know Mike Cimino quite well. I'd met him in New York before he made any films, and I worked on some things with him—or for him, rather—that were never made." (McGrath's archive at the University of North Dakota contains two other scripts they co-wrote—*Paradise* and *Kef*.)

In 1969, when McGrath went to teach at Minnesota State University, he met Cimino again. "I'd hardly gotten started when Mike came out from L.A. He had spent a winter in Fargo, North Dakota, while I worked on a film that he had an idea about. . . . He was living in a little dump beside the railroad tracks, driving his red Jaguar around, and being arrested very frequently . . . nobody in the Fargo police force believed that anybody out *there* had a red Jaguar and would drive it around in wintertime. I told him about Manfred and this book [*Conquering Horse*] and told him it would make a wonderful film, and so he said yes."

Containing the themes of frontier life and the search for masculinity that Cimino would often return to in his career, it is a rite-of-passage story about a young Sioux who cannot become a man until his spiritual vision comes. When it does, in the form of a glowing white mare, he has to risk his life before he becomes Conquering Horse, chief of the Sioux.

Frederick Manfred's daughter, Freya, now a distinguished poet, told me that she remembered Cimino and Carelli coming to see her father in Minnesota about the project in 1970. "I distinctly remember he came in the door with Joann, and I thought she was so beautiful," she said. "Even when they moved through the room they seemed connected. He reminded us of Napoleon—he was so short compared to everyone in my family [her father was six-nine.] He filled the room."

"He had got to Universal and had got them to put up some money, just by, I suppose, jaw-boning," McGrath said. "So, he came out there and I worked on the script—wrote the script." (Cimino's is the only name on the draft of the script I saw.) "The script, everything, was acceptable, all was fine, until they started budgeting it. . . . It was *far* over what had been projected. . . . There was no reason why it couldn't have been a far less expensive film. There was no need for—you know, *hundreds* of Indians." It was going to cost substantially more than Universal's cut-off figure of $1 million. More than that, Cimino wanted to shoot it in black-and-white, and in the Sioux language with subtitles. They canceled the project. Cimino and McGrath never spoke again. "I couldn't reach Mike, and, I don't know, I might not have been on his list any longer," he said. However, Cimino stayed in touch with Manfred for many years and tried to get the project off the ground for the rest of his life. "My father loved Michael and his work. He thought he was the greatest person he had met for years," Freya Manfred told me.

Ever resourceful, Gruskoff moved Cimino sideways onto another of his projects, the science fiction movie *Running Silent*, which had rearranged its title to *Silent Running*. It was the idea of Douglas Trumbull, who had been the supervisor of the groundbreaking special effects in *2001: A Space Odyssey* in 1968 and had worked with Stanley Kubrick for three years on it. While it might seem like a curious move to get a special-effects designer with no experience with actors to direct, there was the possibility that the fairy dust of Kubrick movie's enormous success might land on almost anyone who had worked on it. (John Barry, the production designer of the first *Star Wars* movie in 1977, was similarly given a movie to direct in 1980, *Saturn 3*, from which he was sacked). Anyway, Trumbull was not going to be directing *Hamlet*—*Silent Running* had only four actors.

"I wanted to make a SF movie to say something about the future that would be very much human and very real," Trumbull said. "I'd like to say that in a hundred years, people aren't going to be very different. They're still going to be sort of funky people." He came up with a storyline to capture his vision. "The evolution of the *Silent Running* idea began with a treatment I wrote which involved a man and some drones on a space freighter in deep space. Some conflict happened and he was totally alone with the drones without human contact as he became contacted by aliens in a very dark and abstract way while he's asleep, and the drones play an important role. It was only a treatment, a very fragmentary idea."

There was not much meat on the bones of that idea, and Gruskoff brought in some writers to come up with a more fully rounded story. Dennis Lynton Clark and Robert Dillon delivered a script in June 1970. They followed Trumbull's outline fairly faithfully but fleshed it out. A space freighter called *Valley Forge*, carrying large geodesic spheres containing trees and plants, is told to return to Earth because the freighters are going to be scrapped. The captain does not want to go back and be told to retire, so he steals the ship. He vanishes into the rings of Saturn so it looks like the ship has been destroyed. After receiving some strange signals, he believes an alien craft is trying to get in touch with him. Meanwhile, a recovery force has realized that his ship is still intact, and they try to retake it. The captain puts a drone into one of the spheres and detaches it from his ship minutes before he is killed. The aliens board the sphere and find the drone. The movie ends with the drone producing a photograph of itself and the captain and handing it to the aliens.

The script had some logical flaws, and Gruskoff gave it to Cimino to come up with a new draft. In the Thomas McGrath archives, there is a copy of the Dillon/Clark script with his notes on it, so Cimino had obviously asked his opinion. In fact, Cimino did not like science fiction very much. In a later interview, he said, "I don't find it interesting. I think the world is far too interesting for us to try and make up a new one. . . . Most people who write science fiction are running away from life."

Still, lukewarm though he was about the subject, he took it on. Its major attraction was that, unlike the other projects he had worked on, this one was definitely going to be made. The spaceship sets were already being constructed inside a disused aircraft carrier moored off Long Beach that was about to be scrapped. In the summer of 1970, he was flown out to work on the script at the Beverly Hills Hotel. He was under no illusions about what it was like working on other people's ideas and other writers' problematic scripts: "It's just a job. It's like changing tires in a racing team."

When he talked about *Silent Running* in later interviews, he never mentioned the fact that he had brought Deric Washburn on board to work on it with him. Michael Gruskoff remembered Cimino being overstretched and telling him he would need to ask another writer to help. Because of Cimino's unreliable narration on almost every aspect of his working life, it is hard to figure out exactly who did what on their rewrite, and Washburn admitted that his own memory of the project was rather hazy: "My recollection is that we didn't work together. I wrote it." Nor, he thought, did Cimino do much tinkering with Washburn's drafts. "He didn't say anything. That was Mike's way. Generally speaking, he wouldn't."

Trumbull remembered many conversations with Washburn: "I have my own particular passions about man's place in the universe. And Deric was very much on the same page. He and I got on very well, and he was probably the largest contributor to the whole environmental aspect of the story." It was that aspect that transformed the movie and helped it become an enduring cult classic. Whether it was Cimino or Washburn who came up with it, *Silent Running* discarded its standard sci-fi story and replaced it with something much more original. The geodesic domes that housed trees and plants were no longer a rather irrelevant plot point; they became the central theme of the movie. Both Environmental Rights Day and Earth Day were first celebrated in 1970, and in one stroke, Cimino and Washburn tapped into a new movement. The movie became countercultural—which was exactly what Universal was aiming for with their low-budget slate.

Lowell, the captain of the ship, was no longer a grumpy veteran who did not want to return to Earth and be forcibly retired. He was now a messianic, deranged ecologist who is guarding and tending the wildlife in the domes so it will endure while the forests and plants on

Earth are dying from pollution. The order to blow up the domes and return home sends him over the brink. He is prepared to do anything to stop it, including killing his three crew members, who have no interest in the wildlife and simply want to get back. He goes through the rings of Saturn in order to escape a pursuing spaceship, but when that ship catches up with him, he goes into one of the domes and ejects it as he blows up his ship. The movie ends with him floating through space in the dome, looking after his plants for eternity.

Cimino and Washburn's script is bleak, uncompromising, and powerful. The last two-thirds of the movie after Lowell kills his crewmates is just him alone on his ship going a little mad. To Gruskoff, this did not seem a very commercial notion, even though he and Trumbull loved the environmental theme. In March 1971, a few months before *Silent Running* began shooting, Warner Bros. released George Lucas's first feature, *THX 1138*, starring Robert Duvall. It was also essentially a lone-man-on-a-spaceship story (except it takes place in an underground dystopian world), and it was a flop. While the majority of Kubrick's *2001: A Space Odyssey* had also involved its lead character floating alone through space, it had been a success because the ravishing and expensive visuals meant that its bleakness did not really matter. The problem *Silent Running* had was that—on a budget that was one-fifteenth of *2001*'s—the effects would be much more basic than the ones Trumbull had designed for Kubrick.

Gruskoff decided that he needed some more tire changing on his racing team, and he brought in yet another writer, Steven Bochco. Bochco was a relatively untested TV writer, but Gruskoff thought he had more of a commercial sensibility—his instincts were proven correct, as Bochco later created *Hill Street Blues*, *L.A. Law*, *NYPD Blue*, and *Doogie Howser, M.D.* Bochco made the story more accessible but less interesting. He kept the crewmates in the movie for longer and turned them into raucous space jocks who race against one another in high-tech golf carts. The three drones who helped run the ship were humanized with names—Huey, Dewey, and Louie—and kept Lowell company after he killed the crew. (Trumbull said that George Lucas asked his permission to use some of their characteristics for R2-D2 and C-3PO in *Star Wars*, but in 1981, Universal instigated and lost ["No one has a monopoly on the use of robots in art"] a copyright infringement case against 20th

Century Fox.) The end was changed so that it was Dewey who was sent off in the dome as Lowell blew up himself and the ship. The last shot was of the cute drone watering the plants accompanied by a maudlin song—"Rejoice in the Sun"—sung by Joan Baez.

Gruskoff tried to get Gene Hackman to play the lead, but the buzz on the upcoming *The French Connection* indicated that he was about to become a big (and therefore expensive) star, so he went for Bruce Dern, a modestly successful client of his when he had been an agent, and gave him his first lead part. After Cimino and Washburn had handed in their script, they had no further involvement. Trumbull said, "I got all these drafts and I liked a lot of the pivotal ideas in them, and I merged them all together into one screenplay, which became the shooting script." The final writing credit was "Screenplay by Deric Washburn, Mike Cimino and Steven Bochco."

When he was a successful and sought-after commercials director, Cimino had at least a limited power to achieve his vision. It was not the same when he was an untried writer working as a hired hand on someone else's movie. He knew that he would need to both write and direct in order to retain some measure of control. To do that, he moved to Hollywood and never returned to the world of commercials.

The lure of Hollywood's honeypot—although there often turned out to be little or no honey in it—had existed since the industry began for writers and directors. Classy writers from the East Coast were welcomed there, usually on the back of a Broadway hit or best-selling novel, like F. Scott Fitzgerald, Lillian Hellman, and Gore Vidal. However, happy though they were to take the money, they generally felt they were slumming it. Joseph Heller never talked about working on the Natalie Wood movie *Sex and the Single Girl* in 1964, nor did Richard Yates, author of *Revolutionary Road*, who co-wrote the screenplay for a schlocky war movie, *The Bridge at Remagen*, in 1969.

For directors, it was different. Making movies in Hollywood was regarded as a more prestigious occupation than hack writing—there was the opportunity to work on a much larger canvas. Cimino's move from making commercials to making feature films sounds like an obvious and easy trajectory. In fact, it was the opposite. Many of the New York filmmakers, including Sidney Lumet and John

Frankenheimer, had worked since the 1950s making live television dramas of extraordinary technical complexity. Some, like Arthur Penn, had also directed successful Broadway plays. These were all viable currencies in Hollywood. Making product plugs in New York, however successful, was not. (In England, it was different: commercials directors like Ridley Scott and Alan Parker both graduated to movies quickly—but then both worlds coexisted and fed off each other in London, rather than being three thousand miles apart, as they were in the US.)

Cimino's decision to move to Los Angeles was a bold one. He gave varying reasons for it. One was in his playboy persona, which as usual did not strike an entirely convincing note: "I had been going to California because I was in the business of shooting commercials, mostly beautiful women and beautiful cars, and I think that's why I took this road. I love cars and I love women, so it was an opportunity to have both." The other reason was Carelli. "She said to me, 'I'm sure you could make a film in Hollywood!' 'What?' I said to her. And then she replied, 'There's only one way for you to direct a movie there. You must write an original script and propose it to the biggest star at the time. Then you may have a chance. . . .'"

The odds were stacked against him. I asked George Parker and Francis Grumman, who were both at the heart of the advertising scene in New York in the 1960s, if they knew of any other commercials directors who had successfully gone to Hollywood to make movies. Both of them said that they presumed there must have been some, but neither could think of any. When Cimino sold his first Hollywood screenplay, *Daily Variety* reported, "Architect Sells Script," presumably because being a commercials director was simply too low-rent.

In 1971, Cimino rented a house in Hidden Hills from the British director J. Lee Thompson. In June of the next year, he bought his home in the hills from Richard Nixon's brother Donald for $145,000. His choice of home was perhaps surprising. He had always grandiose tastes—flashy cars and expensive wines—and with his love of architecture, he might have been tempted to buy a house designed by one of the famous modernist Los Angeles architects like Richard Neutra or Frank Gehry. In fact, the one he chose was relatively modest and unexceptional, at least by the showy standards of the movie business. He lived in it for forty-four years, until his death.

Michael Cimino fitted rather uneasily into the new Hollywood when he arrived in 1971. He was not really a movie brat. Al Ruddy, who produced *The Godfather*, was friendly with him and introduced him around. He told me that he felt Cimino was pressing his nose to the window but somehow could not get in. Frank Yablans, then president of Paramount, felt he was always an outsider. He was neither radical nor chic—a rather awkward figure who found it difficult to join the group of cool new filmmakers like De Palma, Scorsese, and Steven Spielberg who discussed Jean-Luc Godard and John Ford movies. "I didn't go to film school, I didn't come from the scene," Cimino said. "I'd rather talk about paintings or read about Kandinsky," all nonexistent subjects in the repertoire of the movie brats.

However, he had the advantage of now being represented by one of the most powerful agents in Hollywood, Stan Kamen at William Morris. His colleague Lenny Hirshan, who looked after Clint Eastwood and sifted projects for him, suggested Cimino write a script tailored for Eastwood. In six weeks, he came up with *Thunderbolt and Lightfoot*, which was the opposite of an auteur project. It was a heist movie made under the rigid studio system and starred an actor who was far too uncool and establishment for the new directors to bother with.

Eastwood had become one of the most reliable and popular actors since he became famous for the Sergio Leone Westerns *A Fistful of Dollars* and *For a Few Dollars More*, which had set in stone his austere, unsmiling, tough-guy persona from which he would never stray far for the rest of career. He had begun to direct his own movies—*Play Misty for Me* and *The Beguiled*—and never had much trouble getting projects off the ground: he had a reputation for being unfussy, quick, and cheap. Eastwood had just made his most popular movie, directed by his mentor, Don Siegel, *Dirty Harry*, which had touched a nerve with its bad-cop vigilante theme, and he was working on a sequel to be called *Magnum Force*.

Eastwood loved *Thunderbolt and Lightfoot*, but Cimino—with not many cards in his hand—had a very ballsy stipulation: he had to direct the movie. Eastwood, never much of a bullshitter, rather liked his nerve and was powerful enough to follow his whims. Throughout his career, he had a reputation for taking a gamble on new talent, whether they were writers, directors, or cameramen. A source close to Cimino told me that Eastwood had said to him, "I'll give you three days. If it doesn't work, I'll get another director." (On *The Outlaw Josey Wales*, he sacked the writer/director Philip Kaufman two weeks into shooting for taking too long to set up a scene and got another director—himself.)

He was committed to making *Magnum Force* first, but he had a problem with it: the scriptwriter was leaving the project. He had hired John Milius, a writer with a fearsome reputation in the generally liberal movie business because he was known to be a gun-toting, reactionary, wild man who kept a large collection of firearms in his house. Eastwood knew he was the perfect person to write another movie about Inspector "Dirty Harry" Callahan, the gun-toting, reactionary, wild-man cop. Milius was often brought in to beef up a script and had done a little rewriting on the first movie (he had come up with the famous line, "You've got to ask yourself one question: 'Do I feel lucky?' Well, do you, punk?) as well as being brought in by Spielberg to write Quint's famous *Indianapolis* shark massacre monologue in *Jaws*. However, after writing sixty pages of the *Magnum Force* script, he was offered the chance to direct one of his own projects, *Dillinger*, about the famous Depression-era gangster. Eastwood, always generous to people he liked, let him go. As usual, he acted quickly and on impulse. He thought Cimino was talented, he liked him, and he was available to take over writing *Magnum Force*.

"At first I said no. I didn't feel used to the genre. But they were very persuasive," Cimino said. It was really Carelli who was the persuasive one. She told me that when he didn't want to do it, she told him he must be crazy. Whatever Cimino felt about the project, he completed it professionally and quickly. Milius, of course, did not like it much: "Of all the films I had anything to do with, I like it least. They changed a lot of things in a cheap and distasteful manner. The whole ending is wrong, it wasn't mine at all." Nonetheless, it became the sixth-highest-grossing movie of 1974. As soon as it finished shooting, the prolific Eastwood went straight into production with Cimino's movie.

The script of *Thunderbolt and Lightfoot* has an arresting start that for a moment subverts the traditional Eastwood persona: he is in a dog

Cimino, Clint Eastwood, and George Kennedy on set (Getty)

collar, giving a fire-and-brimstone sermon in a church, when someone bursts in firing a machine gun. Eastwood is "The Thunderbolt," a legendary bank robber who is being pursued by his former friends, Leary and Eddie, who believe he double-crossed them over money that they all stole. On the run, Thunderbolt is rescued by a young and not-too-bright drifter called Lightfoot, to whom he becomes a reluctant mentor.

Eventually, Leary and Eddie catch up with them. When they realize that Thunderbolt did not cheat them, they decide to do another bank heist. Using Thunderbolt's favorite weapon—an antitank cannon—they pull it off, but Leary steals the money and beats up Lightfoot, kicking him so violently in the head that he eventually dies. The movie ends with Thunderbolt driving off with the dead Lightfoot beside him.

Of all the films that Cimino wrote and directed, *Thunderbolt and Lightfoot* is the one most like an orphan. It is different from his others in style and tone, and it seems the least likely kind of project for him. Of course, it was written specifically for Eastwood, which implies some measure of cynicism, but actually, Cimino was the least cynical of directors. However, the script reads like an efficient but not very original genre piece, patching together bits of other movies—the double crosses, the bank job, the meet-cute of two mismatched characters. It has a perverse kind of *Dukes of Hazzard* vibe with its cornpone characters and on-the-nose, salty vernacular: "Hell, Reverend, I didn't see your ass-backward collar before. I thought you were heat." "We go in as a team, not a busted-up set of tomcats, trying to claw one another's eyes out." The women they run into are all feisty broads in skimpy outfits who are only too happy to hit the sack with the boys. The script is like a pastiche of a genre movie, the kind that Hollywood had been returning to since movies began.

For one of the few times in Cimino's directing life, there was little interference from the producer. Eastwood was running the show ("I'm working with a twelve-year-old kid," Cimino reported him saying), but he respected Cimino and did not try to rein him in creatively. However, the crew was mostly chosen by Eastwood—his usual producer, cameraman, editor, production designer, and stunt arranger. None of them had much more than workmanlike credits, but Eastwood was always smart enough to find people who were both cheap and talented. Cimino was impressed enough by his choices to use many of them again—particularly Tambi Larsen, who was responsible for *Heaven's Gate*'s breathtaking production design.

The movie shot in Montana from July to September, with a schedule of forty-seven days and a tight but not unfeasible budget of $4 million. Jeff Bridges played Lightfoot, and George Kennedy was Leary. Bridges, in spite of being nominated for a supporting actor Oscar in *The Last Picture Show* two years before, did not yet have much confidence, but Cimino had learned early how to make actors feel good: "Mike looked at me and said, 'You know that game tag?' 'Yeah,' I said. 'Well . . . You're it,' Mike told me. He went on to say that this guy, Lightfoot, was no one other than me, that I couldn't make a mistake, or a false move, even if I wanted to," Bridges remembered.

Cimino was careful to make Eastwood happy by keeping things moving as quickly as possible. "I knew that the only way I could keep control of the movie was to be ahead of schedule," he said. There were a few instances when Eastwood felt Cimino had done enough takes ("It's good, let's go."), but, happy with how it was going, he generally let him do it his way. More deferential than he would ever be again, Cimino reported that "I would go to Clint every day and say, 'Hey, boss, you happy with the dailies?' He said, 'Michael, you just keep shooting what you're shooting.'" Cimino would later say that it was the best experience he ever had: "My partner, Joann Carelli, said, 'You better enjoy this, because it's never going to be like this again.' Boy, was she right. It never has been."

The movie was edited quickly, with no fuss. Eastwood's movies never depended much on reviews, but *Thunderbolt and Lightfoot*'s were reasonably good. However, although it made money, there was a feeling that, being a little different from Eastwood's usual movies—his tough-guy persona had softened to the point of geniality—it might have alienated his core audience. Now it is generally regarded as one of Eastwood's most interesting movies. In a large measure, that is because Cimino did something miraculous—he had transformed his derivative script into something funny, powerful, and moving.

Although he follows the screenplay closely, the movie feels quite different. The dialogue that had seemed like pastiche now feels authentic; the predictable storyline becomes quirky and fresh. The relationship between Eastwood and Bridges is very touching—Richard Brody of *The New Yorker* called it a proto-bromance. Cimino brings to the surface their inarticulate but deep bond, so deep a bond for Peter Biskind that he wrote a brilliant deconstruction of the movie called "Tightass and Cocksucker"—probably the first and last time that anyone found subtext in an Eastwood movie. When Lightfoot dies in Thunderbolt's arms in the final scene, it is as haunting as Ratso's death at the end of *Midnight Cowboy*. In the script, a tear comes down Thunderbolt's cheek. In the movie, Eastwood simply pulls his sunglasses down over his eyes and drives away.

The problem for Cimino was that, although the movie was well-reviewed and reasonably successful, it was the least respectable kind of piece—a genre movie—and although he was the writer as well as the director, it was regarded as a Clint Eastwood movie. "This put my ego out of joint a little bit," he later said. More than that, it did not open any particular doors for Cimino—few of the other directors Eastwood worked with ever had much of a feature film career afterward.

Cimino never liked to seem in a weak position and sometimes put an upbeat swing on this period—"I got a lot of offers"—but in unguarded moments, he would be more honest: "It was four years after *Thunderbolt and Lightfoot* and . . . people just forget who you are. Four years and all that work, and nothing. I had the terrible feeling that I had let everything slip by."

In the absence of any directorial offers he wanted, Cimino went back to being a writer for hire, a highly sought-after but menial position, and one in which he never felt very secure. His two earlier passion projects, the script he wrote for Michael Gruskoff, *Conquering Horse*, and *The Johnson County War*, an early version of *Heaven's Gate*, were both unfashionable Westerns and not easy sells—passion is not always contagious in Hollywood, however successful you are. Work-for-hire projects seemed easier—after all, they are the ones that the studios are already enthusiastic about—but soon, like so many others, Cimino found himself in the most overpopulated waiting room in Hollywood: development hell, a place that exists because of the uncertain and mercurial nature of the movie business. The studios' inability to make decisions, the exiting executives and the incoming ones who cancel their predecessors' projects, the casual sacking of writers, the unpredictable flickering green light—all conspire to create a Hollywood version of the myth of Sisyphus: projects are laboriously pushed up the hill only to roll down again.

The project he most wanted to make was Ayn Rand's 1943 cult bestseller *The Fountainhead*, which had sold over a million copies. Cimino had loved the book for years—he had given it to David Freeman, his Yale classmate in the early 1960s. United Artists owned the rights (an earlier 1949 movie starring Gary Cooper and Patricia Neal had flopped), and they commissioned Cimino to write it. His passion for the book is easy to understand. It is about a visionary architect called Howard Roark who nobody will hire because he is so uncompromising. At the end, he blows up one of his buildings because the design has been changed. Cimino was quite happy to let people see the parallels between a visionary architect and a visionary filmmaker: "In architecture, you're not looking at an abstract creation of concrete and steel but at the realization of a man's spirit. The building itself is completely expressive of who you are, just like a movie or something you make."

The book manages to be overblown, trite, and powerful at the same time, particularly in its description of the volcanic, larger-than-life relationship between Roark and Dominique Francon, the only person he considers his equal. Their passion for each other is hysterically operatic and extravagantly sexual. Steven Bach, the United Artists executive who later supervised *Heaven's Gate*, noted with some relief when he met Joann Carelli that "she in no way resembled Dominique Francon." *The Fountainhead* was out of step with the kind of movies the studio was trying to make, and it would also be eye-wateringly expensive. The project, like so many others, slowly evaporated.

Statements that Cimino made about the scripts he worked on at this time all come straight out of the lexicon of Hollywood despair, statements that could have been made—and often were—by writers and directors from William Faulkner to F. Scott Fitzgerald to Orson Welles: "There was a corporate scuffle at 20th Century Fox"; "Because of various political machinations at the studio, the project fell through"; "The movie was three weeks into preproduction and was canceled"; "The studio was going through management changes and the script was put aside."

He worked at Paramount on a project called *Perfect Strangers*, which was aborted after eighteen months' work. A script he wrote with James Toback for 20th Century Fox about the life of the mobster Frank Costello was never given the green light either. He did a rewrite for United Artists of Frederick Forsyth's *The Dogs of War*, to be directed by Norman Jewison, who eventually left the project.

In 1976, Fox hired him to write *Pearl*, the story of Janis Joplin. He was working alongside a writer he respected (not often the case), Bo Goldman, who had written the screenplay for *One Flew Over the Cuckoo's Nest*, but soon another writer, Bill Kerby, was brought on board for an additional draft (in Hollywood, a process variously described as a nip and tuck, tightening and brightening, or a wash and rinse, as if soothing terms will camouflage the brutality of being sacked from your own project). The project foundered when Fox found they could not get the rights to Joplin's songs. Eventually, without many changes other than the character names and different songs, it became a movie about a Janis Joplin type called *The Rose*, produced in 1979 and starring Bette Midler.

For writers, even the projects that do get made can be humiliating experiences. On the eventual movie, there is no credit for Cimino, even though the original script I read is almost identical to the final movie in terms of scenes and dialogue. Only Goldman and Kerby are listed, but the credit process in Hollywood is notoriously unpredictable, and many people have run up against the Writers Guild's arbitration system. Credits were always a fraught issue for Cimino, and there would be lacerating rows about them on four out of his next six films. He deserved a credit on *The Rose*. On the later films, it was much less clear-cut.

In 1976, at the same time he was working on *The Rose*, there was another project he was writing for Paramount that he was also going to direct, and it was the one that came closest to production—ironic, because it is his least interesting script. Called *Head of the Dragon*, it was set in that place beloved by writers—a mythical South American country. It could hardly be more generic. The US government is secretly supporting a corrupt regime against the rebel leader, and the CIA fixer is a glamorous, polo-playing Wasp whose grandfather was president of the United States and whose brother-in-law is secretary of state. He springs a Mafia killer from jail in order to kill the rebel leader, and it ends with a mano-a-mano fight on polo ponies, using mallets as lethal weapons. It was Cimino's desperate attempt to come up with something commercial that might stand a good chance of being made—just as he had with *Thunderbolt and Lightfoot*—but his strengths never really leaned toward the obviously commercial.

In the summer of that year, Herman Blumenthal, the production designer, and his team made several trips to the Dominican Republic, scouting locations and planning set construction, sending back detailed reports to Cimino for his approval. But by September, the project had fallen to pieces, almost certainly because of the horrendous location problems on another movie Paramount was shooting in that country—William Friedkin's *Sorcerer*, the budget of which escalated from $15 million to $22 million.

After a string of disappointments—none of his scripts put into production and few offers to direct—his luck suddenly changed. A month after *Head of the Dragon* was canceled, Cimino took a routine meeting that seemed as if it would be another dead end. However, with a mixture of luck, ambition, aggression, and bloodletting, it put him on a tortuous path to a project that did get made—his epic Vietnam movie, *The Deer Hunter*.

PART II

1976–1981

CHAPTER 5

STALKING THE DEER HUNTER

ON DECEMBER 8, 1978, the day *The Deer Hunter* opened in Los Angeles at the Avco Embassy Cinema on Wilshire Boulevard, Michael Cimino took his editorial assistant Penny Shaw, who had worked with him on the movie and would do so again on *Heaven's Gate*, to the first public screening. Apart from Joann Carelli, Cimino trusted almost no one, but he had grown to both trust and respect Penny, the daughter of the British actor Robert Shaw, who had starred in *The Sting* and *Jaws*. Together they had endured the long, arduous, and fractious process of editing the movie into a shape that would satisfy both the producers and Cimino, who had been diametrically opposed as to the running time of the film.

In truth, of course, Cimino was interested only in satisfying himself, and by a variety of wily and surreptitious power plays, he had managed to get the movie released at his chosen length of 183 minutes, punishingly long for a downbeat movie set in Vietnam. Whatever ticket *The Deer Hunter* was traveling on, it was not a feel-good one, and everyone, not least Cimino, was nervous.

But something unexpected happened outside the theater. "People were just driving up in cars, just a line of cars," Cimino said. "And someone would run out and buy twelve tickets. And someone would run out and buy twenty tickets. This kept going and going and going and going. And then we had the screening, and Penny came running up to me and said, 'You've got to come quick to the lobby.' I said, 'What's wrong?' The ladies' room was filled with women who were weeping and wailing, and I just broke down crying. There were ex-vets who literally crawled up the aisle out of their seats. It was just an astounding reaction."

The screening could have gone either way. The movie had never seemed a sure bet, and it was a tribute to its British producers, Michael Deeley and Barry Spikings, whose London-based EMI Films was trying to break into the US market, that they had been prepared to finance 50 percent (they persuaded Universal to put in the other 50 percent) of what was going to be an expensive and hard-to-market project from a relatively inexperienced director about an unpopular war.

The Second World War was a much more popular one, and during the 1960s and '70s, Hollywood continued to produce a startling number of movies about it. The difference between the two wars was that the earlier one had good guys and bad guys who were clearly delineated. The Vietnam War was altogether more opaque, and the five or so movies that were brave enough (at least by Hollywood standards) to dip their toes into it had varying agendas.

Only one of them was released during the war itself: *The Green Berets*, which John Wayne both starred in and directed in 1968, the halfway point of US involvement. It is unflinchingly on-message—or at least Wayne's version of the message. The US Army is loosely portrayed as humanitarian—warm blankets, medical supplies, and a steady supply of tea and sympathy—while the Vietcong are all vicious killers. At the end of the movie, the cute Vietnamese urchin Wayne has befriended asks what will happen now. "You let me worry about that, Green Beret," Wayne says. "You're what this thing is all about." It was a huge success.

Although there were a few movies about the troubled lives of returning Vietnam vets—notably Travis Bickle in Martin Scorsese's *Taxi Driver*—it would be a decade before the Vietnam War itself was examined in dramatic terms again. Some four years had passed since the US Army pulled out, and there was some presumed "perspective" in play by then. In 1978, four movies about the war tumbled out in quick succession, *The Deer Hunter* among them. Sidney Furie's *The*

Boys in Company C followed young soldiers from induction to tour of duty. The tag line on the poster read "You'll never forget the Boys in Company C" which might be because they are all so recognizable from a host of other war movies. The dialogue, characters, and situations are so familiar that the film might just as well have been set in Germany in 1940.

Go Tell the Spartans was more interesting and took an unashamedly antiwar stance. It starred Burt Lancaster as a war-weary major ordered to defend some South Vietnamese villages with a team of misfit soldiers at various stages of disillusion about the war. Though well-reviewed by the liberal press, it had a limited release and was the least financially successful of all the Vietnam movies.

Coming Home, a passion project from the militant and antiwar Jane Fonda directed by Hal Ashby, was the only one of the movies, apart from *The Deer Hunter*, to achieve any kind of notoriety. Although its poster tag line—"A man who believed in war! A man who believed in nothing! And a woman who believed in both of them!'—suggested a more old-fashioned and conventional movie, it was more subversive than it looked. Jane Fonda plays a dutiful military wife married to a gung-ho captain in the Marine Corps. When he leaves for Vietnam, she begins working in a veterans' hospital and, through her relationship with a radical group of women, changes her views on the war and falls in love with a paraplegic soldier.

There was a sixth Vietnam project that did not end up being realized in the way it was originally intended. In 1974, before Barry Spikings and Michael Deeley got EMI America up and running, they had purchased a curious script called *The Man Who Came to Play*, written by an unlikely pair of writers named Quinn Redeker and Louis Garfinkle, for $19,000. Garfinkle had written a few obscure movies (*I Bury the Living* and *A Minute to Pray, a Second to Die*), and his partner was a handsome actor who had had a reasonably successful career. In a startling piece of actors' versatility, Redeker had played recurring characters in television's two most successful soaps, *The Young and the Restless* and *Days of Our Lives*, one straight after the other.

Everybody—stars, directors, and studios—to whom Deeley and Spikings offered the script turned it down. Maybe that was not surprising:

it was very quirky indeed. It followed two soldiers, Merle and Keys, who make their money by playing rigged games of Russian roulette in Vietnam. Keys fakes his death, and when Merle finally tracks him down, he has become—in an unlikely plot development—successful in the mobile home business. They go into partnership again, resume Russian roulette, and end up playing an unrigged game against each other.

If you happen to be looking for a lighthearted Russian roulette movie, this one will do nicely. It has the tone of a larky buddy movie like *Butch Cassidy and the Sundance Kid*. At the start of the games, Merle behaves like a fairground barker, shouting, *"Puhlllllace your bets!"* People have their heads blown off, but Merle and Keys romp around bickering with each other. The geographical setting of these antics did not seem of enormous importance to Garfinkle and Redeker—earlier drafts had taken place anywhere from the Bahamas to South Dakota—but Vietnam was decided on as the final setting. This was more of a plot point than a political statement, but in order to give the script some local color, they added some astonishingly racist touches. The Vietnamese are described as "very primitive" with "bones in their hair," as if they are spear-carrying natives from an old *Tarzan* movie.

All in all, it was an unlikely project, and it was their kind of British devil-may-care attitude that made Deeley and Spikings continue to hawk it around after so much rejection. As Deeley said, "I intended to stay the course."

THE MEETING THAT Cimino took after the disappointment of *Head of the Dragon* was organized by his powerful agent, Stan Kamen. In Hollywood, meetings do not necessarily indicate a strong desire to meet. They are more of an animal sniff-around, a nervousness about missing out, a desire to see who is hot and may be snapped up by some other studio. Ideas are floated, cards are marked. "We'll get back to you" is not a statement to be relied upon. The status of the writer or director is indicated by the importance of the studio or production company and where the person who has requested the meeting sits in the hierarchy.

Cimino's meeting was with someone of reassuringly high status. Marion Rosenberg was a savvy and street-smart British producer who had worked in the US for a number of years. Deeley and Spikings had hired her to run EMI America while they traveled back and forth across the Atlantic, but in terms of studio importance, it was not Paramount or Universal; it was a small British company trying to become a player in the US—never an easy thing to do. However, they seemed to have access to money, and two of their movies were set to go into production in 1977, Sam Peckinpah's *Convoy* and a Ryan O'Neal thriller called *The Driver*. They had the money for a third project, but for tax reasons it had to begin shooting within the next few months, and they had found nothing that they liked apart from *The Man Who Came to Play*, which everyone else disliked.

In Cimino's later account of the meeting with Rosenberg, he disingenuously said that he mentioned a "notion" he had to her. In fact, it was more than a notion—it was a fully formed story that took him an hour to tell. It was called *The Deer Hunter* and began with the last few days of three blue-collar steelworkers in Pennsylvania before they go to Vietnam in 1968—Michael, Steven, and Nick. All of them are from Russian Orthodox immigrant families and are an integral part of their close-knit community. The day after Steven gets married, they go on a final deer-hunting trip, which is something that has always been their bond. Then they leave for Vietnam.

The three of them are taken prisoner and forced to play Russian roulette by their Vietcong captors. Although they survive, Steven is almost destroyed by the experience. They manage to escape, but then get split up. In Saigon, Nick finds Michael in a secret roulette club, where he is gambling for his life, but before he can get to him, Michael vanishes.

Nick returns home and discovers that Steven is still alive in a veterans' hospital but has lost both his legs. He goes to see him, and Steven tells him that he receives regular amounts of money from abroad. Nick guesses the money must come from Michael, and he goes back to Saigon. He finds Michael in a crowded club where he is again playing Russian roulette, but he seems to have no recollection of Nick. They end up pitted against each other and go through a few rounds of roulette until Michael recognizes him. Then he raises the gun to his head and shoots himself. Back in Pennsylvania, all the friends gather to mourn Michael. Spontaneously, they begin to sing "God Bless America."

Cimino said he was amazed by the reaction: "I still don't know what happened. They said, 'OK. Do it.' I said, 'What do you mean, do it?' They said, 'Do it.' I asked, 'When?' They said, 'Forthwith.' There was no 'We'll get back to you.'" This might be the only time that the word "forthwith" has been used in a Hollywood meeting, and is certainly the quickest sell in the history of movies. However, as Rosenberg told me, it was not a totally accurate account of the meeting, but it played into the myth that Cimino created about himself: that he was a prodigy, that as a five-year-old boy he could draw a perfect circle "like Michelangelo." His brilliant, off-the-cuff pitch for *The Deer Hunter* was the movie equivalent of that. The difference between his story and the truth was that, in this case, he had traced the circle rather than drawn it.

Nobody ever really retires in Hollywood. Marion Rosenberg is in her late seventies and still juggling projects (sharing an office with Jay Kanter—once Marlon Brando's agent—doing the same at ninety-four) and when I met her, she remembered every detail of her bumpy ride with Cimino, especially the way he spun the truth in his favor. She told me a crucial detail he left out of his later account of the meeting: he had already read the script for Redeker and Garfinkle's *The Man Who Came to Play*.

Still trying to breathe life into the project, Rosenberg had sent it to Cimino's agent to see if his promising client might be interested in directing it. Cimino discussed it with Joann Carelli, who told me that they both thought it was the worst script they had ever read. Then, Rosenberg said, he came in a week later for the meeting and told her that he did not want to direct that movie. What he wanted was to write and direct a different movie, one that would jettison everything from the old script except the Russian roulette. Then he gave her his pitch.

Though Rosenberg thought it was brilliant, the go-ahead did not happen as instantly as Cimino described: she had to get her bosses on board. However, it turned out that Deeley and Spikings loved it, too, and they quickly decided it should be the third film on their slate, but they needed it to start shooting by March 1977, not much more than four months away. It would be an impossibly short preproduction period, but Cimino was up for that. He said later that "all the frustrations of the previous four years, all the energy, everything, came together in *The Deer*

Hunter. Nothing was going to stop this. I drove people. I drove myself. The thought of not putting this together, of failing, made me crazy." He was going to make it happen: this project was going to be rolled up the hill and it was not going to roll back down, but the process set in motion an astonishing series of betrayals.

Cimino, despite ignoring the existence of the original script in his later telling, had by some alchemical process transformed the story in an extraordinary way, turning it from ugly duckling into swan, but more importantly for EMI, from base metal into eventual Oscar gold. And he had put it together in a week. Cimino's idea had no tonal similarities to *The Man Who Came to Play*. The characters, situations, and dialogue could not be more different, and in fact became infinitely more ambiguous and frightening.

Where, precisely, his story for the movie came from was unclear at that point. Later there was a plagiarism suit against EMI and Cimino. A writer named Harry Klekas alleged, in a lawsuit that was eventually dismissed, that they had been inspired by an unproduced screenplay of his from 1970 called *The Fields of Discontent*, about Vietnam vets who go deer hunting. Despite the lawsuit's dismissal, Rosenberg, bitter after her experience with Cimino, told me that she would bet on her life that "Cimino read that story at one time or another. There is no way he could have concocted *The Deer Hunter* story in such a short period of time without some frame of reference."

She was right when she said that there was no way Cimino could have come up with the story so quickly, but it was not because he had plagiarized someone else's script. In the short period between reading the Garfinkle/Redeker script and going in to see Rosenberg at EMI with the fully formed movie in his head, he had enlisted some secret help that he neglected to mention to her: he had called Deric Washburn in New York to work on the story with him. They had collaborated amicably on *Silent Running* in 1970 and had been sort-of friends (Cimino's preferred kind) since the mid-'60s. According to Washburn, they had had no contact after Cimino moved to Los Angeles in 1971. Washburn's writing career had not gained much momentum after the movie they wrote together, and he had gone back to his day job as a carpenter. Cimino sent him *The Man Who Came to Play*, and initially they threw around ideas on the telephone—what screenwriters call "spitballing." It was a good way of working for them: "He's thinking what I'm thinking, and vice versa," Washburn told me. "It was real chemistry. Extraordinary."

Cimino always maintained that everything he wrote came from his own personal experience. He said that even *Thunderbolt and Lightfoot*, his genre piece about a bank robbery in the Midwest, came from inside himself, "although it masquerades more easily as a less personal work." He could not allow *The Deer Hunter* to masquerade as anything other than intensely personal, and he carefully laid the foundations of his ownership.

The deer-hunting trip was like one he had done himself when younger, he said. He had been the best man at a wedding that "was very similar to the one in the film." When he was doing "industrials and documentaries," he went to Pennsylvania for U.S. Steel. The "God Bless America" ending, which later caused so much controversy, was inspired by an evening Cimino claimed he had in a Pittsburgh restaurant: "I don't know what provoked it, but suddenly everybody began singing 'God Bless America.' I used it because in a moment like that, people can find a certain degree of solace from making a communal sound." Most controversially, he said that he had served as a medic attached to a Green Beret unit—a claim that would come back to haunt him when the film was released.

Some of these may have been true. He had been the best man at the wedding of a Russian Orthodox friend called Nikanor Chebotarev-ich (Nick, the Christopher Walken character, was named after him). Did he actually go deer hunting? It seems somewhat unlikely that a middle-class kid from the Long Island suburbs would do so, but it's not impossible. He may have been to the steel mills, but nobody remembers him shooting "industrials and documentaries" there. However, it sounded more respectable than shooting commercials.

"Most of the things in the film come from me," Cimino said. The things that did not come from him, although he never acknowledged it, came from Deric Washburn. I drove up to Ojai, eighty miles from Los Angeles in distance, but also on another planet, where Washburn lives a reclusive life with his dog, Zeus. He left the movie business many years ago. Despite the success of *The Deer Hunter*, his screenwriting career afterward was patchy; he was credited on only two movies, both of which were rewritten by others.

Washburn's recollection is radically different from Cimino's: "The deer hunter concept came because I was building a house up in the Berkshires. . . . I suddenly had this scary feeling somebody is watching me and I realized it's a guy sitting on a log in full camo outfit with a fucking gun. He told me that he couldn't afford sneakers for his kids and stuff. Anyhow, I just cried this to Mike on the telephone. The concept of the steel mills came up because I remember talking about Pittsburgh in the wintertime, how beautiful it was with this gray, black, disgusting white snow all over the place."

I asked Washburn where the idea of "God Bless America" originated. "That was me," he said. "I can remember being shocked when the idea came into my head. I remember sitting in the room thinking, 'Oh my God, do I dare to do this?' " He said that Cimino went for it instantly, and Washburn loved his decisiveness: "If you pulled it out on twenty other directors, they would have been, 'I don't know. I don't know. I don't know.' He was completely brave that way."

AFTER DEELEY AND Spikings had given the go-ahead, they had to confront their big problem: shooting had to start in less than four months, there was no script, Cimino would have to immediately go out on the road to find the complicated locations they needed, and no actors had been cast. All the participants remember what happened after this point in different ways, a kaleidoscope of stories that sometimes interlock and sometimes contradict. Of course, it was forty years ago and memories are faulty, but there are also axes to grind because everyone subsequently fell out with one another: Cimino and Washburn, Rosenberg and Cimino, Cimino and Deeley, Rosenberg and Spikings and Deeley, and Spikings and Deeley themselves, who later broke up their partnership.

Rosenberg remembered that Cimino came up with an idea of how to solve the time problem: as if he had just thought of it, he suggested bringing in a writer he trusted called Deric Washburn to write the script under his supervision. Deeley, however, remembered that Cimino said he was going to write the script himself, and without telling anyone, surreptitiously brought in Washburn. His memory on this issue was faulty:

on December 6, 1977, little more than two weeks after Cimino's pitch to Rosenberg, a contract between Washburn and EMI was agreed for him to do a revision of "an existing screenplay" in four weeks, even though no screenplay—only the treatment—existed. It was hard to argue that the Redeker/Garfinkle script was the "existing" one because the Russian roulette idea was the only element that was lifted from it. Washburn was paid $10,000, a bargain-basement price even for a relatively untried screenwriter—the Writers Guild minimum for a rewrite (and this was not really a rewrite) was more than double that at that time.

Deeley recalled something else that was surprising: Cimino was adamant that he would not use the Russian roulette element from the earlier script and that it was only with great difficulty that Deeley persuaded him that it should stay in. Rosenberg refuted this: she was the first person to whom Cimino pitched his vision for the film, and Russian roulette was already an integral part. Anyway, why would Cimino want to jettison the one original thing in the old script?

But any film that is nominated for nine Oscars and wins five will set in motion a feeding frenzy of argument about how it was created and who helped it along its way most. Deeley, in saying that he persuaded Cimino not to throw out the most famous element of the film, put himself in prime position as a crucial participant. Rosenberg, instrumental in the instigation of the project, was not mentioned in Deeley's autobiography at all.

At the beginning of December, Cimino flew Washburn out to Los Angeles, and, ensconced in the Sunset Marquis hotel, they fleshed out the story and characters of the film. Then Cimino left him alone to write the script while he went on a search for locations with Rosenberg, by then the film's associate producer. Cimino later said, "I called him [Washburn] every single night from the road, from Ohio, from the steel towns, from Chicago. I was calling the dialogue into him every night." Washburn remembered Cimino calling him only occasionally. "At the end of every day," Washburn told me, "one of Mike's assistants, or sometimes Joann, would come in to take the day's pages and they were gone. I didn't have any copies." Carelli was now deeply involved in the film, although her precise role was not defined and never really would be. One of her eventual credits was as "Production Consultant," which can mean almost anything.

In the meantime, Cimino's road trip with Rosenberg, who he would later describe as his "location assistant," was not going well. At the start of the project, he had been easy to deal with. "He was a sweet little lamb," Deeley said. "Never would he have a confrontation face-to-face." Now he had changed. Carelli told me that she had once given Cimino a piece of advice: he should go into a meeting and ask for ten things and come out with the four he really wanted. Now he wanted to come out with no less than all ten things. Looking for the steel town where the film starts, he found eight places in four states that had elements that he wanted to incorporate into his single fictional town, Clairton. He insisted on using all of them. He wanted to shoot the deer-hunting scenes in the mountains of Washington State, way across the country. There was only one Russian Orthodox church that Cimino was prepared to use for the elaborate wedding sequence—one that would be the cause of vicious disagreements during production and afterward—and it happened to be in Cleveland.

One of the central conflicts of the movie business is that the studio wants a director with a vision and then complains about how costly that vision is. Rosenberg and Deeley were not happy about the difficult and expensive logistic problems Cimino's demands would cause, even though splitting locations is not an uncommon practice—on *Jaws*, the difficult shark sequences were divided between Martha's Vineyard and Florida. But, as often happened with Cimino, his ideas were pricey but brilliant. However complicated it was to merge the towns into one, Cimino's cherry-picking of the parts he wanted created a rich and detailed setting that rooted his characters organically in a specific place and community.

By now, the cost of the location trip was well over the budget that EMI had agreed. Rosenberg told me that she sensed trouble early on when Cimino ordered a $350 bottle of wine while they were having dinner. He told her that "they"—EMI—would pay. Later, Rosenberg said, Cimino told her he was buying Robert De Niro an expensive hunting jacket on the budget, but the next day he was wearing it himself.

Cimino wanted to use archival news material in the movie, as well as to show it to the cast and crew so they would get some idea of the reality of the Vietnam War. Rosenberg told me that she went to New York to sort out the footage (she reacted furiously when I told her that Cimino said that this was one of Carelli's major contributions). Much of it was in poor condition, and Rosenberg knew that they would have to expensively restore the parts of the footage they wanted to use, but Cimino demanded that every bit of film (according to him, three million feet) should be cleaned up whether they used it or not. When she objected, Deeley overruled her. Rosenberg would not be the first executive that Cimino rendered powerless.

Thom Mount, the young president of Universal that was co-funding the movie, quickly became involved in the problems. One of the most urbane and civilized figures in Hollywood, Mount talked to me in the unlikely location of the coffee shop at an out-of-the-way Whole Foods, with his little dog's leash tied to the table leg. *The Deer Hunter* was an early baptism by fire for him. He told me that he had heard Cimino was being "difficult" and arranged to talk to him on the phone—a call that had to go through Joann Carelli first. Mount realized quickly that Cimino was running the show. He felt that Deeley and Spikings were not strong enough producers to be able to handle him, and he called their boss, Lord Lew Grade, the chairman of EMI, to ask that they be replaced. Grade, financing 50 percent of the movie, refused.

By January 1977, Cimino was back in Los Angeles. On the twenty-eighth, Washburn delivered the script he had started on December 6. It was credited as "An original screenplay by Michael Cimino and Deric Washburn," presumably an act of courtesy by Washburn, who never denied Cimino's contributions. A few days later, Cimino and Carelli invited Washburn to dinner at "a cheap restaurant off the Sunset Strip." Not for the first time in meetings they took together, Carelli did the talking, and according to Washburn, she said something extraordinarily brutal, even by the standards of Hollywood, where the sacking of writers is regarded as inconsequential collateral damage: "Well, Deric, it's fuck-off time." (She flatly denied to me that his sacking happened that way.)

In *One Shot*, his comprehensive book about the making of *The Deer Hunter*, Jay Glennie takes the view that no formal sacking was needed—Washburn was always going to leave the project because his contract only stipulated four weeks' work, That is not how Washburn remembers it. Specifying a time period in a writer's contract is simply to establish a delivery date (as it turned out, Washburn was a not-unreasonable two weeks late). After a script is handed in, the studio has a contractual option to commission further drafts (movies almost never go into production without many of them), but the writer may be sacked off the project if the first draft is deemed unacceptable, as Cimino and Carelli always fiercely maintained Washburn's script was.

Whatever happened, the one thing that is not in question is that Washburn was off the picture. He returned to New York and, once again, resumed his carpentry job. He never spoke to Cimino or Carelli again. The row over who had written what simmered on for many years. Each side took up their position, Cimino's the cruelest: "I could not believe what I read. It was written by someone who was mentally deranged. He was totally stoned on scotch, out of his frigging mind. He started crying and screaming and yelling, 'I can't take the pressure, I can't take the pressure!' He was like a big baby." Washburn said, "It's all nonsense. It's lies. I didn't have a single drink the entire time I was working on the script." Anyway, if Cimino had dictated the script to Washburn from the location trip, as he said, why did he find it so terrible when he and Carelli first read it?

Cimino said he completely rewrote the Washburn script in six weeks while he was on the road, but it's hard to imagine how there would have been time. He and Rosenberg left for their long location trip—in a typical Cimino exaggeration, he said they traveled 150,000 miles—in mid-December. Washburn could not have delivered a script that he had only been contracted to start on December 6 in time for Cimino to have rewritten it by the end of January. More than that, there is the credit on it: "An original screenplay by Michael Cimino and Deric Washburn." If Cimino, always a compulsive credit-grabber, had rewritten the script himself, he would never have put Washburn's name on it, just as he did not put Thomas McGrath's name on the script of *Conquering Horse*.

In the mid 1970s, the writer/director, James Toback had written a script for Cimino —*The Life and Dreams of Frank Costello*—and was upset that Cimino was "passing [it] around with his name on it, and I don't understand why he's doing it, because we're friends." Even on his rewrite of the Dirty Harry sequel *Magnum Force*, he put only his name on the title page, even though there was never any suggestion, even from

Cimino himself, that he had been hired to do anything other than finish off the script that had been half-written by John Milius, who had left the project. In the credits of the final movie, both their names are there.

After forty years, it was clear that the betrayal was still painful for Washburn, but he retained a kind of counterintuitive admiration for Cimino. "Mike, looking back on the thing, if he hadn't been so dishonest and basically such a crook, that movie would never have gotten made," he told me. Of *The Deer Hunter*'s nine eventual Oscar nominations, one that it didn't win was Best Screenplay. When I asked Washburn if he felt bitter that Cimino had won Best Picture and Best Director and he had come away with nothing, he gave a graceful response: "I wished that I had got the Oscar, but I didn't. I don't wish that Mike hadn't got it. It deserved everything it got." What he did wish was that they had gone on working together. It was a tribute to the power of Cimino's vision and his strengths as a collaborator (even if he denied having any collaborators) that Washburn—after all that had happened to him—could tell me, "We could've kept working together. We could have done ten movies. I can

First draft screenplay cover (Author's collection)

still remember the pleasure of working with Mike. My God, he was a rare thing. If he had called me anytime in the last forty years to do a script with him, I would have dropped everything."

After the January draft, there were at least four others until the movie began shooting a few months later. On the second draft, Washburn's name was gone and the credit was "Original Screenplay by Michael Cimino."

There is something in the mindset of a particular kind of director—the ones whom French critics call an auteur—that a movie must be entirely theirs. It is not enough to own the house; they must own the furniture and drapes as well. Hitchcock never thanked a writer or cameraman—his were always "Hitchcock" films. Pauline Kael wrote a long diatribe against Orson Welles's appropriation of credit for the script of *Citizen Kane*. Robert Altman was so incensed that Ring Lardner Jr. won the Oscar for Best Screenplay for *M*A*S*H* (and that he did not win Best Director) that he immediately gave a press conference saying the script was his own work.

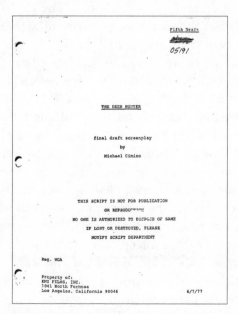

Fifth draft screenplay cover (Author's collection)

Scripts go through many drafts. The Writers Guild rigidly specifies the exact paper colors to be used to indicate the changes—blue for pages that have been altered in the second draft, pink for the third one, and so on until salmon for the eighth. What is curious is that the eventual shooting script of *The Deer Hunter* would have been almost colorless. The differences between the first script delivered in January and the later drafts before the movie went into production in June are surprisingly few.

There are some alterations, but by no stretch of the imagination could most of them be described as anything other than light tinkering. There is one substantive change: in the pitch and the first script, Michael (the Robert De Niro character) stays behind in Saigon, playing Russian roulette, while Nick (Christopher Walken) goes home and later returns to Vietnam to find Michael. In the final film, it is the other way around. The alteration is handled in the easiest and quickest way possible: the names are simply transposed so that what was originally Michael's dialogue is now Nick's and vice versa. Cimino would have made this change, and it was a smart one. The De Niro character is clearly the lead, and the movie works better if he is in it all the way through, rather than vanishing for half the film.

The other changes are very Cimino. Always fixated on the nature of masculinity in both his life and his movies, he macho'd up the script. When Michael is asked if only one shot is needed to kill a deer, he replies, "Definitely," in the first version; in subsequent drafts, the response is "Two is pussy." When asked a question, Axel (one of the deer hunters) always says, "For sure!" This gets changed to "Fuckin' A" in every instance. The line "There's times I swear I think you're not normal" becomes "There's times I swear I think you're a faggot." "Jerk" is always changed to "asshole."

By February, however the script was created and whoever had created it, Cimino was ready to begin casting. They started in New York with Patricia Mock, a casting director Cimino had worked with on *Thunderbolt and Lightfoot*. But Cimino, as was often his way, brought in someone more prestigious—Cis Corman, a legendary industry figure who cast for Scorsese and Barbra Streisand. Despite Corman's heavyweight presence, Carelli told me that she did a lot of the casting herself. This is probably something of an exaggeration, but there was no question that—despite her undefined role—she had become involved in every decision Cimino made about his work. Thom Mount called her Cimino's "shadow government."

According to Cimino, "The first person we approached was De Niro. He's the only one who saw the script." It was a smart choice: he had won an Oscar for *The Godfather Part II* and had been nominated for *Taxi Driver*. "I liked the story and the dialogue," De Niro said. "It was so simple. It seemed so real to me." For $1.5 million, he accepted.

It plays into the perceived omnipotence of directors that magisterially they choose who they want in their movie and then always get their man. In reality, this is rarely the case. As Irwin Winkler, producer of more than sixty movies puts it, "Actors you want are unavailable, too expensive, don't like the script, don't like the director, don't like the location, don't like their co-star, don't like the studio, don't like the wardrobe, or they do like their wife and kids and have . . . promised . . . they'd stay home for a while." John Travolta turned down *An Officer and a Gentleman* and Richard Gere came in; Leonardo DiCaprio was offered the lead in *Boogie Nights*, but Mark Wahlberg played it.

It was no different with *The Deer Hunter*. Thom Mount told me that another actor, Roy Scheider, had originally been offered the part of Michael and had accepted it. Sid Sheinberg, the powerful CEO of Universal, wanted him because he had just starred in the most successful movie Universal had released in years—*Jaws*—and might act as a good-luck charm in this difficult-to-market movie. Sheinberg was used to getting what he wanted—his wife, Lorraine Gary, a minor TV actress, had been shoehorned into *Jaws* to play Scheider's wife.

Cimino, who, with Carelli's help, always had a sure eye for casting, was less convinced. Within weeks, Scheider was gone. He said he left the project because he disagreed with the ending—he did not want his character, Michael, to travel halfway across the world to Saigon to rescue his friend, only to have him kill himself. Thom Mount said the reason was much simpler than that: ever manipulative, Cimino made it clear that he did not really want Scheider, and the actor was unwilling to be in a movie under those circumstances. The resourceful Universal allowed him to pull out on the condition that he did *Jaws 2*, which he had originally turned down.

Once De Niro was in, he committed himself totally to the project, with an eye for detail that equaled Cimino's. His personal copy of the script was covered with questions, notes, and suggestions. Together, they visited some of the locations—the steel mills, the veterans' hospital, the local bars. De Niro was also helpful in the casting. He suggested that the steel worker who was showing them around, Chuck Aspegren, should be cast as one of the deer hunters. "If you're fool enough to ask me," he said, "I'm fool enough to take it." He never acted again, but he gave a performance of extraordinary authenticity.

At three days' notice, Meryl Streep had replaced the lead actress in Bertolt Brecht and Kurt Weill's *Happy End* at the Brooklyn Academy of Music in April and got an ecstatic review from the *New York Times*. De Niro took Cimino to see the play, and they offered her the part of Linda, even though she had had almost no film experience at that point. Her boyfriend was John Cazale, who had played Fredo in *The Godfather*, and Cimino wanted him to play Stan, despite the fact that he was suffering from terminal lung cancer. In order to be with him, Streep accepted the part, although she secretly felt Linda was rather a generic character—just "the vague, stock girlfriend."

However, there was a problem with Cazale: no insurance company was prepared to give him cover because of his illness, and EMI were nervous. All films carry a giant insurance policy that will cover the cost of expensive reshooting if equipment is faulty or one of the cast gets ill. The actors all have a medical examination before shooting to check that they are in good health. When Harrison Ford broke his ankle during the shooting of *Star Wars: The Force Awakens* in 2014, production had to be closed down for three weeks with a giant payout. When Oliver Reed died halfway through the shooting of *Gladiator*, the costly reshoots to explain his sudden absence were covered by insurance.

"Those morons, those so-called producers" insisted that Cimino come up with an alternative script to use in case Cazale died during shooting, and he finally "cobbled together some absolutely dreadful piece of shit." In fact, callous though they may have sounded, EMI were not idiots—they were simply acting responsibly. Without insurance, they needed to have a contingency plan so they would know what would have to be changed in the story if Cazale was unable to complete his part.

Later, everyone wanted the credit for making sure he ended up in the movie: Cimino said he would have quit if he was not cast. There was a story that De Niro had paid for the insurance himself, which Spikings denied: "What makes anybody think that Robert De Niro has any special edge in the insurance business?" EMI, he stressed, had always wanted Cazale and were happy to go with him uninsured. In the end, Cazale made it through the film with no problems.

Cimino had originally been interested in Brad Dourif to play Steven, whose wedding ceremony starts the movie, but finally he chose another actor, John Savage, who was desperate for work after a promising early career had been derailed by a bad motorcycle accident. Robert Duvall was in the Broadway production of David Mamet's *American Buffalo*, and he recommended his co-star Savage to the director. One night, Cimino and De Niro came backstage to see him. Savage told me he could sense their bond: "Together they were like family—simpatico. It felt like they were saying, 'We have the answer to the world.'" They didn't talk about the film much, but Savage could tell he was being sized up. He got the part ("I felt I was being enlisted"), and the day after the play closed on June 11, he flew with his wife and children to Pennsylvania, where the movie was about to start shooting.

Carelli told me that when they were casting, she liked to watch the actors coming down a long corridor toward the casting office because they were themselves. When they walked through the door, they became someone else, and she felt that she didn't see them naturally. Christopher Walken, who had played Diane Keaton's brother in *Annie Hall*, was one of the actors who made the walk, and she instantly knew he was right for Nick, the soldier who stays behind in Saigon to play Russian roulette. They had already seen Richard Gere and Jeff Bridges for the part, but no decision had been made. Walken said, "I walked in and he [Cimino] asked me who I'd like to play. I named about four of them, but I figured if I was lucky I might get to play Stan [John Cazale's part]. I never expected him to cast me as Nick. It was just too good a part."

Carelli said that she never influenced Cimino during casting. She told me that she wrote Walken's name on a piece of paper and put it in

Cimino's pocket and then got him to look at it after he had chosen the actor. Carelli expressed no surprise at this to me—the depth of her and Cimino's synchronicity was never in doubt.

By then, Carelli was involved in every aspect of the movie. Thom Mount told me, "The good news was that it would never have got made without her. The bad news was that it was made with her." Spikings, who in some ways took a sunnier view of the making of the movie, said that he thought she was "sensible" and "good counsel" for Cimino. However, her ruthless and aggressive protection of Cimino alienated Mount, as well as many others. He said that working with them was "like a drive-by shooting." The fact that nobody knew precisely what her role was gave her a curious kind of authority. Was she the secret producer of the movie, or was she only there because she was, as many people presumed, Cimino's girlfriend? Because the extent of her power was not defined, it seemed as if there might be no limit to it.

Carelli told me, talking about Cimino in the present tense as she always does, that she never understands why people think Cimino is difficult, but it was soon apparent to EMI and Universal that she was the only person with whom he was not difficult. Rosenberg and Deeley discussed ways of controlling him and sensibly decided to hire an experienced producer, Robert Relyea, who had wrangled difficult directors and knew how to run large-scale, demanding, and sometimes out-of-control movies. He had worked on *West Side Story*, *The Great Escape*, and *Bullitt*. He took the job, but in a short while he was gone. He refused to discuss with Deeley and Rosenberg the reasons for his departure. They could only presume that after working with Cimino for a few weeks, Relyea, one of the toughest producers in Hollywood, was humiliated by the fact that he knew that this was a director he would not be able to rein in.

Deeley later said, "For a man of Bob's integrity to quit a picture at this stage of preproduction was a serious blow." They had to come up with another solution quickly, because Deeley was heavily involved with producing Sam Peckinpah's *Convoy*—a movie that was in free fall before shooting even started—and Spikings was mostly in London running the EMI office there. They hired a less substantial figure than Relyea, John Peverall, who had recently been sacked by Stanley Kubrick from *Barry*

Lyndon and had worked on B movies like *The Vengeance of Fu Manchu*. Deeley described him as "a straightforward Cornishman," but Cimino did not care how straightforward a producer was or where he came from: he hated them all. Within a matter of weeks, Peverall had been sidelined by the director.

There was more casting to be done in Los Angeles. Although a large production office had been set up by EMI, Cimino insisted that he needed to have a separate one at the expensive Beverly Hills Hotel. More than that, he wanted to stay there as well. When Rosenberg asked why he could not live at home, he said that Carelli's brother, Arthur, was staying, and he was "too noisy." Again, Deeley did not back her up. Cimino also landed EMI with a giant liquor bill, charging them for crates of scotch. He liked to be "hospitable," he said.

By the time shooting started, there was another casualty: Rosenberg was fired from EMI by Deeley and Spikings, although she retained her credit as associate producer on the movie. She told me that because of their mutually hostile relationship, she guessed that Cimino might have played some part in her abrupt departure. She has had a successful career since, but after forty-five years, she was still bitter: "I always swore that if I ever saw Michael again, I would throw a glass of wine in his face," she told me. "I was invited to a party at [Quentin] Tarantino's, and I heard that Michael would be there. By the time I got there, he had gone and I'd lost my chance."

THE DEER HUNTER went into production on June 20, 1977, in Mingo Junction and Weirton, on both sides of the West Virginia–Ohio border. It had taken months to secure the cooperation of the U.S. Steel Corporation to film the furnace scenes, and the production was forced to take out a $5 million insurance policy to cover the actors working at the blast furnaces. The cast arrived a week before shooting, and some of them were put up in the Holiday Inn, which was way out of town. Rutanya Alda, cast at the last moment to play John Savage's pregnant bride, told me that she thought Cimino had cleverly organized it that way because there was nowhere to go and the cast could hang out and get to know one another.

Cimino on the set (Photograph courtesy Patty Nelson Haglund)

As on many movies that shoot on location, there was a kind of collegiate spirit. John Savage told me, "It was a lot of fun. It was an organized party. We were singing, dancing, hanging out, hugging." The actors all loved working with Cimino and felt that, although he seemed shy, he was warm and generous toward them. Rutanya Alda said, "He was a real pleasure. He cared about the actors. I couldn't have had a happier experience than working with him." But actors tend to buy into their director—the movie equivalent of Stockholm syndrome.

The crew, more expendable than actors, are a better acid test, and Cimino was much less popular with them: he could be dictatorial and rude. Carelli, too, was difficult and offhand, and an actor told me they tended to avoid her. She saved her charm for the actors. Savage said, "Being in that movie with the spirit of Michael and Joann . . . I loved him, I loved her. She was a tough lady. I heard stories of her pulling financial and business people by the tie over a desk. I think she's incredibly gorgeous too. Attractive and smart. She and Michael were just so devoted." But their devotion had a downside for some: One of the actors said, "You had to be careful. If you were on Carelli's bad side, you would be on Cimino's as well."

The movie was set in the fall because that was when the deer-hunting season started. However, when filming began, it was late June and the weather was sweltering. The actors were drenched in sweat; Meryl Streep's hair had to be constantly dried; the false sideburns one actor wore kept falling off.

There was another problem: all the trees and foliage were lush and green, and the leaves had to be painstakingly removed from large areas and—according to some—painted fall yellow and reattached to the trees. Directors often like to exaggerate the production troubles that they have managed to solve—ones that would, of course, have daunted anyone else—but in fact, while the problems on *The Deer Hunter* were difficult, they were no worse than on many movies. David Lean, another famously autocratic director, tried to film a countryside scene for 1970s *Ryan's Daughter*, but because of weather problems, he decided to plant a huge wildflower meadow inside a warehouse and had butterflies and birds brought in.

But production complications have a knock-on effect. By the time Cimino had filmed the steel mill sequences and town scenes in the various locations he had chosen, the movie was over schedule and over budget. He assured Spikings and Deeley that he would be able to catch up, but when the filming shifted to Cleveland for the wedding sequence, the problems continued. The difficulties Rosenberg and Cimino had in finding and securing St. Theodosius Cathedral had been worthwhile. In keeping with Cimino's rigorous quest for authenticity, it was based on a church in Moscow, with wall-to-wall paintings depicting the Old and New Testaments in proper sequence. It was also huge, but Cimino, of course, had never been planning an intimate wedding for his characters. Scale was what he always wanted.

In the script, the wedding is about ten pages long, maybe fifteen minutes of screen time, and it became the first of many pressure points on the production. It was soon clear that the wedding was not going to be the brief character introduction it appeared to be on the page—it was going to be nothing less than a huge set piece that would define a whole immigrant community. Cimino always professed not to know much about movies and rarely talked about directors who had influenced him—he liked it to appear as if his talent had arrived fully formed with no help from anyone else—but later he did mention the extraordinary ballroom scene that was the climax of Luchino Visconti's *The Leopard* in 1963. Although Cimino's was an immigrant wedding and Visconti's was an aristocrats' ball, their sequences showed societies on the cusp of change and were elegiac farewells to a dying way of life. Both were conceived on the most grandiose scale, and both would be the subject of rows over their length. Thirty-five minutes were cut out of Visconti's scene when his movie was released, and Cimino would later fight passionately to keep his wedding intact.

He said that he wanted to shoot the wedding and the party afterward as if they were "a documentary with actors, something as intimate as a home movie." He had a forensic eye for detail, and he made sure—expensively—that everything was authentic. The party was filmed in Lemko Hall, which was down the road from the cathedral and was a popular wedding venue for the community. The priest was a real one. The catering was not just prop food; it had all been locally prepared. The wine bottles were not filled with juice nor the vodka bottles with water, as they normally are in movies—Cimino was quite happy for the guests to get authentically merry. The band was comprised of local musicians. The actors had to be taught dances like the *korobushka* and the *troika* quickly. Rutanya Alda, playing the bride, had to pick it up in four hours practicing in a hotel corridor. She told me she asked Cimino why he had presumed she would be able to learn the movements in such a short time. He always knew how to bind actors to him: "Because I trusted you," he said.

The 250 extras required for the sequence did not have to be taught how to dance or how to behave at a wedding: they were all Russian Americans from the local community, drawn from three different parishes, wearing their own clothes. They were paid $25 a day with an additional $2 if they brought a dummy box that looked like a wedding gift. Taking authenticity further than even Cimino had expected, many of the packages contained real presents, like toasters and china.

The movie took over the community. Trucks and generators and actors' trailers were parked all along the street; there was the constant squawking of walkie-talkies and more than one hundred crew members milling around, picking their way over the generator cables that powered the giant lights that heated up the already sweltering hall. Every day, filming started at 7:00 A.M. and continued until 8:00 P.M. and was as fraught as shooting any movie on a giant scale with so many extras can be. Cimino rarely lost his temper on set, but he was rigorous in his attention to detail. When there was a problem with the bride's dress, he shouted at the costume designer, "You've had weeks to get this right—if I was Coppola, you'd have got it right."

Generally, he was brilliantly organized and knew exactly what he wanted and how to get it, working with assistant directors he trusted to control the huge crowd. He tended not to break up the action into short segments that would be edited together later—he liked to shoot in long master shots with multiple cameras that would give an uninterrupted vista of the talking and dancing and drinking. Naturally, as always with Cimino, this was not the most time- or cost-efficient way of shooting—moving 250 extras back into their original positions for each new take was agonizingly slow.

Soon there was panic back at EMI and Universal as the schedule kept expanding. On movie sets, there is a daily call sheet that outlines

Cimino, De Niro, and Streep (Alamy)

exactly what specific scenes are to be shot that day. The breakdown for the wedding sequence was much vaguer because it was really one long scene taking place in, more or less, real time, so it was hard to establish what was meant to be filmed on any given day.

The director tries to "finish" the day—complete all the scenes on the call sheet—but if he falls behind or there are weather or technical problems, the unshot scenes are shunted into the next day with a consequent domino effect. But Cimino did not think he was falling behind—he just had his own schedule, which happened to be different from the studio's. Filming took longer because he simply shot—very efficiently—at his own pace. Deeley believed, probably rightly, that Cimino had always planned to expand what the script had indicated would be a fifteen-minute sequence into one that lasted for an hour and fifteen minutes in the first cut. "This plan was to be advanced by stealth rather than straight dealing," he said. Later, Cimino told his assistant, Penny Shaw, that he had a technique for dealing with studios: "Tell them what they want to hear and then do what you want."

Although the dailies were watched by the producers, Thom Mount at Universal had an uneasy feeling that Cimino was shooting a great deal more material than was being sent back to Hollywood. Something had to be done to rein him in. Rutanya Alda remembered that the actors were told that they would not be shooting the next day. Three men arrived in Cleveland from Los Angeles, one of whom was Barry Spikings. The gossip among the crew was that the picture was going to be shut down.

Spikings told me that he had taken Cimino aside and said that he thought he was going a little crazy over the wedding sequence. Cimino replied that in the finished movie, "It would last no longer than the flicker of a candle." Deeley believed that his fellow producer "hadn't faced this sort of problem before and that Cimino was skillfully manipulating him." Spikings and the others returned to Los Angeles, and shooting resumed at Cimino's stately pace. Although there were many more disputes to come over the wedding, it would end up as one of the most indelible sequences in the movie. On the last day of the shoot, Cimino saw an old man crying and asked him why. "It was such a beautiful wedding," the man said.

As soon as filming ended in Cleveland, Cimino, the actors, and the crew flew in a chartered plane to the other side of the country to

Cimino in Washington (Alamy)

shoot the two deer-hunting sequences that take place before the men go to Vietnam and after they return. The unit went from the heat of the Ohio summer to the freezing cold of the Cascade Mountains in Washington, nearly fifteen thousand feet above sea level. Cimino, an unlikely peddler of spiritual enlightenment, always professed that he found regeneration in the wild. "The mist is a gift from the mountains," he said. "These are gifts that are given back to you because of your respect and love if you believe that all things have spirit." In fact, the mist proved to be not much of a gift. It came and went, causing problems when it came to getting shots to match. The deer proved troublesome as well.

Normally in a movie, trained animals are used because they are docile and easy to control. Cimino did not like the deer that were provided: "These little deer arrive. They looked like Bambi. I went crazy. The name of the movie is *The Deer Hunter*. We needed big deer. I told them there would be a revolution in theaters if we killed Bambi." Finally, two large and indocile specimens were located in a game reserve in New Jersey. Cimino had them shipped across the country, and it took thirty men to carry the crates containing the deer up to the location. Cimino filmed in Washington for four grueling weeks before the unit flew to Bangkok. The deer-hunting scenes were the last that the ailing John Cazale shot. He died six months later.

ON AUGUST 20, THE crew flew to Bangkok. Although Cimino desired authenticity above all else, it was impossible to get permission to film in Vietnam. Francis Ford Coppola faced the same problems on *Apocalypse Now* and had to shoot in the Philippines. For Cimino, Thailand proved to be a nightmare. Although he was largely responsible for the schedule and budget problems while shooting in the US, the difficulties he faced in the Far East were not always of his making.

Cimino was not the first director to underestimate the complications involved in making a movie in an underdeveloped country without an indigenous film industry. Shooting in somewhere like Spain or Norway would mean that only a reduced crew needed to be flown out because experienced technicians—construction teams, electricians, costume assistants—are already working there, and local rates are cheaper. More than that, most people can speak English. Not so in Thailand: most communication had to be done through interpreters. To recruit extras and organize transportation and permits, the production had to rely on local fixers, whose ability to fix was often in doubt. It was hard to keep track of the budget because payments were made in cash. However much preparation they had done—and *The Deer Hunter* had had a crew out in Thailand for months organizing the shoot—it was a journey into the unknown.

As soon as they arrived in Bangkok, they hit their first big problem: the extreme weather. The monsoon season had come early, and the rain was torrential. On many occasions, Cimino was forced to stop filming. There were other difficulties: many crew members got sick. One of the production managers was injured by a train. The city was under a military curfew, so for much of the shooting, armed police hovered around the edges of the set. Cimino had managed to get the cooperation of the Thai army, but there were constant rumors that a coup was about to happen. The military's supreme leader, General Kriangsak Chomanan, helped to procure the vehicles, weapons, and aircraft the production needed. Spikings remembered that the general suddenly asked for all the equipment back, and when he protested, Chomanan said, "Barry, please—you're making a movie. I have a military coup, but it won't take long. There'll be a few people shot on Sunday, and then you can have the stuff back."

One of the impressive things about Cimino was that he took these kinds of problems in stride and was immune to pressure or angry producers. Working harder than anyone else, he never lost his focus or his eye for detail, however difficult it was to achieve the desired result. When there were problems trying to control the rafts they were using on the River Kwai, he asked one of the production managers, "What would David Lean do in this situation?" The production manager replied that Lean "would have been understanding." "Well, I'm not fucking David Lean," Cimino said.

As sometimes happens in movies, the constraints called for the kind of creative thinking that benefited the picture. Because of the unpredictable street lighting and generator problems, Vilmos Zsigmond, the visionary Czech cameraman (suggested by Carelli) who had shot *McCabe & Mrs. Miller* for Altman and *Deliverance* for John Boorman and would work again with Cimino on *Heaven's Gate*, had to overdevelop the film to compensate for the low-light conditions, a way of shooting that brought with it many risks. As the footage had to be sent back to Los Angeles to be developed (another problem with countries without a movie industry: they do not tend to have reliable labs) and Cimino never saw it, they had to take the chance that what they had shot would be usable. In fact, the way Zsigmond had to shoot the movie created an extraordinarily intense effect, a kind of chiaroscuro with the visible grain that is often seen in news footage. It highlighted the characters in a sea of darkness that might be hiding many dangers and vividly portrayed the precariousness of Saigon during the Vietnam War.

Some of the Bangkok scenes were giant set pieces that involved shooting at night on the river and in streets that they attempted to clear of everyone but the seven hundred extras who had been hired. However, because of the huge interest the film caused, Zsigmond remembered that six thousand people turned up to watch. Cimino had originally been told that filming could not go beyond the start of the curfew at 1:00 A.M., but the sheer size of the crowd made it impossible for the police to get them off the streets, and he was able to shoot through the night. Although he had never worked on this scale with this many extras before, Cimino and his team were brilliant at controlling the crowd and getting the shots he wanted. As in the wedding sequence, he used multiple cameras shooting from a distance to reveal the giant vista of nighttime Bangkok, achieving an almost documentary realism. Zsigmond said, "When you see the first shot of the big crowded street, you think you are watching stock footage, but when the camera comes in to pick up Chris Walken in the crowd, you know this couldn't be stock footage."

The last sequence to be shot in Bangkok before heading north was the final, terrifying confrontation, when Michael finds Nick playing Russian roulette in a secret room behind a bar, surrounded by raucous gamblers feverishly betting on the outcome. Cimino tended to do many takes, but the end of this scene was improvised in one. Cimino's only direction was to say to De Niro and Walken, "You put the gun to your head, Chris, you shoot, you fall over, and Bobby cradles your head," and it turned out to be perhaps the most devastating moment in the movie.

Charles Hubbard, now a successful producer in England, was living in Thailand teaching English and spoke a little of the language. He told me he applied to be a runner on the movie and was hired. They sent him up-country to Kanchanaburi a few weeks before the main unit arrived to shoot the difficult river sequences there. Hubbard felt that everything had been as well organized as it could have been in a difficult and unpredictable location, even though, as usual, the local fixer seemed to have his own agenda. He had the improbable name of Prince Billy, and said he was related to the royal family. According to Hubbard, he was sleeping with one of the accountants and had access to the safe. It was clear that money was changing hands, but it was impossible to tell how much and to whom it went, and what services were meant to be provided. Hubbard had little interaction with Cimino but was impressed with how he worked.

When Cimino and the crew arrived in Kanchanaburi, Hubbard was surprised to see that he had an armed bodyguard who slept outside his bedroom. He presumed that this had been organized by Prince Billy, who liked to imply that they were filming in an extremely dangerous area and only he could protect them. Hubbard told me that he didn't see much of Carelli, but there was a certain amount of gossip among the crew about her mysterious relationship with Cimino. Hubbard admitted that nobody "had any idea how that structure worked."

According to Carelli, John Peverall, the soi-disant producer who was meant to be in charge, never left his hotel room. She told me that the only sign of his presence was an increasing line of room-service trays along the corridor. By then, the movie was even further over budget and behind schedule, and EMI were panicking at the thought of Cimino shooting a producer-less movie under such difficult conditions. Barry Spikings said that he realized hiring Peverall was a mistake: "Cimino ate him, and the crew had lost confidence in him."

Once again, Spikings flew out to the location to sort it out. But, just as after his Cleveland visit, nothing much changed. He was sympathetic to Cimino—much too sympathetic, his partner Michael Deeley felt. Spikings said afterward, "We knew we were making something important to America and the world. And you just had to back that vision. You had to support him."

Cimino was shooting in an isolated region, and the local villagers were nervous about what filming would involve. They proposed that a small Buddhist temple should be built by the side of the river. Art departments on movies are always good at constructing a quick set on a moment's notice, and on the first day of shooting there, Cimino—still in his spiritual mode—said he led prayers at dawn to bless the day's work.

Although the up-country sequences were shot after the Bangkok scenes, they are the first introduction to Vietnam in the movie. In one of the most startling transitions since Stanley Kubrick cut from a prehistoric ape throwing a bone in the air to a spaceship floating through space in 2001: A Space Odyssey, Cimino cut from one of the steelworkers in a bar in Pennsylvania playing a mournful Chopin nocturne to a village blowing up in Vietnam.

Perhaps there should have been more prayers in the Buddhist temple: the scenes on the water proved to be a nightmare. While the weather was unbearably hot, the river was freezing. "You want it to look authentic," De Niro said, and shooting under such realistic conditions made it impossible for it not to be. Michael, Steven, and Nick are taken captive by the Vietcong and are kept in submerged bamboo cages. John Savage, who played Steven, told me he was alarmed having to improvise around rats and water snakes in the fast-moving current. Still, actors like a bit of method, and it was a matter of pride that they all did their own stunts.

Eventually the men escape and begin a terrifying trip—both in reality and in the movie—floating down the river, clinging to a log. Every movie that has been filmed on water, like *Deliverance* or Kevin Costner's *Waterworld*, has proved to be grueling because the water is impossible to control. On *The Deer Hunter*, cameras on the shore and on rafts, some moving and some anchored, covered the action, but after each take, everything—including the actors—had to be laboriously pulled back upriver to the first position. Of course, none of this fazed Cimino, who, as usual, was undaunted by the challenges and put the actors through their paces—hitting rocks, going over a waterfall, nearly drowning—over and over again until he got what he wanted.

It would be harder to shoot such sequences now because regulations have become more stringent, but Cimino had the most experienced stunt coordinators working with him, including the legendary Buddy Van Horn, who organized all the action on Clint Eastwood's movies and had worked with Cimino on *Thunderbolt and Lightfoot*. The function of the stunt coordinator is not only to plan the sequence with a scrupulous concern for safety, but also to troubleshoot at lightning speed if something goes wrong, as it often does—and it did on the river sequence in *The Deer Hunter*.

John Savage told me that even after forty-five years, the terror of shooting the scene where a chopper tries to pick up the three friends from the fast-moving water has never left him. A rickety rope bridge had been strung across the river, and the men grab hold of it when they see a US helicopter coming to rescue them. It was flown by Thai military pilots who were not experienced with this kind of complicated stunt sequence. More than that, they spoke no English, so Cimino had to use a walkie-talkie to communicate with the interpreter on the ground, who relayed the instructions back to the pilot. As the helicopter came in, one of the landing skids went under the cables strung across the bridge, which the three men were hanging on to.

Shooting the helicopter sequence (Alamy)

The bridge was pulled up into the air and began to tilt dangerously. The stunt coordinators sprang into action and climbed out onto the runners of the helicopter and managed to disentangle the cable. Cimino, pragmatic as ever, said, "I was trying to make all this work. I had the cameras rolling. It was insane."

Cimino then filmed the sequence as it was meant to happen, which was really no less dangerous. The three men hang on to the skids of the helicopter as it rises high into the sky. Christopher Walken manages to clamber into the cockpit. John Savage is too weak and falls, and De Niro jumps after him because he sees him drowning. Savage told me that they shot this fifteen times.

On November 4, 1977, filming ended and the crew returned to the US. The budget for the whole movie had doubled from $7.5 million to $15 million, but Cimino was quick to point out that it "had nothing to do with excess or lack of discipline. This was a highly disciplined project from the beginning." Not so financially. Charles Hubbard remained in Thailand to sort out the tattered remains of the secretive fiscal structure of a movie shot in a country with a cash economy. Import orders had not been signed, nor bank guarantees ratified. Receipts for petty cash were almost nonexistent. Hubbard told me that, in the undercover way that had operated throughout production, he would sit in one room while a mysterious fixer, whom he was not allowed to see, signed the guarantees in another room.

In 2002, the DVD of *The Deer Hunter* was released, and Cimino—who had given few interviews since the disastrous release of *Heaven's Gate* in 1980—agreed to record a commentary. After twenty-five years, he had an amazing recall of the movie and gave a typically mercurial performance that contained his usual grandiose mixture of fact, fiction, and hyperbole. Everything, he said, was "real"; in the scenes where John Savage is playing bingo in a wheelchair in the veterans' hospital, "Nobody knew we were filming"—which would be a hard act to pull off with a large crew, cameras, and a lighting rig. The fight scene at the wedding was inspired, he said, by his uncle "slugging his wife because she was dancing with someone else" (one of the few references to his mysterious family he ever made). Unbelievably, he appeared to remember the names of many of the Thai extras and which villages they came from. There is one unusual detail he recalled that was unlikely to be featured in a commentary by most directors: when a Thai dancing girl crossed the screen, Cimino said, "She was my girlfriend for a while. She wrote me the sweetest letter." Nor would they have criticized a collaborator: he wanted to settle a score with someone he felt had exaggerated his contribution: "I get annoyed when cameramen take credit for a shot. They just come in for sixteen weeks. I've been working on it for two years. Now they're called directors of photography—they're cameramen. Sorry, Vilmos!" When he talked about the Vietnam War, he began to weep. He ended by singing "God Bless America" in a strangled voice, echoing the famous last scene of his film.

There was one record he particularly wanted to set straight: "The person who really produced the movie was Joann Carelli." She was not credited as such, only as an associate producer and production consultant—the only person on the poster and in the credits, apart from Cimino, who was mentioned more than once. He had fought hard to get this through EMI. Spikings told me that he felt he had been "weak" in allowing it.

CHAPTER 6

THE BODY COUNT

ONCE BACK IN Los Angeles, Cimino began looking at the footage, much of which he had not seen, with his editor, Peter Zinner, who was given the job because of his work on *The Godfather* for Coppola. Penny Shaw was brought on as a junior editorial assistant and would work closely with Cimino for the next four years. Shaw was in charge of collating six hundred thousand feet of film, about one hundred hours. In those days, before the advent of digital editing systems, "cutting" was literally that: strips of film laboriously cut up and then spliced together with tape. To change anything, the strips had to be unpasted and then put together in another configuration.

In the past, editing had been a more streamlined process because directors tended to shoot less—David Lean cut *Lawrence of Arabia* in twelve weeks. Because of the sheer amount of footage shot by multiple cameras, it took Cimino the same amount of time to simply view it. For the first few months, EMI left Cimino to work on a first cut, what's generally regarded as a work in progress that producers will discuss with the director and then agree on changes.

When Spikings and Deeley saw Cimino's first cut running at three and a half hours, they were pleased: they thought there was "a riveting film" within it and presumed that it would be honed down to around two hours. They soon realized that it was not a "first" cut and that Cimino was not interested in their input— Cimino regarded it as his final cut. Thom Mount, the president of Universal, said that it "was a continuing nightmare from the day Michael finished the picture to the day we released it. That was because he was wedded to everything he shot."

But regardless of the length, Universal, who was distributing it, was a great deal less enthusiastic about the movie than EMI. Mount told me that Lew Wasserman, the longtime boss of Universal, liked nothing about it. Sid Sheinberg, the executive who had wanted Roy Scheider for the De Niro role, was no more enthusiastic. So pessimistic was Mount that Deric Washburn told me that Mount brought him to LA to see the movie—the first time he had any involvement since his sacking by Cimino and Carelli a year before—and was asked by Mount whether he thought there was any point releasing it.

All this was a problem for Deeley and Spikings. The US was going to be their major market, and they did not want to be in a situation where the distributors had no faith in the movie and would release it in a halfhearted way. Normally the distributor will guarantee a certain amount of money to be spent on marketing and advertising and agree to a minimum number of theaters that will show the movie. This was not included in EMI's contract with Universal. Deeley made an attempt to take the movie away from them. In secret, he sounded out United Artists, probably the most artist-friendly studio in Hollywood, which had an impressive record of marketing "difficult" films, like *One Flew Over the Cuckoo's Nest*, but in the end, Universal refused to let it go. Always more finance-led than artist-led, they had done a deal with CBS, who acquired the TV rights for $3.5 million. As Universal's contribution to the budget had been around $4 million, they realized that if they spent as little money as possible on the marketing and release of the movie, they could make up the minimal difference.

Despite their lack of enthusiasm, however, they still wanted to get the movie into a shape they could live with. Cimino refused to budge over the length. The predictable area of contention was the wedding sequence, which had seemed so economical in the script but was now running for an hour and fifteen minutes in his long cut. He said, "The first places people attack are those scenes that involve character development. A film lives, becomes alive, because of its shadows, its spaces, and that's what people wanted to cut." For Mount, the trouble was that the wedding had become "a cinematic event unto its own." He was less interested in character development than pace. The problem for Cimino was that his contractual final cut—the right to release the film the way he wanted—depended on it running for two hours or less. Even though Deeley and Spikings told Cimino that they would agree to increase the length by half an hour or so, he still insisted on his long cut, even though he knew that EMI and Universal might exercise their right to take the film away from him.

This was a high-stakes game, and one that Cimino, as usual, was prepared to play. Thom Mount brought in Verna Fields, the veteran editor who had pulled *Jaws* into shape. "Verna was no slouch," Mount said. "She started to turn the heat up on Michael, and he started screeching and yelling."

Then he appeared to back down. "The thought that I would be removed and someone else would take over made me physically ill," Cimino said. In the end, he did cut the picture back to 183 minutes by taking half an hour out of the wedding sequence, but everyone still thought it was too long. Spikings and Deeley secretly brought Cimino's editor, Peter Zinner, into the cutting room over a weekend to do his own shorter version of the sequence. Cimino may have disliked Verna Fields being foisted on him, but he did not feel betrayed by her. Zinner was different—Cimino had chosen him and expected loyalty. He gave Spikings and Deeley a choice: Zinner or Cimino. He knew how to fight a war of attrition, and Spikings and Deeley wearily agreed that the editor should go.

Now, despite thinking it was too long, something changed for them: they had come to the realization that *The Deer Hunter* might just be a masterpiece. The industry always liked auteur movies, and—when they were successful—could bask in the warm glow that came from backing an artist. If they sacked Cimino and insisted on the Zinner cut, they might not appear as talent-friendly as they would have liked. They would have an auteur movie on their hands without an auteur.

However, despite Zinner's departure, his cut was still in play. There were now his 160-minute version and Cimino's 183-minute one.

Universal was insisting on the shorter version (which they would have liked to be even shorter) because it would be possible to fit in more screenings per day. Cimino demanded what he thought was his contractual right to screen a public preview of his version. Universal refused. They argued that his right of final cut was predicated on a two-hour cut of the movie, and because he had not delivered it, he had no right to preview his long version.

Universal cared much less than EMI about their reputation within the artistic community. They were too powerful, too prolific, and too profitable to worry much. However, nothing stays secret for long in Hollywood, and Cimino was not keeping quiet about the row. He had managed to get a print of his long version out of the cutting room and was storing it secretly at Technicolor's labs, where he was showing it to influential industry friends. For the first time, that elusive thing known as "Oscar buzz" began hovering around town—the movie's kind of epic Americana was always attractive to the Academy. Someone who particularly loved *The Deer Hunter* was Irwin Winkler, a producer who had the rare gift of making movies that were often both prestigious and profitable, like Sydney Pollack's *They Shoot Horses, Don't They?* He had known Cimino and Carelli casually for some years, and he and his wife, Margo, were among the few people who had occasionally been invited for dinner at their house.

Cimino organized a screening for him and described the preview problem. Winkler, now nearly ninety, is another Hollywood producer who is still working, and he told me how moved he had been by the movie. He called Ned Tanen, the powerful head of production at Universal, and said, "I tell you what I'm going to do: I'm going to take out a full-page ad in *Variety*. It's going to be signed by Scorsese, Sydney Pollack, Francis Coppola, and it'll say that Ned Tanen will not let Michael Cimino have a preview of this movie. Tanen said to me, 'You would do that?' and I said, 'Absolutely, I would do that.'"

It takes a certain amount of nerve for a producer to take on a studio head, but Winkler had two unusual qualities in Hollywood: integrity and clout. He had just shepherded the unproduced screenwriter and bit-part actor Sylvester Stallone through *Rocky*, a movie that cost $1 million, grossed $225 million, and won the Oscar for Best Picture.

Anyway, he told me, he had never liked Tanen much, and he wanted to make the gesture not just for Cimino, but also for De Niro, with whom he was about to start shooting *Raging Bull*. A big success for De Niro would help his boxing movie—as violent and depressing as *The Deer Hunter*—which had proved a nightmare to get off the ground. At the end of the call, Tanen said to Winkler, "OK, well, if it's that important, he can have his preview." He added, "But it will be a disaster." There was also a catch: Universal insisted on two previews, the long version and the short one. Whichever played better would be the one released.

The preview situation was not the only thing proving problematic for Cimino during the long days in the cutting room. Firstly, there was the music: Carelli told me that she had met the distinguished English composer Stanley Myers when she had worked in London in the late 1960s and had recommended him to Cimino. Myers had done some temp tracks for the movie but had not yet come up with a main theme. Carelli remembered a piece of music he had written called "Cavatina," and Cimino loved it. The difficulty was that it had already been used seven years before as the theme for another movie, a little-seen MGM picture called *The Walking Stick*, and the studio, not Myers, owned it. Despite the fact that it was eccentric to recycle music from another movie, Cimino did not care. He wanted it, but EMI dug in their heels about paying an exorbitant price to MGM for the license to use it.

A bigger problem was that Deric Washburn had resurfaced. He had been out of the loop back in New York, but when Thom Mount had shown him the movie, he thought it was brilliant and wanted his part in its creation to be recognized. However, his name was nowhere to be seen on the credits: it was billed as "Original Screenplay by Michael Cimino." After his sacking by Carelli and Cimino months before, and now seeing his contribution unacknowledged, he went to a lawyer and demanded a Writers Guild arbitration.

On the surface, it appears to be a simple procedure: the various drafts written by the competing writers are submitted along with documentation and then forensically compared. A writer must be deemed to have contributed at least a third of the script to be awarded credit, but smaller contributions are sometimes acknowledged as "Story by." In practice, however, it is known to be an extraordinarily imprecise process, particularly if there are many writers involved—on *The Flintstones* movie in 1994, the arbitration had to sort out the contributions from an unbelievable thirty-six writers who had worked on it. There are numerous examples of writers unfairly denied credits—Gore Vidal on *Ben-Hur*, Joss Whedon on the Keanu Reeves movie *Speed*, and Cimino himself on Bette Midler's *The Rose*. One of the other reasons the screenplay credit is so fought over is money: a writer gets paid for his work whether the movie is made or not, but if it gets green-lit, there is a substantial production bonus paid out when credits are agreed. If there is one writer credited, he gets it all. If there are more, the bonus is divided pro rata. There's an urban myth that a disgruntled writer once turned up at the Guild's offices waving a gun.

It operates behind more closed doors than the Vatican. A panel of three Guild members, their names kept secret, makes a decision that is handed down with no explanation of how it was reached. In *The Deer Hunter* arbitration, the original Redeker/Garfinkle *The Man Who Came to Play* script was examined, as well as Washburn's and Cimino's work. There was a puff of white smoke: the Guild decided that the credits should read "Screenplay by Deric Washburn, Story by Quinn Redeker & Louis Garfinkle and Michael Cimino & Deric Washburn."

Cimino did not pull any punches: "In their Nazi wisdom," he said, "they didn't give me the credit because I would be producer, director, and writer." (In fairness to Cimino, the Guild is always reluctant to add the director to the writer's credit because it is hard to determine whether his work constitutes a rewrite or whether he and the writer have simply worked together honing the script.) He appealed the decision but lost again. Tenacious as ever, he went back and said that there was new material he had not managed to submit at the time of the arbitration that would prove his case.

Washburn's lawyer wrote a withering riposte to the Guild in March 1978: "I was informed that the credit arbitration panel's decision in connection with the screen credits on *The Deer Hunter* was to be re-opened. Mr. Cimino has already submitted a great deal of material. It is inconceivable that only now has he 'discovered' new and relevant material. . . ." Once again, Cimino's claim to be the sole screenwriter was rejected.

One battle was lost, but he was determined not to lose another one: the preview. Cimino had a reasonably good relationship with

Spikings—"Barry Spikings has the most beautiful smile in the world," he said later—and he got him more or less on his side. By doing so, he had managed to put a chink into the producers' close partnership. Deeley, less involved in the shooting of the movie, felt that Spikings had been too soft on Cimino in Thailand. Spikings had also agreed to pay MGM the expensive fee for the use of the theme music from the other movie. More than that, Deeley was furious that he had allowed Cimino to have a producer's credit even though he "had performed none of the traditional producer's functions—rather the reverse." When there was a press conference at the time of *The Deer Hunter*'s release, Spikings suggested that Deeley should not attend because Cimino refused to go if he was there. Forty-five years later, Spikings told me, "I loved Michael," but he was almost the only producer who ever made such a statement about Cimino (he later worked on two unhappy projects with him). Deeley did not love him: "The one flaw I find in my Oscar for *The Deer Hunter* is that Cimino's name is also engraved on it." Thom Mount at Universal was equally uncompromising: "I came away with no respect for Cimino and Carelli. I thought they acted like thugs, entirely greedy and out for themselves."

THE PREVIEWS TOOK place in August. It was agreed that Cimino could choose where he wanted to hold his one, and he chose Detroit. Universal opted for Chicago. At these screenings, the name of the movie is not revealed—it is billed as something like "A Major Studio Preview"—so that the viewers are unencumbered by knowledge or gossip and come to it fresh. That is also the reason why previews are never held in Los Angeles itself, where knowledge and gossip hover in the air. At the end, the audience fills out cards, checking various boxes such as "Did you like the movie?" and "Would you recommend it to your friends?" and then the scores are added up. If the results are bad, reshoots are sometimes done, uplifting endings tacked on, or more thrills added. However, it is not always an accurate system—many movies have had great scores but died at the box office, and vice versa.

Predictably, all the participants had a different version of how *The Deer Hunter* previews went. Cimino's story was that audiences at his Detroit long preview not only responded but were "overwhelmed." He said that the executives at Universal admitted they had been wrong: "It had been a war, but we all came together in the end. I am proud of this film, and so is EMI and Universal." None of the other participants had any recollection of this unlikely rapprochement.

Thom Mount's version of the story was quite the opposite: the long Detroit screening was "the worst preview I had ever seen." He told me that at the end there were only sixty-five people left in the theater, while the short Chicago version had "an enthusiastic response." Deeley concurred with this. Cimino had a different story about the short version: he said that he had sabotaged it. He had bribed the projectionist to break the film after twenty minutes, to take a long time to resplice the film and then start all over again. According to him, the audience was restless, confused, and bored, and gave that version very low scores.

Whatever happened at the previews, the producers were still not sure what version to release. Barry Spikings had come around to the long version. He thought that shortening it would "cut the heart out of the movie." Thom Mount did not agree. As usual, Cimino tried to force their hand. Mount told me that Cimino said that if the short version was released, he would refuse to do any publicity, which was going to be a problem for a movie that needed all the good publicity it could get.

After the acrimonious two years they had worked with him, the producers knew that Cimino tended not to bluff. In the end, they decided to let Lord Delfont, the CEO of EMI in England, who had not been particularly involved in the movie, decide. Lady Delfont, his wife, wept at a screening of the long version, and he decided to go with it. Cimino, employing his usual mixture of determination, divisiveness, and aggression, had achieved almost everything he wanted: his chosen length, the full wedding sequence, and the costly music. While he had lost the script credit battle, it did not affect the movie.

Now stuck with a three-hour movie, Universal still had no idea how to market it. Spikings and Mount, in a desperate move that turned out to be a brilliant one, did something counterintuitive: they hired Allan Carr to help them. He was an overweight, kaftan-wearing, and—to use one of Hollywood's many code words—flamboyant publicist turned producer. Well-liked and generous, he was known for the lavish and wild parties he held at his house in Beverly Hills, where he had installed a permanent disco in the basement. He had produced *Grease*, a movie so different from *The Deer Hunter* that it could have been in Sanskrit. He seemed to be the least likely person to respond to Cimino's serious and grueling movie.

When Spikings and Mount talked to him about it, he asked them why he would want to work on "a long movie about poor people who go to war and get killed." They screened it for him, and quite unexpectedly, he found himself weeping. He loved it without reservation and said, "It is an incredible movie. I want to run the marketing campaign. I know exactly how to sell the movie." He was the only one who did.

The timing was good for Carr: he had not yet started shooting his follow-up to *Grease, Can't Stop the Music* (a disastrous attempt to make stars out of the Village People, as well as Caitlyn Jenner, then a hunky Olympic decathlete star with zero acting experience), and he leapt at the chance to take on a very different kind of project. Thom Mount told me that Universal agreed to pay him an eye-watering fee of $500,000.

It was worth it. The campaign he conceived was unusual, but it turned out to be astonishingly effective. Brilliant though Carr thought the movie was, he believed it would seem off-putting to a general audience without a lot of help because it was long, grim, and violent. He was determined to win awards and was a tenacious lobbyist. It was only later that the function he served was given a name—"Oscar consultant"—and became an actual profession that changed the way movies were positioned at awards season. Now, DVD "screeners" are sent out at awards season, or the voters are allowed to stream them, but in those days, Academy members had to actually go to a theater to see the movies. Daringly, given the movie industry's traditional antipathy toward television, Carr wanted to organize a unique broadcast of *The Deer Hunter*. Lew Wasserman, the longtime and dictatorial boss of Universal—such a revered and God-like figure that even when I recently spoke to him, Thom Mount talked about him as "Mr. Wasserman"—thought that it would decimate *The Deer Hunter*'s box office to show it on TV before its release. But Carr was persuasive—he wept in front of him and got his way.

With the broadcast, Carr was not trying to reach a large audience; he wanted to target a relatively small one. The Z Channel, with ninety thousand subscribers, was a small pay cable channel in Los Angeles started in 1974 by a visionary movie obsessive called Jerry Harvey. It specialized in the obscure and forgotten, and only movie buffs—many of whom were Academy members—watched it. Carr knew that the showing of an unseen and prestigious studio movie would be a big event for them.

The methods he used, unheard of then, became the standard way of burnishing a potential award-winning movie. It was usual to release a movie in many theaters at once, but Carr decided to give *The Deer Hunter* a limited initial release, showing it in one theater in New York and one in LA for a single week in December (movies had to be released before the year's end to qualify for the Oscars in April) and then withdrawing it until a fuller release after the hoped-for nominations early in the New Year. He knew that releasing it in two theaters for a week would severely limit the audience—and that was exactly what he wanted. He was positioning it as "exclusive," like a limited-edition book or a club that was hard to get into: "Everybody would be asking if you saw it, were you one of the five hundred people . . . ?" Carr made sure that Lauren Bacall, Rudolf Nureyev, and Andy Warhol were among that number.

More than that, he bought full pages in the trades, headed "For Your Consideration" and listing all the categories—editing, cinematography, screenplay, direction, acting, and so on—that were eligible for nominations. Later, Miramax's Harvey Weinstein, a compulsive Oscar hunter, copied Carr's methods with enormous success.

The campaign for *The Deer Hunter* emphasized its "controversial" nature. Playing that particular card can be a double-edged sword: it worked for movies like *The Exorcist* and *Last Tango in Paris*, but Louis Malle's *Pretty Baby*, with Brooke Shields as a child prostitute, and *Caligula*, which had hard-core sequences added to the movie, were disasters. Carr made it seem as if it would be an act of bravery to dare to see *The Deer Hunter*. The posters contained a warning: "Due to the mature nature of this film, under 17 requires accompanying parent or guardian. There will be strict adherence to this policy."

The prerelease buzz was a nice taster, but everyone connected with *The Deer Hunter* knew that success would depend on the reviews. For less substantial movies, they were not so crucial, but for an "important" movie about an unpopular subject, the right kind of reviews were vital.

• • •

AS IT TURNED out, the reviews for *The Deer Hunter* could not have been better, which is not to say that they were all positive, but even the bad reviews were good for the movie. It aggressively divided opinion—critics loved it or hated it, but none of them felt indifferent, which was always a box-office killer. Good or bad, the reviews made it sound daring and interesting, and it continued to be feverishly debated in op-ed pieces long after its opening.

Vincent Canby, in the *New York Times,* called it "a big, awkward, crazily ambitious, sometimes breathtaking motion picture that comes as close to being a popular epic as any movie about this country since *The Godfather.*" The *Hollywood Reporter*: "No point in beating around the bush. For me, *The Deer Hunter* is *the* great American movie of 1978." *Chronicles* magazine: "The first serious art in two decades to emerge from the Hollywood film boutique." *Time*: "It shoves the audience into hell and leaves it stranded without a map." Jonathan Rosenbaum in *Take One*: "Try and imagine a boneless elephant sitting in your lap for three hours." *The Village Voice*: "Massively vague, tediously elliptical and mysteriously hysterical." Pauline Kael, the most decisive and influential film critic in the US, could not quite make up her mind: "His new film is enraging, because, despite its ambitiousness and scale, it has no more moral intelligence than the Eastwood action pictures. Yet it's an astonishing piece of work."

At first, the movie had seemed broadly controversial, but it soon became specifically controversial. As the journalist Michael Herr, who had written about the war in his celebrated book, *Dispatches*, and who co-wrote both *Apocalypse Now* and *Full Metal Jacket*, said simply, "Vietnam is awkward." There were many accusations of racism. The Australian war correspondent John Pilger was outraged by the portrayal of the Vietcong. He felt that Cimino presented "a suffering courageous people as sub-human Oriental brutes and dolts." Cimino's line, not entirely unracist in itself, was that he was not being anti-Vietcong: the other side "could just as well be Eskimos"—as if the soldiers were simply all-purpose ethnics. With the national tide having turned against the war, many critics wanted the atonement of equal-opportunity atrocity, some acknowledgment of US war crimes. There is one scene where De Niro turns a flame-thrower on a Vietcong soldier, but it reads as a heroic act—unlike My Lai—because the man has just thrown a hand grenade into a pit where Vietnamese villagers are hiding.

The Deer Hunter managed the unlikely feat of offending both right-wing and left-wing factions because Cimino seemed to take no stance on the war itself. The first group disliked the movie for not applauding the conflict, while the second objected to the fact that it did not condemn it. There was some floundering among critics: In *Chronicles* magazine, Eric Shapearo wrote, "Is *The Deer Hunter* an anti-war movie? The problem starts with the *Iliad*. Was the *Iliad* anti or pro war?" Cimino would not be drawn on the subject either at the time of its release or later: "My role is limited to allowing you to draw your own conclusions. I will not do it for you."

However, Cimino was not always so inscrutable: there was one element about which he was adamant conclusions should not be drawn. A few forensic critics detected a homosexual subtext to the movie: Peter Biskind, one of the most distinguished film critics in the US, said, "If it is about anything, it is about doomed male love. Its mixture of repressed homoeroticism, violence, and patriotism embrace the very worst aspects of American culture, those that led to Vietnam in the first place." Pauline Kael noted that the movie depicted "a physical-spiritual love between men which is higher than the love between men and women." When asked about this insinuation at the time, Cimino was adamant that it did not exist. Thirty years later, he was still denying it.

There were two other areas that proved controversial. The first was the ambiguous ending, where the characters sing "God Bless America," a scene that was construed in different ways. Because the song was rendered in an unemotional way with no histrionics or tears, the pro-war faction believed that it was ironic and therefore unpatriotic, while the other side regarded it as quite the opposite: a distressingly patriotic acceptance of the war in Vietnam and the traumas that the three soldiers had endured.

The second area caused a hysterical debate that never went away: the Russian roulette. The problem was that nobody believed it had ever happened. In the *Los Angeles Times*, the war correspondent Peter Arnett said, "In its twenty years of war, there was not a single recorded case of Russian roulette. The central metaphor is simply a bloody lie." Cimino was adamant that it had taken place. He said that he had press clippings from Singapore confirming incidents of Russian roulette during the war, but he never shared the actual evidence. As ever, he was backed up by Joann Carelli: "That happened there . . . Yes." Still justifying himself in 2002, he reported that he had just received a letter from a journalist saying that there had recently been an incident of Russian roulette on the Laotian border, but the document was never produced.

There was less comment about those scenes from Vietnam vets. Some were very moved by the film. Having seen the atrocities committed by both the Vietcong and their own side, they might have agreed with Cimino's belief that "anyone who was there would agree that anything you could imagine happening probably happened."

Nearly all the commentators described the Russian roulette as a "metaphor," or sometimes obscurely as a "synecdoche," but just because it is not true does not make it either of those things. It is not hard to spot a movie metaphor because they tend to be rather obvious, but this was something different. Cimino was almost the only person who did not see any kind of metaphor: "Try not to look for symbolism in the movie because there is none." It's hard to see what kind of metaphor the Russian roulette could be other than a general reflection on man's inhumanity to man, no more "symbolic" than the firing-squad deaths in Kubrick's *Paths of Glory* or James Mason walking into the sea in *A Star Is Born*. Most viewers had never seen anything as horrifying and violent as the brilliantly shot roulette scenes, and whether the game actually happened in Vietnam or not, it seemed more comforting to regard it as a metaphor—a way of achieving some much-needed distance.

Whether those sequences are metaphorical or not, whether they are true or not, *The Deer Hunter* would not be the first movie that played fast and loose with historical fact. The bridge portrayed in *The Bridge on the River Kwai* spanned a river some miles away from the actual River Kwai, and it was not blown up by the British soldiers who were forced to build it. Mel Gibson's *The Patriot*, set in the American war of independence, has a completely invented scene in which civilians are locked in a church and burned to death by the British. Critics were not overly exercised about those fabrications.

However, while it was one thing for the contentious parts of the movie to be fictional, it was quite another for the director's life to be similarly fictional. Before *The Deer Hunter*, Cimino did not have much of a profile in Hollywood. *Thunderbolt and Lightfoot* had not needed much publicity because there was a preexisting Clint Eastwood fan base, and what little there was focused on the star rather than on the director. Now, having shot to fame with such a controversial and much-debated personal statement, Cimino had a forum. The publicity about him and the movie, triggered by Allan Carr's campaign, was overwhelming.

Now, as he would continue to do until his death, Cimino began to invent an alternative Cimino in interviews, maybe the one he would have preferred to be. Joann Carelli saw it a different way. She told me that, because he had been subjected to such vicious lies about himself by journalists, he was turning the tables and being willfully obfuscating. In fact, his variations on the truth began long before journalists turned hostile after *The Deer Hunter*. Whatever his intentions were, he created a kind of Russian doll narrative of his life that would confuse and infuriate people for the next forty years.

It started in an interview with the *New York Times* journalist Leticia Kent the week before the movie opened. She described him as "Michael Cimino, 35, a self-described workaholic . . . He is serious; speaks calmly and sometimes inaudibly; frequently parries a question with a question." The interview veered from the exact to the imprecise: "He is vague about how many siblings he has. But Mr. Cimino does reveal that he [grew] up in New York City (borough unspecified)." He was more open about his education at Yale: "Mr. Cimino first wanted to become a fine artist, but that didn't seem, in his words, 'quite respectable,' so he studied architecture and art history instead; just short of his doctorate, he dropped out of Yale." Of great relevance to *The Deer Hunter*, he told Kent that "he joined the Army about the time of the Tet Offensive in 1968 and was assigned to a Green Beret unit training in Texas, but was never sent to Vietnam."

A few weeks after the *New York Times* interview, there were rumors that Tom Buckley, the famous journalist who had covered the war for the *New York Times*, was writing a devastating critique of Cimino and *The Deer Hunter* for the April issue of *Harper's*. On February 12, a few days before the movie opened in multiple theaters across the country, *New York* magazine reported that Cimino was considering litigation against Buckley and Lewis Lapham, the editor of *Harper's*. His press agent was concerned that Buckley would write that Cimino "had made certain biographical misstatements to Leticia Kent." However, Buckley had already listened to tapes of the interview, and he did not mince his words: "Cimino said what he said to Leticia. Apparently he lied to her and his press agent."

When his *Harper's* piece was published, it was as devastating as Cimino had feared. Buckley was unrelenting. He hated the movie, which was fair enough—many people did—but his loathing of Cimino seemed to be unmotivated. "People often abandon uncongenial identities when they go to Hollywood . . . Pimps and prostitutes transformed into poets of the cinema. The former maker of commercials, adept in dramatizing one brand of detergent over the others, must have felt right at home." Buckley called the movie Cimino's "narcissistic fantasy" and said that he was "as insulated from reality as the Marquis de Sade." He, too, seemed almost hysterical about the distressing subtext that he, like some others, detected: "A pornographically violent sado-masochistic fantasy with strong elements of homosexuality."

However, what was most damaging was Buckley's forensic unpicking of what Cimino had said to Leticia Kent: "Cimino wasn't thirty-five when he talked to the *Times*, he was a few months short of forty . . . Cimino did indeed attend Yale, and received a master of fine arts degree in 1963. The university has no record of his having done any work at all toward a doctorate [in architecture and fine art.]"

The most sensational thing that Buckley revealed was that "according to the Pentagon, he enlisted in the Army Reserve in 1962, not 1968." The difference between the two dates was crucial. The US involvement in the Vietnam War had not got underway in 1962—troops were not deployed there until 1965. The Tet Offensive in 1968 was one of the most dangerous and vicious parts of the war, and by moving his service up to that year, he implied that, even though he was not sent to Vietnam, he had been at least involved in the conflict. In fact, in 1968, he was at the height of his career in commercials.

Buckley was merciless: he revealed that Cimino's service in the Army Reserve in 1962 lasted only five months. "A small number of Special Forces troops were assigned to Vietnam as advisers in that relatively quiet period. Cimino may have seen a couple of them in a chow line . . . but he never wore the Green Beret himself."

In one of the few times in their life together, even Carelli broke ranks: "It's hard to tell with Michael. I don't know where this comes from." In the end, Cimino's threatened litigation against *Harper's* never came. While he would sometimes talk about his time in the army later, he was much vaguer and would never be drawn into specific details about dates or places. "I can't shake off *The Deer Hunter* even now. I have this insane feeling that I was there, in Vietnam." Then he added a statement that could have referred to his whole life: "Somehow the fine wires have got really crossed and the line between reality and fiction has become blurred."

Other journalists began to look into Cimino's "misstatement" about his army service. This was a different kind of controversy from the fevered opinion and debate that had been good for the movie. Thom Mount at Universal was concerned. "I know this guy. He was no more a medic in the Green Berets than I'm a rutabaga." He did not care much about Cimino's personal reputation, but the movie was important for him and the studio. He did the sensible thing and went to see Mr. Wasserman.

Lew Wasserman, in his forty-year career as a top agent and boss of Universal, was an old hand at sorting out messy and damaging situations that the talent had got themselves into. He was a fixer on a grand scale. Mount told me that Wasserman called in a favor from one of his impeccable political contacts, who set up a special Pentagon telephone number. At the other end was someone who would confirm that Cimino had, indeed, told the truth about his military career.

By the time *Harper's* was on the newsstands, there was better news for Cimino and his movie. On February 20, four days after it had opened wide, the Oscar nominations were announced: *The Deer Hunter* was up for an astonishing nine awards—Best Picture, Director, Sound, Actor, Supporting Actor, Supporting Actress, Film Editing, Original Screenplay, Cinematography. Fonda's *Coming Home* was nominated for eight. It was symptomatic of the deep-seated ambivalence about Vietnam that Cimino's and Fonda's differing takes on the war could be equally lauded and indicated that the Academy preferred to sit on the fence. The multiple Oscar nods were a more newsworthy story than its director's tactical reboot of his past and army service, and anyway, *Harper's* was regarded in Hollywood as a magazine read only by East Coast intellectuals.

The ceremony took place on April 9 in the Dorothy Chandler Pavilion. Cimino gave a disingenuous description of that day, what would now be called a humblebrag: "I was measuring somebody's outfit at Western Costume Co. and the chauffeur had to remind me, 'Michael, you've got to go home and change.' I said, 'For what?' " If his story is true, he must have been the only filmmaker in the history of Hollywood to have forgotten the fact that he was up for Best Director and Best Picture.

Outside the theater there was some publicity-rich picketing, and the police arrested thirteen members of the Vietnam Veterans Against the War. At the same time, the Hell No, We Won't Go Away Committee was handing out newspaper and magazine articles critical of the movie. After getting through the heckling crowd, Cimino then found himself sharing an elevator with Jane Fonda, who was up for seven Oscars for her film, the uncompromisingly antiwar *Coming Home*. She had already labeled Cimino "a right-wing fascist" and now "she wouldn't even look at me." It was not the only embarrassment of the evening. Nominated for Best Screenplay, Deric Washburn had flown from New York. He told me that Cimino and Carelli did not speak to him. In an awkward display of solidarity, they sat alongside Barry Spikings and Michael Deeley.

The awards began to pile up. First, Best Sound, then Best Editing to Peter Zinner, who had betrayed Cimino by doing a secret cut of the wedding sequence. Afterward, the editor was graceful: "We had our differences at the end, but he kissed me when I got the Academy Award." Cimino not so much: "Zinner was a moron. I edited *The Deer Hunter* myself." Vilmos Zsigmond won Best Cinematography, then Christopher Walken for Best Supporting Actor. It did not win Best Original Screenplay (*Coming Home* did), which might have been just as well: the award is accepted by all the writers involved, and Cimino would have found himself onstage with Washburn as well as Quinn Redeker and Louis Garfinkle, who also attended the ceremony.

The penultimate award was for Best Director, and Cimino's name was announced. His face was curiously blank as he went up to the stage and accepted the award from Ali MacGraw and Francis Ford Coppola, who called him "my colleague and *paisan*." Cimino looked genuinely moved,

Cimino, Jane Fonda, and Jon Voight with their Oscars (Alamy)

and his words were equally graceful: "At a moment like this it's difficult to leaven pride with humility. But I am proud to be here and proud of our work, proud to be part of this tradition." Then there were the thank-yous. The first one was to his "dear and very special associate, Joann Carelli." It was unusual to mention someone who was credited as a nebulous "production consultant" before thanking the producers and actors—even the inevitable supportive mothers are normally left to the end. When he did get to the other thanks, he acknowledged only Barry Spikings and not the sidelined Michael Deeley or the hated John Peverall.

The last and most prestigious award to be handed out was for Best Picture. There was a huge cheer when John Wayne, already dying from cancer, came onstage to present it. The right-wing Wayne was reading from a prepared auto-cue script, so he was not called on to express his own unflattering opinion about the Cimino and Fonda movies. When he opened the envelope and announced *The Deer Hunter* as the winner, there was enthusiastic applause from the audience. Allan Carr, several seats along from Cimino, began to cry.

The Best Picture award is accepted only by producers, so it was lucky that Cimino had managed to persuade Spikings halfway through the shoot that he should be credited as one. He, Spikings, and Deeley all climbed on the stage. The Oscars were laid out on a table, and Wayne handed out the statuettes to the three of them. Then there was an awkward moment: Wayne looked confused because there was still a fourth Oscar on the table. "One more?" he said uncertainly. Deeley went over and whispered to him that John Peverall was "unable to attend." In Peverall's long career, *The Deer Hunter* was his only producer credit. It was unlikely that he had, like the director, forgotten the date. In the moments since his first award, Cimino had gotten more into the swing of the Oscar tradition. When he leaned into the microphone, he used the kind of phrase adored by winners: "I love you all madly." Spikings and Deeley spoke briefly. Neither mentioned the director.

THE DEER HUNTER has never lost its power. It is still remembered as the most influential and visceral of all the Vietnam movies. The London *Independent* commented, "*Apocalypse Now* was released in 1979. Oliver Stone's Vietnam trilogy was to follow along with Kubrick's *Full Metal Jacket* but *The Deer Hunter* was where it all began." There are people who remember, in a kind of where-were-you-when-Kennedy-was-shot way, the place and the day they first saw the movie. Its resonance can partly be explained by the fact that the movie was set in both Vietnam and the US, unlike the others, which were set wholly in one or the other (*Coming Home* never left California), and its settings gave it a unique context. For many, there was a personal connection. Jean Vallely wrote in *Rolling Stone*, "My brother Timmy had been blown up in Vietnam. How could this have happened? Nobody understood. Nobody wanted to. And then I saw *The Deer Hunter*. Michael Cimino got it right."

Soon after its release, Cimino got a phone call: "Joann said to me, 'Michael, there's someone calling you from Washington.' I had never had a phone call from Washington before. It was a Vietnam vet called Jan Scruggs on the line. 'I've just seen *The Deer Hunter*,' he said. 'Because of that movie I'm determined to get a memorial built.'" Scruggs proposed an obelisk thirty feet high with the names of the dead inscribed on, but his idea was strongly opposed. For the next two years, he lobbied and fought to raise the money and was finally successful. The Vietnam Veterans Memorial was unveiled on November 13, 1982, and Cimino went to Washington to see it.

While the success of *The Deer Hunter* was an unexpected triumph for everyone connected to it, Cimino was the person who deserved it most. All directors are, of course, "responsible" for their movie (and nobody believed that more aggressively than he did), but he had done something extraordinary. Even if Washburn's contribution was much greater than Cimino would ever acknowledge, he had come up with a detailed outline of a hugely complex movie in a week, had gotten a finished screenplay written in little more than a month, then pushed it into production in four months. That was almost unprecedented in Hollywood—Kubrick's *Barry Lyndon*, for example, involved years of research and a ten-month preproduction period. Cimino's three-hour movie was shot in four and a half months. Kubrick's took a year.

Of course, Spikings and Deeley believed in the project, and Universal liked it enough to finance half of it, but that does not imply any real certainty on their parts. The random and mercurial nature of the movie business does not inspire much of it: there are no sure bets. In a more logical universe than Hollywood, the choices that EMI made might have seemed foolish. They believed in the Quinn/Redeker script, but they chose to allow an untested director to railroad it into a different and seemingly uncommercial movie. Then, when things got difficult in Cleveland, they considered closing down the production but chose not to. They allowed the budget to almost double, and finally, they allowed Cimino to keep the full wedding sequence, which meant releasing a three-hour movie that nobody had much faith in.

In fact, all the "wrong" decisions turned out to be right, but Deeley and Spikings did not know that at the time. They might have had a fragile faith in it, but they did not have certainty—as nobody really does in Hollywood. Cimino, on the other hand, did, and his certainty was of a messianic, take-no-prisoners kind that was both impressive and destructive. He would have said that the end justified the means, but others who had been in his firing line might not have agreed. A producer said to me, "If you want a nice experience on a movie, hire a Sunday School teacher to direct it." Sometimes directors need to be monsters—anyone working on a John Ford or Erich von Stroheim movie would not have had a more pleasant time than they would have done with Cimino—but at the end of the process, he had created a movie that was unexpectedly brilliant and surprisingly profitable. In the end, it grossed nearly $50 million, the same as *Coming Home*.

Of course, Cimino had needed assistance to achieve his vision for *The Deer Hunter*, but he would never acknowledge the contribution of anyone except Carelli—and it was Cimino, rather than her, who demanded that acknowledgment. She—at least to me—was unconcerned about anyone's opinion on what she had or had not done on any of his movies. Within the mysterious confines of their relationship—their "secret world"—it was hard to decipher the variety of ways in which she had enabled him. Looking at the footage of that Oscar ceremony in 1979, you can see her sitting next to him in an elegant white dress. When Francis Ford Coppola announced that Cimino had won the Best Director award, Joann Carelli's face betrayed little emotion. She and Cimino did not turn to each other in astonished Oscar surprise. When he got up, she went to touch his back as he passed in front of her and there was a smile on her face. The award did not seem to be a surprise to her: her certainty about the movie was as great as Cimino's, but it was the last time that their certainty would be so well-judged.

At the same time as the Oscar ceremony was playing out in Los Angeles, there was as much excitement in the small town of Kalispell, Montana, 1,300 miles away. A throng of people had gathered in the large bar of the Outlaw Inn to watch the live broadcast. There had been a lot of drinking, and the crowd was raucous. When *The Deer Hunter* was announced as Best Picture, they went wild. This was a film crew that had been in preproduction in Montana for several months, finding locations, casting five hundred extras, and building the complicated sets for a film called *Heaven's Gate*, which was to be directed by Michael Cimino for United Artists.

The day after the Oscars, Cimino flew up to Kalispell, where the film was to begin shooting in a few days' time. With him was Carelli, no longer production consultant, now the sole producer. Together they were going to make the movie that Cimino had been trying to get off the ground for nearly ten years—one that the success of *The Deer Hunter* had finally kick-started. Carelli's wise advice that he should ask for ten things and settle for the four he wanted had been a long time ago. Now the number of things he was going to ask for was infinite, and he would accept nothing less than every single one of them.

CHAPTER 7

OPENING THE GATE

ONE OF THE scripts Cimino had been working on when he arrived in Hollywood was *The Johnson County War*, about a little-known frontier conflict in Wyoming in the early 1890s between American landowners and the European immigrants they believed were stealing livestock. What was unprecedented about the conflict was that the systematic killing of the immigrants was endorsed—at least tacitly—by the president.

Cimino said that he came across the story while researching the history of barbed wire (he never said why he would be doing such an unlikely thing), which had been used extensively in the West to keep cattle-rustlers out. The Johnson County War was not quite as obscure as he sometimes made out. Frederick Manfred, the author of *Conquering Horse*, had written about the conflict in his 1957 novel, *Riders of Judgement*, which Cimino must have read. The British director Michael Winner had developed a project on the same subject, and there was also a television movie in development called *Invasion of Johnson County*, finally made in 1976. Over the space of eight years, Cimino's own script evolved, through several drafts, into *Heaven's Gate*.

The final version of the script begins in 1871, as James Averill, full of passion and hope, graduates from Harvard. The movie then flashes forward twenty years, when, his wealthy East Coast background left far behind him, he has become a marshal in Johnson County. He finds himself on the other side of the law from his old friend Nate Champion, who has become a vigilante for the Stock Growers Association, which has drawn up a death list of 125 thieving immigrants. Champion and Averill are also in a triangular relationship with Ella Watson, who runs a brothel and accepts stolen cattle from the immigrants as payment. When she is raped as punishment, Averill and Champion kill the perpetrators. Champion refuses to participate any more in hunting down the people on the death list and is killed. The war escalates and ends in a battle between the mercenaries hired by the Stock Growers Association and the immigrants. There are heavy casualties on both sides, but the US Army arrives to save the remaining mercenaries. As Ella and Averill prepare to leave Wyoming for good, she is shot. There is an enigmatic epilogue set ten years later, when Averill is sailing on his yacht off Rhode Island, haunted by his memories of Ella and the conflict.

The first version of the script, written in 1971, differed in some respects from the final one: there was no prologue and epilogue. Averill was not a marshal but a district judge. Although there was still a triangular love affair, Nate Champion worked for Averill and was not on the other side of the law. The project was optioned by David Foster, an independent producer who had made Robert Altman's *McCabe & Mrs. Miller* and Sam Peckinpah's *The Getaway*. They offered the role of Averill to Steve McQueen, but although he liked the script, he had little confidence in Cimino as a director. United Artists had dabbled with it for a while, and then 20th Century Fox picked it up and commissioned a rewrite, retitled *Paydirt*, which was much closer to the final movie, although it still did not have a prologue and epilogue. However, Jere Henshaw, the head of production at the studio, felt that "the overall impression one was left with was one of depression because the three protagonists did not survive and died in a very bloody and nihilistic way." Foster eventually dropped the project: "People liked the script, but no one was willing to take that shot to let Mike direct."

In the spring of 1978, although *The Deer Hunter* would not be released until December, the heat around Cimino was rising. Barry Spikings, the only producer who had been supportive of him during and after the shoot, was talking it up enthusiastically. Cimino was also showing the print he had quietly taken from EMI during the rows over the length of the movie. Danton Rissner, the head of production at United Artists, had seen it, and in May, he proposed to his boss, Andy Albeck, that they should offer Cimino a two-picture deal. That kind of deal sounds better than it usually is for unproven directors. Experienced ones have more cards in their hands and are in a better negotiating position. For the others, there can be some downside. Projects are offered to the studio, but they can turn down any ones that they do not like—the director has no automatic right to make anything—and if a movie is made, the fees will have been prenegotiated. However, it means that a director is a step closer to the decision-makers and—in an insecure town—his talent has received some kind of recognition. The studio may also pay a retainer, will commission scripts, and maybe provide an office and some staff expenses. If a director were interested in this kind of deal, United Artists was an good place to have one.

It was unlike most studios because it was not actually a studio in the conventional sense of the word. They did not have a physical presence as others did. There was no giant and expensive backlot—20th Century Fox's was fifty-three acres in Culver City—that needed to be filled with "product" shooting in it. More than that, United Artists was small, with much less bureaucracy: decisions were made quickly, and projects did not generally languish. They also charged no overhead—other studios might add 15 percent or more to a movie's budget—and their method of calculating profits was much more transparent and fairer than most studios' accounting practices. Best of all, they had a long tradition of being talent-friendly—mostly because it was talent that had created the studio.

In 1919, four of the most powerful and wealthy figures in the industry—Charlie Chaplin; Mary Pickford; her husband, Douglas Fairbanks; and D. W. Griffith, the director of *Birth of a Nation*—wanted to have more control over the pictures they made, so they created their own studio. However, it soon became clear why studios tended to be run by hard-nosed moneymen rather than the talent: the creators of United Artists were more interested in show than business. They were all at the peak of their careers, so they could be choosy about the projects they made, but there were not enough to produce a viable cashflow for the studio. In the end, they did hire a businessman called Joseph Schenck to run it and find other talent to work with. Like many of the people who came to Hollywood in the early years of the industry, he had managed to segue from an unrelated career (he had been a pharmacist) to a career in the movie business.

He did a deal with Samuel Goldwyn (originally a glove salesman) to distribute the films, and slowly United Artists became a more solid and profitable operation. However, by the '30s, Schenck had left to form 20th Century Fox with Darryl F. Zanuck. By then, two of the original founders had significantly diminished careers: Mary Pickford was too old to play the kind of roles she had become famous for, and she and Douglas Fairbanks had divorced before his death in 1939. The third, D. W. Griffith, had sold his shares in 1932 to stave off bankruptcy. Only Chaplin retained his star power, but he was far from prolific, and he and Pickford had also fallen out acrimoniously. The studio limped on until the early 1950s, when two smart ex-lawyers, Arthur Krim and Robert Benjamin, made a proposal: if they managed to turn United Artists around, they could buy 50 percent of the company. They did so very quickly and later bought the other half of it.

The 1950s and '60s became a golden age for the studio. Krim and Benjamin did not tend to work with unproven talent. Instead, they formed strategic relationships with established and fiscally responsible directors and producers. Because they made sure that the projects were in experienced and trustworthy hands, they did not have to interfere too much. They offered attractive deals that worked for all parties—tangible profits and part ownership of the movies. Over two decades, they worked with star directors such as Stanley Kramer on *High Noon* and *It's a Mad, Mad, Mad, Mad World*, Otto Preminger on *Exodus,* and Robert Wise on *West Side Story.* They had a close relationship with Billy Wilder, and later Woody Allen.

In 1967, Krim and Benjamin merged United Artists with the Transamerica Corporation, a conglomeration of various businesses that included insurance, car rentals, and airlines, in return for $180 million of Transamerica stock. They were not the only studio to go corporate—in 1966, Paramount was bought by Gulf + Western, whose activities embraced publishing, swimwear, and zinc. It wasn't just that filmmaking seemed glamorous to gray-suit businesses—studios tended to own valuable real estate, and their film libraries had the potential of being exploited for television and the new media that was coming.

The upside for Krim and Benjamin was that they had been richly rewarded for twenty years of success. The downside was that it was not so much fun—although their business was technically autonomous, they reported to bosses who had no understanding of movies. In January 1978, they tried to take United Artists out of Transamerica, but they were rebuffed. In retaliation, they did something unexpected: they jumped ship and formed a new company called Orion, which they were going to run on the same lines as their previous studio. It was United Artists under a pseudonym. They took most of the creative staff with them, as well as the talent relationships. It was a hastily reconfigured United Artists that was talking to Cimino about a deal.

The new team that Transamerica hired to run the studio did not have the track record or prestige that Krim, Benjamin, and their lieutenants had. Andy Albeck, a genial United Artists lifer—he had been there for thirty years as vice-president—was elevated to the top job. Danton Rissner, who had been with the company since 1970, was made worldwide head of production. Neither he nor Albeck had much industry profile. In turn, Rissner hired two new production executives from 20th Century Fox, Steven Bach and David Field, who were to work out of New York and Los Angeles, respectively.

The reason Danton Rissner was interested in making a deal with Cimino was simple: the new United Artists needed prestige and product: nothing going into production seemed very exciting. With such an undynamic and unproven team at the helm, the studio was not at the top of anyone's list for submitting projects to, and the talent who had respected Krim and Benjamin so much gravitated to Orion. Woody Allen, despite a charm offensive by Albeck and Rissner, left as soon his last United Artists movie had been released.

They did have one important continuing franchise—James Bond—and one sort-of franchise, which was the *Pink Panther* series, but there was no real guarantee of any more of them because of the volatile relationship between director Blake Edwards and star Peter Sellers, who had fallen out. But those two franchises were linked with the old United Artists, and anyway, they were not really prestigious and were never going to be Oscar fodder. With the buzz around *The Deer Hunter,* a deal with Cimino looked very attractive (although others—particularly Steven Bach—were not as keen as Rissner). Inevitably, before long, the problems with those kinds of deals surfaced: UA wanted Cimino to direct the script he had written with no great enthusiasm—Frederick Forsyth's mercenaries-in-Africa novel *The Dogs of War*—but Cimino was not going to follow *The Deer Hunter* with such a schlocky and workmanlike project. He refused. What he wanted to do was *The Fountainhead,* and while Rissner was initially enthusiastic, nobody else was, and he had to do some embarrassing backtracking.

In order to maintain confidence in the Cimino deal, he suggested that Bach and Field see *The Deer Hunter.* It had to be a surreptitious screening, and the only way it could be arranged, of course, was through Joann Carelli, who was as elusive then as she is now. Bach managed to track her down with some difficulty by going through a succession of private numbers and answering services. On August 16, she brought the film to their office in New York without Cimino, who was in Los Angeles. Field knew them a little, but Bach did not. At the screening, he found her attractive, low-key, and businesslike, not the "dragon lady" people had warned him about.

Like almost everyone who had seen the movie, they were knocked out by it. Bach said that he found it "absorbing, repellent, touching, brutal, confusing, stirring, and *long.*" As they were leaving, Carelli asked if *The Fountainhead* was dead. When Bach acknowledged that it was, she said, "Mike has a lot of ideas. You should talk to him."

Rissner, despite being only thirty-eight, had had triple-bypass heart surgery and was recuperating at home in Malibu. Albeck asked Bach to go to Los Angeles and work alongside David Field to cover for Rissner. Bach wrote to Cimino to tell him how much he had loved *The Deer Hunter* and suggested that they should talk. On September 17, they met for lunch at the Polo Lounge in the Beverly Hills Hotel, a classic movie hangout place that was safe ground—establishment, but not too stuffy.

Carelli, of course, accompanied Cimino. Bach found them both good company—Cimino soft-spoken and modest, Carelli courteous and friendly. Despite the constant battles he was having over *The Deer Hunter* with Thom Mount and Michael Deeley—the contentious previews had been only a month before—Cimino spoke calmly about the movie. He was quietly confident that he would get his way because he knew his way was right. Bach made a very perceptive comment about him: "If there was a ruthlessness, it stemmed not from recklessness but from conviction." At the end of the lunch, Carelli opened her shoulder bag and handed Bach the script of *The Johnson County War*. Cimino told him that he thought he could come up with a better title.

In fact, a couple of weeks earlier, Stan Kamen, Cimino's agent at William Morris, had let Danton Rissner see an "unofficial" version of the script, because it was already being looked at by other studios. 20th Century Fox had first refusal because they had commissioned a rewrite by Cimino a few years before. Out of politeness, Kamen had shown it to Universal because of *The Deer Hunter*, and he let Warner Bros. see it as well. What Kamen was offering was a "package" that included Cimino to write and direct, Carelli to produce, and Kris Kristofferson to play James Averill. Naturally, Kamen represented them all.

Not long after he sent the script to UA, everyone else began to turn it down—20th Century Fox did not like the script any better than they had before; Warner Bros. were initially keen but were not convinced that it was commercial and did not want Christopher Walken, who Cimino had decided should be the second lead; Thom Mount at Universal said that under no circumstances would he ever work with Cimino again. In classic agent style, Kamen subtly implied to United Artists that the project was still in play at some of the other companies.

Cimino's existing deal at the studio was one that would allow him to develop projects, and Kamen insisted that because *The Johnson County War* had been written before the deal, had the key players already on board, and was ready to go into production immediately, it should be not be part of Cimino's two-picture deal with its fixed—and significantly lower—fees. He was asking for $750,000 for Cimino, $100,000 for Carelli, and $850,000 for Kristofferson. It was a high fee for the actor, but he had just come off starring opposite Barbra Streisand in the hugely successful remake of *A Star Is Born*. Kamen was also demanding pay-or-play deals—they would all get paid whether the movie was made or not. A budget had already been done: Cimino and Carelli believed that they could bring the picture in for $7.8 million.

At United Artists, the reaction to the script was rather cool. Rissner liked it but was worried that the powerful sales department might veto it. Some of the script executives did not like it. One of them, Steve Bussard, felt that there were too many characters and not enough time to develop them properly. The ending, in which the protagonists were killed, was "downbeat." He said, "If it were not for Cimino, I would pass," and that was the problem they had: reject the script and lose Cimino. Steven Bach, too, was keener on Cimino than the script.

While the deliberation was continuing, a significant event happened at the company. Rissner had been working part-time since July while he recuperated from his heart operation. In mid-September, his doctor told him that unless he quit his job, there would be serious health consequences for him. Albeck called Bach and Field to his office and jointly offered them Rissner's head of production job. They would be of equal status, and no picture would be made without both of them approving it. If there was disagreement, Albeck would have the final say.

The team at United Artists were still unsure about *The Johnson County War*, but the situation now changed. Bach and Field decided to go for Kamen's deal. It would be a preemptive strike for UA and would prove to the industry that the two new heads of production were decisive and dynamic. Against a lot of competition from other studios—not strictly true, of course—they had landed one of the hottest directors in town, who was going to direct his epic vision of the Old West for them. The very reasonable budget of $7.8 million was appealing, too, although Lee Katz, UA's senior production accountant, expressed some doubts. It seemed that Cimino's movie was going to be that rarest of beasts: a commercial auteur movie at an attractive price. On September 26, Bach and Field called Stan Kamen and agreed to the deal that he had proposed, with two amendments: they wanted another rewrite of the script, and the budget would be no more than the figure Cimino and Carelli had given them: $7.8 million.

In the movie industry, a deal agreed is an engagement rather than a marriage. It is—as lawyers say—"subject to contract," and its negotiation can take months of arguing over the small as well as the big print, and both parties can theoretically walk away. In reality, the closer the project gets to starting production, with other deals with actors and crew agreed and large sums of money spent, it is harder to do that. However, there was at least a formal agreement between Cimino and UA now. As the call with Kamen was finishing, Bach remembered that he and Field "made triumphant eye contact."

Both would be key players in the *Heaven's Gate* saga, and Bach, who died in 2009, would write a book about the making of the movie in 1986, *Final Cut*, a gossipy but coruscating saga that is widely regarded as a film industry classic, along with two other famous books about the making of individual movies: Lillian Ross's *Picture* in 1952 (about John Huston's *The Red Badge of Courage*) and Julie Salamon's *The Devil's Candy* in 1991 (about Brian De Palma's disastrous *Bonfire of the Vanities*.). However, the difference between Bach's book and the others is that they were impartial. Bach was intimately involved in Cimino's movie, and he turned out to be a rather unreliable narrator, accurate about the facts but more dissembling about his colleagues and the attribution of blame. The fractured relationships on the movie extended to the book about it: Bach's fellow executive, David Field, refused to be involved in it.

Bach and Field were an odd combination. They had known each other for a while from their previous jobs at 20th Century Fox, but they were more work friends than hangout pals, and they had had their differences before they were given the joint job. Originally, Bach had been senior to Field and was sometimes not shy about pointing it out. When they had a disagreement about which of them should telephone a particular writer, Bach said to him, "I don't have to ask your permission to call anybody. I outrank you in this playpen."

They were very different personalities. Field was a quiet, reflective (Bach called him "moody") Princeton intellectual, immensely literate and serious. He had an unusual sideline for a producer in Hollywood—he was a poet. Although Bach was good at his job, he was attracted to the superficial glitz of movie life. He loved lavish expense account meals and staying at the best hotels. Because he oversaw European production, he traveled a lot and insisted on flying Concorde. Field was different: he loved movies more than he loved show business.

He left the industry a long time ago and has almost never spoken about *Heaven's Gate*, an experience that altered his life, as it did for so many others. Nobody in Hollywood seemed to know what had become of him—people in the business generally have no interest in people who are out of the business—but eventually I found an email address for him. I was surprised when he called me almost immediately. He was very guarded but agreed to see me, and a few days later, we met in a location that was typical of Field: a bookshop, in a small Santa Monica market.

He told me something that Bach had said to him lightheartedly when they first started their joint job: "I give the best yes in the business. You give the best no." That could have indicated a complementary good cop/bad cop vibe, but in fact, it put them in differing camps and would have a devastating effect on their handling of the *Heaven's Gate* crisis that was soon to come.

Bach's tendency to say yes had a subtext: he did not like confrontation much in a business where confrontation is a given. He and Field soon ran into a problem. One of Bach's passion projects was *Cuba*, a *Casablanca*-like romance set during the Cuban revolution that was about to start shooting in Spain. It starred Sean Connery and would be directed by Richard Lester, an American based in London. Both were on pay-or-play deals, and they were both happy with the script. Field was not and wanted to cancel the picture, despite the deals in place.

The movie was European, and because Bach had been in charge of production there and had brought the picture to UA, it was really his problem to solve. He knew he would have to fly to London and read the riot act to Lester and Connery. Field told me that Bach begged him to come with him because he did not want to confront the powerful director and star on his own (not the way that Bach described it in his book). After an agreement to rewrite the script and many reassurances from Lester, Bach said, "I was prepared to take the gamble and hope." Field was not a man who believed much in the power of hope, and he still wanted to close the picture down. The decision was left to Andy Albeck—a man who also liked to say yes—and he vetoed Field. The movie went ahead and flopped badly.

In the meantime, Field was discussing script changes with Cimino. He told me that one of the problems he had with it was the lack of context: it was unclear exactly where the Kristofferson character came from and why he was in Wyoming. Field—always good with script—suggested that Cimino imagine Kristofferson as a Harvard rich boy (the actor had actually been to Oxford) who, in contemporary terms, has joined the Peace

Corps in Vietnam in order to do good. Cimino ran with it and added the Harvard graduation prologue. Now the Kristofferson character's version of pro bono was to support the immigrants against the cattle barons of Johnson County. In his book, Bach maintains that Cimino came up with the idea himself. He also changed the title to *Heaven's Gate*, the name of the roller-skating rink that the immigrants have built.

The movie was now in formal preproduction, which meant money was being spent. Crew members were being hired; Cimino was doing location scouting. Shooting was to start on April 16, 1979. Like *The Deer Hunter*, the equally ambitious *Heaven's Gate* was being put together in a remarkably short time, not much more than four months, but Cimino was pushing it forward with his usual drive and commitment, a commitment that did not welcome any constraints. When the deal had been done with him in September, he had been merely "hot." Now his stature was growing exponentially. *The Deer Hunter* had opened with a roar of publicity and acclaim in December. On February 20, the nine Oscar nominations were announced. Its five wins would come in just before shooting started.

Naturally, there were budget problems. Bach talked of them as if that was unusual. In fact, every movie that is heading for production will have nervous money discussions. He rightly called a budget "an estimate of an estimate." The original one had been prepared in September, before any real production groundwork had been done, and now that actual costs were coming in—a larger amount of extras than originally planned, higher location fees, increased travel costs—a new one had been prepared by Cimino and Carelli's production team that came to $11.5 million. Lee Katz, UA's accounting supremo, was just as doubtful as he had been about the original $7.8 million budget, mostly because he did not believe that Cimino would be able to shoot the movie in the proposed sixty-nine days. The price of the prologue and epilogue, which everyone wanted, had to be factored in as well. In an internal memo Katz described it as "a budget made with a crystal ball." One of the most worrying increases was down to the United Artists sales team: they wanted the movie to be ready for release by December to qualify for the Oscars, an absurdly short amount of time. Quick costs money in the movie business: there would be a high cost to this accelerated postproduction schedule. There had been a year between the end of production and the release of *The Deer Hunter.* On this movie, there would be fewer than five months—assuming that Cimino did not exceed the sixty-nine days of shooting. It was asking a lot of him, but, although noncommittal, he agreed to think about it.

In the meantime, much of the casting had been done by Cis Corman, who had worked on *The Deer Hunter.* Jeff Bridges, Christopher Walken, John Hurt, Brad Dourif, and Mickey Rourke were all on board, but there was a major problem: with six weeks to go until shooting, the main female role of Ella was not yet cast. The obvious actresses with box-office draw had been approached but turned it down—Jane Fonda, Diane Keaton, and even Raquel Welch. One of the reasons was that Kristofferson had been given contractual first billing and no major actress would have agreed to be below him on the credits and posters.

Cimino came up with someone from left field: a French actress, the twenty-five-year-old Isabelle Huppert. She had had a reasonably successful career in Europe, but not as a lead actress. However, in 1978, she had starred in a Claude Chabrol movie about a young girl who poisons her parents. Carelli said that when Cimino was doing the casting, she told him that she had seen a French film called *Violette Nozière,* and Isabelle Huppert was incredible in it. Cimino's version was that he had discovered Huppert himself—"I found myself at the corner of Madison and Fifty-Ninth, where there was a little movie theater. I saw this name Isabelle Huppert, and it was love at first sight." Carelli was characteristically unconcerned that Cimino had taken the credit for finding her.

Field and Bach were horrified. They had realized that they might have to accept a lesser-known American actress, but an unknown French one was quite different. (In fact, Huppert had already been in one American movie, three years before: Otto Preminger's *Rosebud.*) Bach also felt that not only did she have "a face like a potato," but she probably did not even speak English. Cimino said that he already talked to her: she did.

Bach and Field gave him a flat no. Cimino had been reasonably cooperative up to that point, but he refused to accept their position and threatened to go over their head to Andy Albeck unless they went to Paris to meet Huppert. Bach and Field made a compromise—Bach spoke good French, and he would telephone her. After he had, he reported that he "didn't understand one word of English she spoke." In the end, the always conciliatory Albeck felt that they should go to Paris anyway, just to make a gesture to Cimino that they were not the kind of people who rejected creative ideas out of hand. Field and Bach made one stipulation to Cimino: if they were not convinced by Huppert, their decision would be final. He agreed.

He, Carelli, and Christopher Walken were already in Paris doing publicity for *The Deer Hunter* when Bach and Field flew out at the end of February. Walken was going to read some of the script with Huppert. When they met in Cimino and Carelli's suite, she was already there. Bach said, rather cruelly, "She didn't have a face like a potato after all. She looked like the Pillsbury Doughboy got up in a shapeless cotton shift." He felt that she read indifferently in stilted and heavily accented English. Although they did find some charm in her, the answer was still no, but their decision was not given to Cimino and Carelli until dinner the next night.

Despite what he had agreed to with Bach and Field before they went to Paris, he refused point-blank to accept their decision. He was not prepared, he said, to make his movie with people as insensitive and untalented as them. He was going to move the picture to Warner Bros. They did not know whether this was a bluff. (In fact, Cimino had already talked to the studio, but Robert Shapiro, then head of production, told me that they had not taken Cimino too seriously—they felt he was just trying to engineer some kind of bargaining position with United Artists.)

Here, Bach's and Field's stories diverge significantly. In his book, Bach reported that they went back to their hotel, where they called Albeck to tell him what had happened. Albck was philosophical, telling them that it didn't matter too much who starred in the picture because the real star was Cimino. He said that they should go with Huppert.

Field's story is quite different. He told me that, outraged by Cimino breaking his word, he gave the director forty-eight hours to back down or he would advise pulling the picture even though it would cost the company around $3 million for the pay-or-play deals and costs they had already committed to. Cimino refused. When Field was back in California and Bach in New York, he called Albeck and told him that they should cancel *Heaven's Gate* and get out while they still could, not least because he felt that, with or without Huppert, the budget was certain to rise, maybe as high as $15 million. They discussed it for some time.

Albeck did not seem too worried about the budget—he had talked to their international sales people, who thought they could gross $25 million just from outside the US. He decided that they should accept Huppert. There would be no backup for Field. He told me that he had discovered later that Bach had been silently on the line saying nothing. Field knew at that moment with inexorable certainty that they—and he—had lost all power over Cimino and his movie. He told me that it was at that moment when he knew he should have resigned from the company.

Cimino had thought about United Artists' desire to rush through postproduction in order to have a Christmas release that year, a hope that had been discussed in February. In the meantime, contracts had been going back and forth between United Artists and Cimino's people: his agent, Stan Kamen, and his lawyer, Eric Weissmann, a legendary industry figure who had represented actors from Elizabeth Taylor to Gene Wilder and directors like Altman and Scorsese. On March 21, three weeks before shooting was to start, United Artists received a revised contract not only with some significant additions but with a request/demand that the contract be signed no later than the twenty-third. There were the usual ego stipulations, maybe more outrageous than some but by no means unknown. Cimino wanted huge weekly expenses, as well as what is called a possessory credit—"Michael Cimino's *Heaven's Gate*"—but so did every other big director. He also demanded that his name be the same size as the title of the movie on credits, posters, and theater marquees, and UA would have a legal obligation to enforce this in their agreements with theaters. That would mean that Cimino would have legal redress against UA if he found himself by chance in, say, El Paso or Wichita and saw that his name was smaller than the movie title on the marquee. More than that, he wanted total control and approval over the advertising campaign and the poster design.

But the crucial new clause concerned the Christmas release. Yes, Cimino would agree to do his best, but there was a major caveat: he would not be responsible for any budget overages if it cost more to achieve it. That, in some ways, was fair enough (UA, after all, were the ones who were asking for an early release) but there was more—he would not be responsible for the excess "even if it is finally decided that it is not feasible to complete and deliver the picture in time for such a release." As it would be impossible to work out which added costs were caused by forcing an early release through and which were due to other reasons, like director profligacy, it meant that Cimino could go overbudget if he felt like it with no restraints, which removed the biggest stick a studio can normally wield over a director: penalties for him if the budget is exceeded. In these instances, he would not literally have to pay the money back, but some of his fee could be withheld or his profit percentage reduced. With the Huppert decision, Cimino had essentially gained complete creative control. Now, if UA agreed to the revised contract, he would also have financial control.

The negotiations had become a game of bluff: Who was going to blink first? In hindsight, UA was in a stronger position than they believed. Cimino was threatening to move the production to another studio, but this would realistically be hard to achieve (and there was little evidence that any other studio was really interested at that point). For one thing, it would have been impossible to start shooting in three weeks because another studio would not be geared up to do so. With a delay, it could mean that the actors and crew Cimino had chosen might not be available. On top of that, another studio would be obligated to repay United Artists the money they had already spent, at this stage maybe as much as $4 million. There would also have been bad publicity, probably more harmful to Cimino than to UA. They might have seemed like philistines unable to see a great director's vision, but they could have survived that—since the industry began, creative people have always seen the studios as essentially philistine. He, however, would be seen as autocratic and difficult and—most terrifying to the money people—cavalier with a budget (the stories about the problems of *The Deer Hunter* had already circulated around town).

Carelli seemed curiously absent during the contract negotiations, which was unusual for a producer. However, she was an unusual producer. Agreeing to her appointment had always been a strange move for United Artists—she had never produced a big (or small) movie before. While courtesy producer credits are fairly commonplace, nobody expects those producers to actually produce. Tom Cruise's former agent, Paula Wagner, had a credit on many of his movies. Robin Williams's second wife, who had once been his children's nanny, was producer on five of his projects.

The difference between them and Joann Carelli was that they shared the role—there was always an experienced producer on board as well.

Although Carelli had been part of Stan Kamen's "package" back in September, Cimino had fewer cards in his hand then—*The Deer Hunter* was three months away from opening, and it was uncertain how it would go. Nobody was in any doubt that she was indispensable to Cimino, but it would have been feasible—although they would have kicked up a fuss—to insist on a powerful fellow producer. Irwin Winkler told me, half-jokingly, that he thought United Artists were "too mean" to hire one. More than that, the associate producer—the line manager of the crew, who responsible for anticipating budget problems—was the enormously experienced Charles Okun, but he had known Cimino for fifteen years and had worked on his commercials. On this movie, the associate producer would be answerable to the producer, who would be answerable to the director. There would be none of the usual checks and balances—the impartial view—normally provided by those roles.

But there is a certain irony here. Carelli was tough and charismatic—qualities that a good producer needs. With her formidable intelligence and flame-thrower personality, she would have been a brilliant producer for the most difficult director in Hollywood, but working with Cimino in their "secret world" was another matter.

With a few light tinkerings (his giant weekly expenses were reduced somewhat), United Artists caved in to Cimino's demands. Both he and the studio professed delight that they had agreed on a mutually beneficial contract. In reality, they were like a celebrity couple trapped in a loveless marriage who have to put on a united front for publicity purposes. Cimino even presented David Field with a handsome pair of cowboy boots as a start-of-production present.

In his book, Bach says that on Field's copy of the contract, next to the crucial budget paragraph, he had written and underlined the word "OK." It seems an irrelevant note for Bach to add—it had no legal status—unless it is to imply that, in the crowded pool of United Artists' responsibility, Field was just a little bit more guilty for caving in. In fact, though they might not have scrawled it on their contracts, they had all said OK. Cimino had stared resolutely in their eyes, and they had all—Bach, Albeck, Lee Katz, Field—blinked first.

CHAPTER 8

THE CIRCUS COMES TO TOWN

KALISPELL IS IN the heart of hunting country. So keen is it to establish its macho credentials that there is a large stuffed black bear watching over the luggage carousel in its small airport. Of the many rifle stores in the area, one of the most popular is Machine Gun Montana; Flaming Arrow Archery provides broadheads for hunting wild turkey. The tourists who do not come for the hunting head for the million-acre Glacier National Park, which was where Cimino was planning to re-create Wyoming's Johnson County, where the range war between landowners and immigrants, which would serve as the subject of *Heaven's Gate*, had taken place in 1889. Kalispell, some thirty miles away, was the obvious place to base the hundreds of crew members. They were not a natural fit with the virile hunting locals, who presumed the visitors would be pampered Hollywood hippies, and they were initially regarded with a certain amount of suspicion.

There is no particular reason why a small town in Montana should change much over forty years, and Kalispell has not. The Outlaw Inn, where most of the *Heaven's Gate* unit stayed, is still there, and that was where I stayed too. By coincidence, I arrived there on October 9, 2019, forty years to the day that Cimino's movie finished its troubled shoot. In 1979, the crew filled all of the hotel's rooms, but when I was there, almost none of them were occupied. I saw only three other guests. The large bar and the busy steak restaurant have closed because the inn lost its liquor license. These days, it is not a popular place to stay. An unhappy visitor posted, "Two rats checked out as we were checking in. The shower head is falling out of the wall. Ghost village."

While many movies, including *Cattle Queen of Montana* and *The Missouri Breaks*, had been shot in the state, none had ever taken over a small town the size of Kalispell, whose population in 1979 was around ten thousand people. Montana had always been keen to encourage filmmaking because it provided employment for local contractors, boosted retail businesses, and indirectly encouraged tourism by showing off its spectacular scenery. There was even a film office, which had been run by a man called Garry Wunderwald since 1977.

He told me, "I had had a call from Michael six months before the film was starting shooting. He wanted to come to Montana to look at the scenery. He had looked at Wyoming, but he did not want to shoot there because the mountains weren't impressive enough. I was pretty well sworn to secrecy, and I met with him. He said he wanted to go to Glacier National Park, so we did. Michael would come out one week, and then Charlie Okun would come the next."

Wunderwald was determined that the movie should come to Montana, and he provided an enormous amount of cooperation to ensure that it did. "I knew the park people, but I was thinking to myself, 'This is going to be real hard because they're really tough on filming, certainly something of this magnitude with all the construction needed,'" he said, but in the end he convinced them, and they issued permits that had very rigorous stipulations about what Cimino could and could not do.

Wunderwald also organized the hiring of the seventy cars and trucks the production would need, made sure that the Outlaw Inn would welcome the huge crew, and found warehouses to store the props and the vast wardrobes of costumes. The train sequences were crucial to the movie, and when Cimino did not like Kalispell's railway station, Wunderwald found a much better one in Wallace, Idaho, which was just about close enough—a three-hour drive—for the main locations to stay in and around Kalispell. He found a seven-foot antique potbellied stove for the roller-skating set and even helped Cimino find the exact model of black Jeep that he was looking for. "Joann liked it really well, so he gave it to her. I said, 'Michael, you've just given away a Jeep.' 'Oh,' he said, 'I'll buy another one.'"

It was worth Wunderwald's time and trouble. Over the seven months of filming, 2,500 locals were employed as extras, and 150 local carpenters were hired in four separate construction crews. More than that, a well-paid crew of three hundred arrived in town from Hollywood to spend money. Wunderwald remembered the dry cleaners being swamped, the photo labs developing miles of negatives, and the bars and restaurants filled to bursting point. The man who owned the local car wash made so much profit that he built a second one after filming ended. The president of Kalispell's chamber of commerce reported that United Artists had pumped nearly $14 million into the area's economy. As the *Kalispell Weekly* said in its down-home way, "The movie has fattened many a wallet."

For many people in Kalispell, this invasion by the movie crew was the most electrifying thing that had ever happened to them. I had put a notice in the local online newsletter saying I was writing a book about Cimino and asked—without much hope—if anyone had any memories of something that happened forty years before. I received nearly fifty emails from people who had worked on the movie, some for a short time and some for the entire length of filming. They all wanted to talk, share scrapbooks and press clippings, and reminisce. It became clear that nothing as exciting had ever happened in the town before the movie, and in the forty years since, nothing had equaled it.

Tony Gaznick was in charge of hiring extras, and Cimino's instructions had been predictably precise: they were all to have an immigrant Eastern European "look," less definable for the women, but for the men tall, thin, dark-haired, and bearded. Word got around Kalispell quickly, and many people were desperate to be part of such a glamourous-sounding experience. (Buck Torenson, the owner of the Outlaw Inn, had begun advertising it as "Home of the Stars.") Tina Buckingham was one of the most determined: after being rebuffed by the front desk of the Outlaw Inn, she pushed her way onto the closed set, convinced an assistant director to give her a shot, and landed a role as an extra.

Bryan Buchanan told me, "I was a grad student in Kalispell study-ing media arts, and Tony asked me to help him sort out the extras. Then he told me they needed someone to be Kris Kristofferson's stand-in and offered the job to me. I quit college and never went back."

Kona Luke lied to get on the production: "I responded to an ad saying they were looking for extras. We went to the Colt 44 room of the Outlaw Inn, my seven-year-old son and I, and we listened to their spiel. They told me the various ins and outs of the movie, and they said, 'Nobody pregnant.' I did not tell them I was two months gone, and they hired me and my son. I took him out of school. Kris Kristofferson and Jeff Bridges befriended him and taught him how to play chess in the trailer." She had to stop being an extra when her pregnancy began to show, but then she acted as her son's chaperone instead, which meant that she could still go to the set every day.

Brian Wood, who had a student job as a night manager at the Four Seasons Motel, heard about a casting call from the overflow crew who were staying there. "A young lady interviewed me," he told me, "and the next thing I knew I was wearing a big blue full-length wool coat, the one that Burt Reynolds had worn in *The Man Who Loved Cat Dancing*. Filming went on so long that I didn't get back to school that fall because it was such fun. *Heaven's Gate* was a huge part of my life."

The locals were fascinated to meet the actors. They liked some more than others. "We found some of them tough to get to know, and some not worth the effort. Chris Walken gave us the impression that he does not really dwell here on earth with us mortals . . . like, who needs it, man?" Kris Kristofferson was going through a painful divorce and did not mingle much. However, everyone liked Jeff Bridges, who was always happy to be photographed with the extras: "He's a very friendly, self-confident, and regular guy."

Apart from extras, the movie needed experienced local horsemen as well, particularly for the climactic battle scene, which would require hundreds of them. Rudy Ugland, in charge of all the horses and rid-ing, said, "We had a hundred and fifty wagons and over a hundred saddle horses. We took portable corrals with us, and we had semis loaded with hay hauled in every two days, and we fed all the horses by hand." The wranglers Ugland brought with him were enormously experienced—several of them had worked on the famous chariot race in *Ben-Hur*—but they operated in a different way from the Montana riders, and there was often friction.

A local, Pamela Dylina, told me, "We called ourselves 'The Bohunk Cavalry' ["bohunk" being slang for an immigrant from central Europe]. There were about twenty-five of us. We got so disgusted because we were all experienced horsemen. We would come to work, and the wranglers would have my saddle on someone else's horse and they were telling us which ones to ride. We told them to bug off. They finally left us alone, and we made cracks about California wranglers not knowing what they were doing."

Carol Eads had come to live in Kalispell a few years earlier "because the horses and hay were cheaper." She loved the outdoors life. In the Mexican restaurant we met at, she told me, "I've been called Annie Oakley pretty much all of my life. I'm a pretty good shot. I could hit that light from here." On Easter Sunday, the day before shooting started, "My husband and I rode to church. I had no idea about the movie—none, zero—and I looked across the field and said, 'Those are too slick to be Montana horses. They look like movie star horses.' Lo and behold, they were! Jeff Bridges and Kris Kristofferson were being taught to ride. I said, 'Are there riding parts?' and they say, 'Let's see what you can do.' I'm pretty much a coward, but I jumped logs and I ran around trees. I came to a slid-stop and jumped off. They said, 'You're hired.'"

Local drivers also had to be found to ferry the actors and key crew members around. Van Robinson, a member of the powerful Teamsters' union, the organization that controls the use of trucks and cars in movies, told me, "I kind of got interviewed, and the guy said, 'Turn up in the morning.' Later that evening, I turned on the TV and it was the Academy Awards, which I find kind of boring, so I changed channel. The next day I showed up and the transportation captain said, 'You go up front and pick up Michael Cimino,' and I said, 'Who's he?'"

One of the most complicated parts of preproduction was the building of the sets. A construction crew had been in Kalispell for three months working with the local carpenters who had been hired. The sets were huge: the fictional town of Sweetwater, where the immigrants lived, was constructed by the lake in the Two Medicine camping site

The roller-skating set (Alamy)

and included the exteriors—a large church and a huge meeting hall. Sweetwater had to be built on elevated platforms so that the ground surface would not be damaged. The exterior of the Heaven's Gate Roller Skating Arena, which gave the movie its title, was also built there. Their interiors—the rink was a hundred feet long and forty-two feet wide—were built at Snowline Acres on the outskirts of Kalispell.

The largest and most ambitious piece of construction was the transformation of Wallace, Idaho, into an 1889 version of the town of Casper, Wyoming, a process that had begun several months before filming started. Wallace was the place proposed by Garry Wunderwald because its railroad station was more suitable than Kalispell's. Cimino was going to shoot the first sequence of the movie proper there (after the flashback of the Harvard graduation, which takes place twenty years before the main action), when Kris Kristofferson as James Averill arrives by train from the East.

The old station and its buildings were preserved and had become a museum, but what made it more unique was that the railway track came right into the town. Joseph Stanley, one of the location managers on the

Wallace, Idaho (Author's collection)

Wallace becomes Caspar, Wyoming, 1889 (Alamy)

movie, said it was "a gem—the only place where a railroad station looks right down the main street of a town." It was perfect for a director who liked to do things on a grand scale—with cameras high up on cranes, you could see almost the whole town in the frame: station, tracks, and most of Sixth Street.

Naturally, using Wallace was not a cheap option. Fake shopfronts of the period had to be attached to the buildings for a block and a half of the street. To hide Food City, the town's largest supermarket, an entire three-story facade was erected. Telegraph poles and electric lines had to be put all the way down the street, which was covered with dirt and gravel to hide the asphalt. More than that, all the shops had to be bought out—they were recompensed for the income they would have generated if they had been open for the planned two weeks of shooting. In fact, just in case filming fell behind, the production reserved the Wallace location for an additional two weeks as well.

To make Wallace look like the bustling and crowded Casper, eighty teams of horses were brought in, as well as their carriages. There were a thousand extras used, and the huge amount of costumes had to be stored at the nearby Silver Hills High School, which the production had hired. And then there was the train: an ex–auto body shop owner in Colorado had bought it for the Lee Marvin Western *Cat Ballou* in 1965 and now rented it out for other movies. Because the engine had a different gauge from modern trains, it could not be driven to Wallace; rather, it had to be transported by train itself. It weighed forty tons and had to be lifted onto a flatbed truck by two huge cranes. Some tunnels along the way could not accommodate its massive size, so a circuitous route through five states had to be found to avoid them.

It was an entirely characteristic Cimino operation. His extraordinary attention to detail might have been expensive, but the Wallace scenes were the most visually spectacular in *Heaven's Gate*. Bryan Buchanan, Kristofferson's stand-in, told me that he was stunned when he arrived at the dressed location for the first time. This would not be the last time that Cimino's grandiose and costly vision created such an unforgettable sequence.

CHAPTER 9

KURTZ IN KALISPELL

AS THE CREW in Kalispell were finishing the set construction for the start of shooting on April 16, Steven Bach, David Field, Andy Albeck, and Lee Katz had still not decided how to handle *Heaven's Gate*'s budget problem. They met on April 10, the day after *The Deer Hunter* had triumphed at the Academy Awards. In one way they were jubilant: its five wins boded well for their movie being nominated for Academy Awards, assuming Cimino could stick to the sixty-nine-day filming schedule so the film could be released in December. However, Cimino's victory seemed to put even more cards in his hand while they were negotiating the budget.

Since Katz had sent his memo at the end of February, in which he described Cimino and Carelli's budget of $11.5 million as being "made with a crystal ball," nothing much had been done. United Artists had neither approved it, nor turned it down. Technically, the movie had not been green-lit, but that made little difference. With a week to go before shooting, they were on a train that was almost impossible to get off of. With his forensic accountant's mind, Katz had always known the budget was way too low, but his job was simply to present the information: it was up to the others to decide how to proceed.

He was almost certain that Cimino would not be able to complete the movie in sixty-nine days even if he wanted to, and there was no evidence that he did. Each additional week of shooting would cost around $500,000, and because they had agreed to the deal that removed any financial penalties for Cimino if the movie went over budget or schedule, there was no incentive for him to stick to any figure, whether it was arrived at with a crystal ball or not. Field, going by gut instinct rather than by the math, guessed that the sum they would end up with might be at least $15 million. Katz, going by the math, agreed with him.

They had two options: to agree with Cimino's palpably inaccurate figure and hope that when he went over budget, as he almost certainly would, he might be embarrassed and rein in his ambition. However, that did not seem very likely with Cimino—embarrassment was not in his repertoire. They could also tell him that they were going to increase the budget to $15 million, in the hope that if he was given the sum they thought the movie would cost, he would stick to it. That did not sound much like Cimino either. It would also mean that—for the first time in movie history—a studio was giving a director more money than he was asking for. Katz summed it up succinctly: "We seem to be in the ironic and paradoxical position of not trusting the gentleman with our money and therefore insisting that he take more."

The other option, of course, was to cancel the movie, but nobody was very keen on that. Anyway, if you looked at it a different way, a cost of $15 million was not an outrageous sum for such a prestigious and grand project. *The Deer Hunter* had cost more or less the same, and that had worked out pretty well. Coppola's *Apocalypse Now*, with its horrendous production problems in the Philippines—typhoons, replacing Harvey Keitel with Martin Sheen, and then closing down production for a month because Sheen had a heart attack—had increased its cost to $25 million and was still heading upward.

At heart, Albeck, Field, and Bach were moviemakers, and this was a movie they wanted to make. Field was the most passionate of them, and he seemed to have a better understanding of Cimino's mercurial personality than they did. "I had a lot of respect for Michael," he told me, "and I had no respect for him at all." He did not trust Cimino himself, but he trusted that he could make a great movie for United Artists. In the end, they agreed to approve the $11.5 million budget and to keep quiet about the $15 million, but they let Cimino and Carelli know that they had some worries about the lower budget. They were hoping for the best, but their lack of transparency made them look weak. Bach imagined what Carelli must have thought: "If they didn't believe this humpty-dumpty budget was real, why did they approve it? And if they didn't believe it, why should we sign it?"

Now in Kalispell, ensconced in the Outlaw Inn, she was angry about it. She and Cimino were particularly outraged that in his budget memo Katz had used the words "crystal ball." It was disingenuous of him to put it that way, but it was oversensitive of them to be offended by it. The truth is that any budget—whether for a movie or the construction of a house—is just an educated guess. You hope you have a good crystal ball and some reliable alchemy—ironically, the brand name of the industry-standard software package used to create a budget is called Movie Magic.

The more accurately a movie has been planned, the more accurate the budget. A hired-hand director would simply be given one and told to make it work. That had happened with Cimino on *Thunderbolt and Lightfoot*—if a location was too expensive, he, under Clint Eastwood's whip, had to find a cheaper one. However, by then Cimino was anything but a hired-hand director, and United Artists' feeble whip was not having much effect.

The additional problem with *Heaven's Gate* was that, like *The Deer Hunter*, it had a far shorter preproduction period than similarly ambitious movies because United Artists insisted on it hitting the December Oscar nomination deadline. Inevitably, there were a lot of unknown elements, any one of which could have an exponential knock-on effect. If Cimino had not yet chosen a location for a crowd sequence, he would not know its size or the cost of the extras needed to fill it. If more extras were needed, additional transport would have to be called in, and more horses and wranglers would be required for them. The cost of catering (calculated on a per-head, per-day basis rather than a flat fee) would increase as well. If the location was farther away than planned (some of them on *Heaven's Gate* were a three-hour drive each way), the working day would be longer and everyone would go into overtime.

These tended to be the producer's and the production manager's problems, but they might expect a director to be reasonably cooperative.

Cimino was not. He was simply demanding, and that was going to be their biggest problem. As Steven Bach said in his book, "Carelli was worried about Charlie Okun's [the production manager] ability to say no to Mike. She worried that Charlie had the same anxiety about her." They had both worked with Cimino for many years—Okun had been an associate producer on *Thunderbolt and Lightfoot* and *The Deer Hunter*, as well as on the commercials in New York—but Bach noticed a certain amount of rivalry between him and Carelli, "as if each needed to demonstrate to Mike a superior, deeper loyalty and affection."

They had to cope with Cimino often changing his mind, in no way an unusual thing for an ambitious director to do. However, there would normally be enough slack in a budget to accommodate a few changes. Cimino's were more than a few. For example: the Wallace location. The cost of getting a train was budgeted at $15,000, but because Cimino insisted on the one he found in Colorado, the cost rocketed to $150,000. (Clint Eastwood would have told him to find a cheaper one.)

In the script, the whole sequence was much less complicated. Averill arrives at the station and walks down the platform, talking to his friend Curly (EXT. CASPER RAILROAD DEPOT—DAY). The next shot in the script is Averill going to a store to buy a gun (EXT. CASPER, ZINDEL'S STORE—DAY.) The stage direction is simply, *"Averill crosses through side-street traffic towards Zindel's."* At no point does the script read, "EXT. CASPER RAILROAD DEPOT AND MAIN ST—AERIAL SHOT—DAY *We follow Averill as he leaves the railroad station, walks through hundreds of people, horses, and carriages and heads down Main St. past many ornate shop fronts."* Cimino could have dressed one store to be Zindel's and had a lot of extras and horses in front of it, through which Averill would pass and then enter the store. It might not have been as spectacular as the sequence Cimino shot, but it would have worked and, of course, been a fraction of the cost. As Bryan Buchanan told me, "Originally Cimino was only going to shoot in the train depot at Wallace. Then he decided, 'I'm the guy now, I'm going to take in this whole town here and I'm going to buy out Safeway's a year's worth of back wages so I can build this facade.'"

In fairness to Cimino, his was not the first huge movie to have a budget that floated on quicksand. If there was ever a final budget on David Lean's *Lawrence of Arabia*, nobody remembers seeing it. For Cimino, it was a very simple transaction and a fair exchange: United Artists would give him all the money he needed, and in return he would give them a masterpiece, a pearl beyond price. The trouble was that the pearl was beyond their price.

Cimino started shooting slowly and continued slowly. Each setup took such a long time to prepare that he had fallen five days behind after six days of filming. His meticulous, detail-heavy direction did not lend itself to speed: he would spend hours moving the extras around into different groups, plucking them from one and seeing what they looked like in another. This was an expensive way of getting the right canvas, but it gave those sequences an amazingly rich texture. When cut together, the footage he had shot that first week would last two minutes—on a "normal" movie, you would be expecting two minutes a day.

The detailed schedule worked out for the movie—originally agreed on by Cimino—showed what scenes were meant to be shot on any given day, but there was also a daily progress report issued that outlined how many of those scenes had actually been shot, how many setups had been done, and how much film stock was used. A simple comparison of the two documents would show the divergence, but communication with Kalispell was bad—fax machines were not used then, and the rooms at the Outlaw Inn did not have telephones, so people had to queue up at the phone booth in the lobby—and it took a few days for the reports to arrive in Los Angeles. However, in that first week, United Artists were under no illusion how much trouble they were in. On April 22, only six days into shooting, David Field flew to Kalispell.

DESPITE WRITING *FINAL CUT*, which gave a forensically detailed description of the making of *Heaven's Gate*, Steven Bach later revealed (but not in the book) that he went to Kalispell only "a few times" during the shooting, despite the fact that he and Field were joint heads of production for the studio. Before they got the jobs, Field had been more responsible for West Coast projects and Bach more for East Coast and European ones, and in their new setup, those arbitrary divisions might have lingered on in their minds even though Andy Albeck had told them, "You will have equal authority and equal responsibility." Their geographical distance was no longer relevant.

Although Bach in New York and Field in Los Angeles were in regular contact, there was now a wariness in their relationship: Bach said, "Feelings of unrest, if not dissension, were close to the surface with Field, Stolber [who was in charge of business affairs], and me." A certain waspishness toward him can be detected sometimes in Bach's book—"Field's melancholy asserted itself thickly." "I had the advantage of access [Bach and Albeck were both in New York] but it was a threat to Field." He gleefully reported how upset Field was when another UA executive called him "Sammy Glick"—the hero of Budd Schulberg's novel *What Makes Sammy Run?*, a heartless movie producer who will step on anyone to get to the top. It could hardly be a less-accurate description of Field, with his patrician air and passion for movies rather than power. After learning of Bach's silent presence on the phone call Field made to Albeck about canceling the movie after the Isabelle Huppert incident, Field had every right to worry about the trust between them.

In fairness to Bach, during the long and painful playout after *Heaven's Gate*'s disastrous opening in November 1980, he did not exonerate himself from responsibility for what happened. However, in his book he subtly distances himself: he asserts that the movie was going to be "a West Coast project and David would be in charge." In fact, Bach had been instrumental in bringing Cimino to United Artists, and had been equally in charge during preproduction, when it looked as if the movie was going to be a prestigious, award-winning success. In a meeting when they were discussing how to watch "every penny" of the budget, Bach said to Field, possibly as a joke, "*You'll* be watching every penny. I have no intention of going to Montana."

He freely admitted that he and Field were inexperienced in dealing with production problems on such a massive scale—as Field put it to me, "We were not Darryl F. Zanuck"—but the subtext of Bach's book is that, as it was not quite *his* movie, he was just part of the general corporate responsibility, as if there was strength (rather than weakness) in numbers. Whatever blame was liberally handed out after the release of the movie, it was Field who was on the front line during its making. Even if Bach had spent more time in Kalispell, saying no to Cimino would not have played to the strengths of a man who gave "the best 'Yes' in the business."

WHEN FIELD ARRIVED in Kalispell, he did not just receive a frosty welcome—he received no welcome at all. Cimino refused to see him. Field informed Bach, "He told Joann he doesn't want to talk to anyone from UA. He's pissed off about Lee's budget memo." The next day, Field and Carelli drove for two hours from Kalispell to the Sweetwater location, where the crew had already gone into overtime. Bach quoted Field as saying, "When shooting ended, I walked over to intercept Michael, and he walked right by me." Cimino was heading for his trailer, where he was to have a massage. "When he came out, he looked right through me, got into a car, and one of the drivers took him back to Kalispell."

Finally, they did talk, and Cimino said that Lee Katz's attitude showed that United Artists had no idea about the difficulties involved in making a movie this complicated. He was sorry that the first week had been so slow, but he told him that the pace would definitely pick up in the second week. With that reassurance, Field flew back to Los Angeles. However, the pace did not pick up.

On *The Deer Hunter*, Barry Spikings and Michael Deeley had found the location in Thailand so inaccessible that communication was almost impossible. No one had quite realized that Montana would be the same. Quite apart from the phone problem, there were no direct flights, and with the change of plane at Seattle or Salt Lake City, the journey could take as much as nine hours. It might well have been on a different continent—or possibly Cimino was simply creating the illusion that it was. Field and Bach knew about the snail's pace of production, but it was hard to ascertain what else was happening, and a succession of wild rumors floated in the air between Kalispell and California for the length of the shooting: staggering amounts of new extras were being hired, and Cimino was adding, as Bach reported in his book, "more horses and wagons, hats, shoes, gloves, dresses, top hats, bridles, boots, roller skates, babushkas, buck-boards, cows, calves, bulls, trees, and thousands of tons of dirt"; there was extensive on-set cocaine use, paid for by $50,000 that had been stolen from the budget; Cimino had burned down one of the sets to see how it would look and then had it rebuilt overnight for the next day's shoot; he had bought a 156-acre ranch on the north fork of the Flathead River out of the budget and had installed an irrigation system. It was hard for United Artists to know which, if any, of the rumors were true, but as Joann Carelli said, not unreasonably, "If he did all of those things, how come he's not in jail?"

One thing they did know was how much it was costing. The finance people at United Artists had arranged a regular draw down with the movie's production accountants, who were paying the costs of the crew, extras, and set building (the people working on the movie were technically not employed by the studio—they were under contract to Partisan, Cimino's company). As United Artists had always known that the budget of $11.5 million was going to end up at what they estimated to be $15 million, it was not a surprise when the draw down had to be increased. However, with the languid pace of shooting, they realized with panic after only two weeks that the $15 million itself was going to be exceeded.

On April 27, Andy Albeck, Dean Stolber, who was in charge of contracts and legal issues, and Bach had a conference call with Field, who was in Los Angeles. They discussed their options: they could simply go on funding it, as 20th Century Fox had done on a picture in 1962 with a similarly skyrocketing budget—*Cleopatra*—which had risen from $4 million to an unprecedented $22 million but had, after many years, made its money back. They could try to control and contain the budget, as they had done with *Apocalypse Now*: Lee Katz had worked with a reasonably cooperative Coppola to reorganize the production, which was in disarray from the various disasters that had befallen it. However, that was not quite as bad a situation as the Cimino movie, because in Coppola's contract—unlike Cimino's—he was responsible for some of the overages.

The third and most brutal option was to shelve the movie. While a studio cutting their losses in that way is rare, it does happen. A few years before, three weeks into shooting, Warner Bros. canceled and never resumed the expensive *Bogart Slept Here*, a very high-profile project starring Robert De Niro, written by Neil Simon and directed by Mike Nichols, because nobody felt it was working. In 1962, 20th Century Fox sacked Marilyn Monroe from the chaotic *Something's Got to Give* after four weeks because she was repeatedly sick and then rehired her and planned to delay production for two months while she recovered. A few weeks later, she died. They decided to abandon the movie rather than recast it. However, some of the losses were covered by an insurance payout because of Monroe's death.

On *Heaven's Gate*, there would be no such payout—nobody had died—and United Artists, fully funding the movie, would have had to take the entire hit if they canceled the picture. Also, it was hard to work out what the precise cost of abandonment would be, even with Katz's crystal ball. All they knew was that it would be huge. Without much expectation of success, they decided on the *Apocalypse Now* control-and-contain option, even though they had no real idea of how they would manage to do that—and, of course, they knew Cimino well enough to know that he would be the opposite of cooperative.

David Field returned to Montana. Cimino was still shooting the Sweetwater scenes at Two Medicine, and he and some of the actors and crew were staying at the nearby Glacier Park Lodge. Field told me that when he arrived, he asked the desk clerk for Cimino's room number and was told that he had been instructed not to give it out or put phone calls through to his room. Field had to sit in the lobby and wait for Cimino to appear. When they finally talked, Field told him he had to speed up production. The next day, he saw Cimino alone in the dining room eating breakfast and asked him why he wasn't shooting. Cimino replied, "You know so much, why don't you direct it?"

The first stage of the contain-and-control attempt was to send a numbers person to Montana. It would be too contentious to send the hated Lee Katz, so United Artists dispatched his second-in-command, an experienced British production hand called Derek Kavanagh. He took a long, calm look at the paperwork. Forensically analyzing the schedule, the footage shot, and the slow pace, he came to the conclusion that the movie would finish shooting on January 3. It was now the end of May, three weeks before the movie had originally been scheduled to end.

At the beginning of June, Field and Bach flew to Kalispell together, the thinking being that Cimino would consider the arrival of two people more serious than just one. Bach said in his book, "I had consented readily to the trip (though I dreaded it)." There was no alternative other than the kind of heavy confrontation he was not keen on. Field knew perfectly well that they would have to bite the Cimino bullet, unpleasant though it would be. They were twin Marlows heading upriver to flush out *Heart of Darkness*'s Colonel Kurtz.

FROM WHAT UNITED Artists had heard about the movie, they would have had every reason to presume from faraway Los Angeles that this was a production in disarray. In fact, it was quite the opposite. It was only the budget that was in disarray. There was no chaos at all. The shooting was calm, beautifully organized, and professional. It just took a long time. The actors and crew were not only respectful of Cimino, but hardworking and happy. There was an occasional satirical newsletter written by crew members called *Heaven's Dirt*, which stated, "The purpose of this paper is to acquaint us with each other . . . and nurture and develop a positive feeling of unity and community." There were affectionate in-jokes: "The Kalispell Police Department has just released a statement refuting any possibility of saucer sightings reported by Heaven's Gate Band Members." There were references to "Joann 'Why the talk back?' Carelli."

As always with Cimino, the actors believed in him, and he in them. Kris Kristofferson said, "Chris Walken told me he would trust Michael implicitly, so that's the way I went at it. Just do whatever this artist is trying to get done. I just figured it was his creative eye, and I trusted it." Later, in a joint interview in 2005, Isabelle Huppert said, "It's very hard to refuse something with Michael. I'm afraid of horses and I can't dance very well. I can't do anything I do in this movie." Cimino replied, "When you ask a great actress to do something impossible, she just does it."

There was a kind of summer-camp atmosphere. The actors were taught how to ride and had roller-skating lessons. The girls who played the prostitutes spent time in a real brothel in Wallace. People called it "Camp Cimino." There were some reasonably good-natured complaints about the long days—some locations were three hours away, which meant that the crew and actors piled into trucks at 4:00 A.M. and got back at 10:00 P.M.—but, of course, they were going into lucrative overtime almost every day. Everybody was particularly complimentary about the catering provided—good food is a sure way to keep the crew

The purpose of this paper is to acquaint
us with each other better,make our stay
more memorable,and nurture and develop
a positive feeling of unity and community.
The scope is large.We need the asistance
of as many people as possible,both in
the actual contribution of articles
and information and in the production aspects of this paper.
We offer this as a public service in and for the"Heaven's
Gate" community.

Heaven's Dirt (Author's collection)

happy—which involved the gargantuan task of making three meals a
day for several hundred people hours away from the base in Kalispell.

Just as on *The Deer Hunter*, the pace of shooting was considered
slow only by a studio's definition, not by Cimino's. It was not that he
tried to shoot a particular scene in a day but was unable to complete it
and had to run into a second day. He always knew how long it would
take—and that was how long it did take. He knew that it would infuriate United Artists—particularly as everyone came to realize that the

filming schedule of sixty-nine days must have been plucked from the air—but he was unconcerned: he was giving them the masterpiece they had asked for.

Bach described many of Cimino's profligacies as if they were unique in the movie business. There were reports of him stopping filming for hours while he waited for the clouds to be in the right formation, but that was no different—rightly or wrongly—to how other auteur directors behaved. On *Ryan's Daughter*, David Lean waited weeks for the weather in Ireland to be right for a storm sequence. When he realized it would never be satisfactory, he moved the whole unit to South Africa for three weeks and shot the sequence there. It seemed that Cimino had done fifty-nine takes of Kris Kristofferson cracking a bullwhip, but on *Eyes Wide Shut*, Stanley Kubrick allegedly shot eighty takes of Tom Cruise saying, "Yes."

The crew called him "Baby Buddha" (he had put on a lot of weight because after a day of stodgy location food he liked to have a cheeseburger and fries while he looked at the dailies at the end of the day) and

Cimino and Kristofferson (Alamy)

"The Ayatollah." These were not unaffectionate names for him—there is a photo of him smiling next to a big sign saying "Ayatullah Cimino." Generally the crew liked him, even if he seemed rather unapproachable. Mady Kaplan, who played one of the prostitutes in Isabelle Huppert's bordello, told me, "He was not overfriendly, but nor was he hostile. He was solitary, but he was happy if someone approached him. Even though there was an oddness about him, there was a side of him that was tender and caring."

During the scenes set inside the roller-skating rink, where the extras had to wear thick winter coats, the temperature rose to over a hundred degrees. Bryan Buchanan, Kristofferson's stand-in, told me, "The extras got a mud puddle going by opening up a fire hydrant outside the set, and they began throwing crew members into it. Cimino went along with it and got thrown in too. It made him laugh."

Of course, he could flare up if something went wrong. Buchanan said, "He was quiet, but when he had something to say, he made sure you heard it. One time he asked me to come over and I didn't hear him. Well, he jumped me and chewed me up one side and down the other, and I tell you—I had every right to be chewed up." A lot of people who

Baby Buddha (Photograph courtesy Penny Shaw Sylvester)

got that kind of treatment were gone if they didn't do something exactly the way he wanted, like Willem Dafoe, playing a small role in his first film. "I was in a lighting setup, and someone told me a joke, and Cimino heard me laugh, and he turned around and said, 'Willem, step out.' And that was that. I was fired . . ."

The people closest to Cimino tended to get on better with him. Van Robinson, who was hired as Cimino's driver, told me, "I was warned that Michael comes on pretty strong; intense, if you will. As it turned out, he wasn't like that at all. We got along beautifully. I was there for all the shooting. I drove Michael all the time. I was just a poor kid who lived in a trailer home, and that man treated me like his friend. He always had this really nice French wine delivered from LA, and I'd put a couple of bottles in the back of the car. He just thought that was the nicest thing anyone'd done for him. We'd be drinking this fine wine out of paper cups, just chatting about you-name-it. He was the hardest working person there. I used to tease him. I'd say, 'My God, I thought a guy like you'd be wearing silk scarves and have a woman around each arm, but you just work like an animal week after week.' He'd just laugh and say, 'Let's have another glass of wine.' I just thought he was a super personable guy. He was considered to be this little Gestapo guy barking orders, but they didn't know him like I got to know him. Yes, he was intense. He was under a lot of pressure, and one time he railed this guy pretty badly. I didn't say much, none of my business—I was just the lowly driver. He looked at me and said, 'Van, these people will hate me. They hated me on *Deer Hunter* until they got their Oscar nominations. Then they're falling all over themselves to thank me for pushing them so hard.'"

Obviously Robinson got to know Carelli as well. He told me, "I found Joann to be very likable. She didn't look down on me, which she could have done—hey, you're the driver, just shut up and drive—but I never felt she was quite like Michael."

As the filming progressed, Cimino would invite Robinson to dinner. "'Why don't you stay with us, stay with Patty and Penny?' And I said, yeah, OK, and we all had dinner and ended up doing a little dancing."

Patty Nelson, Cimino's longtime secretary from Los Angeles, and his editorial assistant, Penny Shaw, whom he had taken to the first screening of *The Deer Hunter*, were probably—apart from Carelli—the people he was closest to on the shoot. Shaw, after more than forty years living in Los Angeles, has retained a particularly English kind of brisk charm. She is still friends with Nelson, and I met them together at a diner in Santa Monica.

Nelson had worked for Sam Peckinpah and had a job at Paramount in 1977. She saw a posting from a "Writer-Director" looking for a secretary. It was Cimino, who was working on *Head of the Dragon* there, and she went in for an interview: "I talked to Michael. He was really a very charming guy. I thought, 'Yes!' I wonder if Joann was there? She must have been. My boss at Paramount wouldn't let me move over to him, but Michael insisted and told them he wouldn't take anyone else. That's how it started."

Shaw, Nelson, and June Samson, who was the script supervisor (the person in charge of continuity), had all worked with Cimino on *The Deer Hunter*, and along with Sandy Berke, in charge of wardrobe, and the production coordinator, Nanette Seigert, they formed the inner circle of women that Cimino surrounded himself with.

Cimino with Patty Nelson and Mady Kaplan (Photograph courtesy Penny Shaw Sylvester)

In Kalispell, he often had dinner with them at the Outlaw Inn. Shaw told me, "Michael got along with women very well. He loved having us around. We were kind of his shield." To them, he could sometimes seem a vulnerable figure, and they looked after him. Patty Nelson made sure he always had the green scarf he wore as a good-luck charm. He had had it on *The Deer Hunter*, and he told Nelson, "You can lose everything, but you can't lose my scarf."

June Samson was a late addition to the crew. Shaw told me, "Joann didn't want her because she was close to Michael. She said she was too expensive and insisted that he hire a Canadian girl. When she shouted 'Cut' during a shot"—nobody other than the director ever calls that out—"Michael lost it and she was gone. He told Patty to call June and get her to come instantly."

He was often possessive of the women. One Sunday, the only rest day of the week, Shaw went for a long motorbike ride with one of the crew members. Cimino had been trying to find her to look at the dailies—Sundays were the same as any other day for him—and when he found out she had been taken out of Kalispell, he sacked her friend. He liked to look at the dailies with Shaw and the editor, Tom Rolf, late at night because he did not want anyone else to see the footage. They had set up a cutting room in the windowless basement of the Outlaw Inn. It was prone to flooding, and decking had to be put down to raise the equipment off the ground.

Given that the general perception of the movie is that it must have been a nightmarish experience, and that Cimino had become deranged with megalomania, it was surprising to hear Nelson and Shaw say, "We had such a good time with Michael." Just as on *The Deer Hunter*, he seemed to have the iron will of the totally focused, the ability to ignore what lesser studio mortals might perceive as "problems"—budget concerns certainly fit into that category—and concentrate on making his movie the way he wanted with the people he liked and respected.

Patty Nelson had a large album of photos taken during the filming that shows a smiling Cimino hanging out with the crew, laughing with Isabelle Huppert, and looking relaxed. She had pictures of the time he took them to the rodeo in Cheyenne, Wyoming. "Michael said, 'I'll get the transportation,' then he had the jet come and pick us up. We spent

Cimino and Penny Shaw (Photograph courtesy Penny Shaw Sylvester)

the night there. It was great!" she said. In the dozens of pictures that she showed me, there was a curious absence: there was not one photograph of Joann Carelli.

Shaw told me, "She would come in and talk briefly to Michael. She never hung out with anyone." Carelli and Cimino had an office next to their bedrooms on the second floor of the inn where she spent her time when she was not on the set. The rest of the production staff, including Charlie Okun, her production manager, had offices set up in portacabins in the car park of the Outlaw. She said later, "Crew people tend not to listen to a woman telling them to do something. You have to be very firm in what you do and believe in. My motto is 'Power is best used quietly.'" But nobody remembers Carelli using it very quietly. She was not a well-liked figure, but with general ass-kicking and tough decisions to make, the producer is often unpopular, and Carelli, with her take-no-prisoners manner, was no exception.

Those who worked with Cimino and Carelli saw how they operated together, and there was constant speculation about their relationship—on movie sets there is nothing much to do after work other than gossip.

One of the crew told me that there was a general presumption that they were "boyfriend and girlfriend"—a charmingly high-school description of such a powerful couple. On the set they sometimes wore similar outfits, a cowboy hat and boots, which gave them a curious kind of Roy Rogers/ Dale Evans vibe, except for their matching aviator shades, and they drove matching black Jeeps.

A crew member who knew them well made a poignant observation to me: "I thought there was something a little unbalanced about their relationship. He seemed in thrall to her, but she was not always as demonstrative. There could sometimes be a wistful quality in his attitude to her. Nobody knew if they really were together or not, but I wondered if a distance had come between them because maybe the romantic part of their relationship had ended and he was trying to reclaim a golden age."

Some people wondered what it was he needed from her professionally on the movie, given that there was those who felt that she did not do much producing and he made all the decisions. As she made no effort to be liked by anyone other than the actors, people were not inclined to cut her much slack. In fact, this paints a very unfair picture of her and underplays the difficulties she had and the loneliness of her position. (Carelli denied to me that she had had an unpleasant time during the shooting. She told me she felt that she had always done the best job that she could.)

In fact, she battled with Cimino often. She knew the problems of his meticulous and detailed way of shooting. "The script was ninety-eight pages long [actually 132]. To this day I don't understand how this produced a four-hour film," she said later. A crew member recalled angry conversations between them as she tried to rein him in and control the budget. Van Robinson said, "Joann was on the set in spurts. When she was there, they would have disagreements. She'd say, 'Michael, you need to get this scene going.' Michael would want to shoot a scene over and over. 'You've got to work with these people. United Artists are going to come up. You're ticking them off.' Michael didn't listen very well."

Two crew members told me that at one point, Cimino was so angry with her that he refused to pay for her bedroom in the motel. She simply moved all her clothes into the office that they shared and slept on the sofa until she was reinstated. Garry Wunderwald told me, "My friend was the manager of the Outlaw. He saw her often and said that she was stressed all the time." Bach, however, considered her overly enabling: she made it "possible for Michael to achieve a certain effect on the screen. She was a supportive producer rather than a combative one. . . . She provided him with a sort of safety net, the emotional comfort that was necessary." This was not always the case: on one occasion, he and Field were with Cimino and Carelli when she stood up to him. She argued forcefully that he should not use a particular piece of land for filming, and he screamed at her, "Goddammit, Joann, that's the location!" and stormed out, slamming the door. "See what I mean?" she said. "So when is UA going to start backing me up?"

What she felt strongly was that she could not do her job without United Artists' support. Bach reported her saying, "I mean, you gotta take my *calls*, David," implying that although Field was "in charge," he was not doing his job properly. In truth, it was hard to see what kind of backup they could have provided her, given how the situation in Kalispell had deteriorated. The only realistic way to reduce the soaring costs was for them to help Carelli get Cimino to double his filming pace, but, as Field knew, UA's weakness during preproduction had removed any power they had. Later, Carelli said, "We should have said, 'No, Michael, no. You cannot have a thousand extras when you said a hundred.' I would say no, and United Artists would not back me up. I should have walked off." Of course, they could have closed the picture down, but that was not exactly backup—it would simply destroy what they had all wanted to create, and they still clung to the hope that, despite the cost, *Heaven's Gate* might turn into a triumph. Carelli was on her own.

Despite the situation, she did not lose any of her usual firepower in other directions. Bryan Buchanan told me about an evening in the bar at the Outlaw Inn where "we were all partying and drinking and getting loud. Ronnie Hawkins [the Canadian singer whose backing musicians, the Hawks—including Robbie Robertson—had broken off to form the Band] was drunkenly pretending to hump his girlfriend on a table just as Joann Carelli comes in and sees that. She's pissed because she's try-ing to sleep and we're making all this racket and she just screams at us to go to bed, and we did." It was no surprise to anyone that she could take on fifty drunken crew members and win.

Van Robinson remembered Cimino telling him the story of the Donner Pass. "He said, 'Van, let me tell you this: if Joann was up there, she would have been one of them that survived. I guarantee it.'"

FIELD AND BACH arrived in Kalispell on June 6. That evening, after shooting had finished, Cimino took them down into the basement cutting room and showed them some footage, not properly cut-together sequences, but nonetheless a heady taster of the movie. Something they saw in the footage was a little embarrassing: they had been wrong about Isabelle Huppert. She had turned from "a potato" into a ravishing beauty, giving a luminous performance and speaking reasonable English. More than that, they were stunned by the overall look of the movie. Bach said, "The footage was perfectly composed, most of it shot at magic hour [the run-up to sunset] . . . the clouds pink and gold with lingering sun. This was it: the poetry of America." Ironically, their astonishment at the beauty of what Cimino had shot removed one of the options they had: if the footage had been bad, they would have had a reason to close production down. Now, seeing "the poetry of America" on-screen, they could not let that happen, but they hoped they might be able to find a studio to share the astronomical cost of that poetry.

As he had done since the beginning of the project, Cimino was still saying that if they didn't like what he was doing, he could find some other home for the movie. Now they were going to try to find one themselves. If they could not achieve that, they were going to put a new producer answerable to them on the picture, whether Cimino or Carelli liked it or not.

Bach and Field had heard that Barry Spikings, who had produced *The Deer Hunter*, was telling Cimino that EMI would love to take the picture over. Field, taking a tougher line than anyone else at United Artists, told Cimino, "I know what you think of me and how ill-equipped and diminished I am as an executive, so how about this: You've told me how wonderful Barry Spikings and EMI are. If Andy Albeck and Transamerica let me, I'm going to offer him half this movie for whatever it costs to complete, and domestic distribution, so when you get all the awards for this movie, you don't have to see any of us and you can stand up there with him, your pal. If he says yes, I'm out. If he says no, you shut the fuck up and finish the movie the way I just told you.'" In early July, Field flew to Kalispell with Spikings, Spikings's wife, Dot, and Cimino's powerful agent, Stan Kamen, to see some footage and talk about the costs involved in sharing the movie between them. Bach did not come.

Cimino wanted to buy Spikings and his wife a welcome present of cowboy hats and boots. Patty Nelson said she would look around Kalispell, but Cimino felt that there would not be any good enough ones in town. He told her to get the production office to organize a flight to Denver and then hire a limo to go to a shop he liked. It took the whole day, and when Nelson got back, he was angry with her and shouted, "Where have you been!"

With his English sangfroid, Spikings was an unlikely person to wear a cowboy outfit, but he was courteous and friendly and seemed to take seriously the possibility of coming in on the movie. Bach reported that this did not happen, but gave no reason. Spikings told me that they had offered him a reasonable deal—50 percent of the movie for 30 percent of the cost—and he was tempted, but Andy Albeck kept changing the terms, "nickel and diming," and he pulled out.

Field had a different story: before Spikings came up to Kalispell, he—taking a much ballsier position than United Artists normally did—made it very clear that the decision had be taken before Spikings returned to Los Angeles. He agreed but then reneged—he said he had to talk to his boss, Lord Grade at EMI. Three days after he returned home, he said that they would not come in on the picture.

With that option gone, Field moved on to the second part of the plan—imposing a producer from United Artists. He would be Derek Kavanagh, already familiar with the *Heaven's Gate* battlefield. Field dressed up his appointment as a friendly rather than hostile move. Kavanagh would be there just to "supplement Joann and Charlie's efforts to speed up the production." Cimino appeared to take this surprisingly well, and Field flew back to California. The next day, Cimino wrote a memo to him that was posted in the lobby of the Outlaw Inn. It read, "Derek Kavanagh is not to come to the location site. He is not to enter the editing room. He is not to speak to me at all."

They came up with yet another option: replace Cimino with a new director. This was not an unknown strategy when a picture was going badly wrong. United Artists themselves had tried to do while the costly 1966 Julie Andrews/Richard Harris movie *Hawaii* was shooting. They wanted to sack the painstaking George Roy Hill (who two years later directed *Butch Cassidy and the Sundance Kid*) with the more workman-like Arthur Hiller. In the same year that *Heaven's Gate* was shooting, Bob Rafelson, the hip director of *Five Easy Pieces*, was removed from the unhip Robert Redford prison drama *Brubaker* in favor of Stuart Rosenberg.

The replacement option is easier on a run-of-the-mill movie than it is on a huge auteur movie, but it is never a cheap way of putting it back on track. The original director will almost certainly sue, claiming wrongful dismissal; the new director will demand an exorbitant fee. The movie will probably have to close down for a period of time with everyone still on salary while the new director looks at the footage and brings themself up to speed. More than that, the crew may rebel, and the leading cast could refuse to work with them. The more famous the outgoing director is, the more embarrassing it is for the studio. Still, it was worth looking into.

In mid-July, Steven Bach surreptitiously went to see a possible replacement. In his book, he did not mention the name (the Directors Guild forbids a director discussing taking over a project until the existing director is fired). In fact, it was almost certainly Norman Jewison, a director United Artists knew very well—he had successfully directed *In the Heat of the Night* and *Fiddler on the Roof* for them.

Of course, like everyone else in Hollywood, Jewison had heard the rumors about the production, and he and Bach had a cryptic conversation in which they talked about a hypothetical studio asking a hypothetical director to take over a hypothetical movie. Jewison, knowing all the problems of the replacement option (he himself had replaced Sam Peckinpah on the Steve McQueen movie *The Cincinnati Kid* in 1965), succinctly said, "Who're you going to get who can do it and won't make you look like assholes?" The paradox was that, on this kind of project, they did not want to hire a reliable hack director, but it would be a poisoned chalice for the kind of prestigious director they were after. If *Heaven's Gate* turned out to be a success, Cimino would get the accolades; if it flopped, the new director would be blamed for compromising Cimino's original vision. Jewison told Bach that he would advise the theoretical director to turn down the theoretical job on the theoretical movie.

In the meantime, one good thing had happened in David Field's life. He had borne the draining burden of the Cimino flack for months—Bach noted that Field had checked himself into a hospital one weekend because of exhaustion—but on July 21, he got married and left for his honeymoon. Bach had to fly to California and take over his job during Field's absence. He reported that both Cimino and his agent, Stan Kamen, called him to ask if he would replace Field permanently. This was neither as flattering to Bach nor as disparaging to Field as it might seem. "I can't talk to Field," Cimino said, but as he would not talk to Derek Kavanagh, it was not surprising that he did not want to talk to the person who had imposed Kavanagh on him either. Maybe Cimino and Kamen thought that Bach might be softer on the director.

With the replacement option gone, the situation was now critical, and as Field was away on his honeymoon, Bach flew to Kalispell on August 1 to try another tack. He did not want to go alone, as Field often did. He said, "I packed no revolver; I packed Dean Stolber," the head of business and legal affairs at United Artists. It was time to talk contracts.

They met with Cimino and Carelli late in the evening after the day's filming had finished in their shared office on the second floor. There were no preliminaries: at the current rate of shooting, the total cost would be around $35 million. United Artists would continue funding the picture only up to a maximum of $25 million. Stolber added, "We hope you will be the director who brings it in at that figure." That was rather an idle threat, because they had shelved the replacement director option, but Cimino did not know this. What he did know perfectly well was that they could close down the picture, but if they continued, it would be almost impossible to fire him because more than a million feet of film had been shot with many cameras and only he knew how it would fit together.

However, they had two threats up their sleeve that were not so idle. The first was the prologue and epilogue, which had always floated outside the main schedule and budget (they were going to be shot respectively at Harvard and on an oceangoing steam yacht after everything in Montana had been finished). Although they added an enormous texture and resonance to the main body of the film, they could be cut without affecting the story—they were essentially bookends. The cost of them was not included in the sum of $25 million, and Stolber said that they would pay for them only if that was the figure the Montana shoot ended up at.

The other threat was potentially an even greater blow to Cimino. At the current rate of shooting, the film would end up at a length of four and a quarter hours. Cimino's contractual right of final cut was predicated at no more than three hours. If it was a minute over that, United Artists could legally take the picture away and cut it themselves. Although EMI had threatened the same thing on *The Deer Hunter*, Cimino had managed in the end to get his own long cut, but this was a different studio, and *Heaven's Gate* was in far more trouble than his previous film. Cimino, in a corner, said—more convincingly than he ever had before—that he would speed up production. At last, Stolber and Bach were giving Carelli the backup she had always wanted—if it wasn't too late.

The movie was now more than four months into shooting and six weeks beyond the date production had been scheduled to finish, but, in fact, the cards that Bach and Stolber were now playing had been in their hands all along. The irony (which Bach did not later point out in his book) was that they could have put them on the table several months earlier, before the movie spun out of control, and they would have had the effect they seemed to be having now. "He's going to agree," Stolber said to Bach after they had left the meeting. Bach, as usual, passed the buck: "I know. And lucky David gets to enforce all this."

On August 5—the moment his honeymoon finished—Field flew to Kalispell on his own to do some enforcing. United Artists had now decided to make a further stipulation: they were going to formally take over the movie. Technically, it was being produced by Cimino's company, Partisan, and its affiliate, the Johnson County War Company, and the studio was simply funding it. Now the studio was going to produce it themselves. As an inducement to take this further blow, Field said that the budget cap of $25 million would be increased to $27.5 million, and if Cimino came in at that figure, he could shoot the prologue and epilogue at a price to be agreed. Despite that, Cimino's response was to demand that they fire him from his movie. Field told him he could resign instead, if he wished. The difference between the two was simply that, if he was fired, there would almost certainly be a lawsuit for wrongful dismissal, which would probably result in a large payoff; if he resigned, there would be neither, and there was the possibility that they could even sue him for breaking his contract. Cimino backed down and agreed to work with Derek Kavanagh on producing a new and sped-up schedule. Under the new plan, filming was due to finish at the beginning of October, and—to everyone's surprise—Cimino did speed up.

There were other reasons why it would have been hard for Cimino to film much beyond that date: summer had ended, and fall was coming in. It was not unusual for there to be snow in Montana in October, which would have compromised the continuity of the movie. On top of that, John Hurt, the British actor who was playing Jim Averill's friend Billy Irvine, was due to start filming David Lynch's *The Elephant Man* on October 15, and he was not going to miss it. (Isabelle Huppert had already pulled out of a project she was meant to be doing in France.) Hurt had had enough of Montana—he had worked for one day in the previous ten weeks. Originally contracted for sixty-nine days, he ended up staying for nearly seven months. When he returned home, he bought a place in the country and named it Overtime House.

CHAPTER 10

THE RETREAT FROM MOSCOW

AS THE WEATHER began to change, so did the atmosphere in Kalispell. The circus had stayed too long in town. The first signs of the rift between the production and the town had been in June, when there was a problem filming in Glacier National Park. Shooting on the Sweetwater town set at Two Medicine was due to finish on June 10, and the scenes were completed on time. They were due to move on to another location at North Fork when Phil Iverson, the superintendent of the park, rescinded their permit to film there. Cimino was incandescent with rage. Garry Wunderwald, who ran the Montana Film Office, told me that, "He called me at one in the morning and called me every name you could imagine. I was trapped in the middle, but I understood what the park were saying."

There were a variety of accusations. "The problem was an accumulation of little things," Iverson said. "Michael said everything was spelled out in the beginning, but we found that there wasn't as much detail as to what alterations to the natural setting there would be." Wunderwald told me, "Some of the crew members were maybe using sprays not supposed to be used in the park system. They were supposed to bring in dirt from inside the park, but then they brought in loads from different areas of a different type."

Cimino and Carelli held a meeting with the local press on June 13 at the Outlaw Inn. Predictably, they did not take a conciliatory approach. "Iverson is exhibiting a total isolation from the community of northern Montana—maybe the same isolation President Nixon exhibited in the Oval Office," Cimino said aggressively. "I do feel that he has achieved publicity at my expense to a degree which approaches libel. I find it hard to believe that two hundred art people can cause more damage in the course of several weeks than two million tourists can do in the course of a year." The row quickly spread beyond the park personnel: Wilbur Werner, a member of the North Central Montana Council, said, "I was appalled at the thousands of tons of material and equipment they had brought in. The physical effects . . . will have a devastating effect for years to come." His anger might have also been fueled by a crew member refusing to let him enter the area where they were filming the Sweetwater scenes because it was a closed set—a policy that most movies follow.

It is quite probable that the production did cause some damage to the park, inevitable with complicated set construction and many people and trucks moving around. That, of course, is why location fees are so exorbitant—and they were for *Heaven's Gate*. It is tacitly accepted that there may be an element of collateral damage during any kind of filming, and on this production an insurance bond costing $50,000 had been taken out.

The community, always sensitive about the park, which was a pre-eminent symbol of the greatness of Montana, may have overreacted: three days after filming had finished at Two Medicine, it was reported that "between 75 and 80 percent of the cleanup work is complete. Buildings have been removed and the dirt on the parking lot is just about all off," but the damage between town and film had been done. There was a feeling, at the very least, that the movie people were behaving in a disrespectful way to Kalispell and its inhabitants. Cimino felt that they were being disrespectful to him: all he had been trying to do, he said, was "to show off the spectacle which is Glacier National Park to the millions of persons who may never have the chance to see it." He estimated—probably not inaccurately, for once—that the forced change of location and schedule would cost the production $750,000.

What had once seemed exciting and fun to the townspeople began to feel less so. The early days when the *Hungry Horse News* reported excitedly, "Oscar-winning director likes Montana!" were ending. Resentments began to ferment even though there was a show of support from local businesses: the Outlaw Inn and the local Chevrolet dealer took out an ad in the local newspaper thanking and praising Cimino. However, they were simply benefiting financially from the movie—they were not working on it.

There was an open letter in the paper to Tony Gaznick, who was in charge of recruiting extras: "We were told sanitation facilities would be provided. . . . It was not until six weeks after we began shooting that running water was provided for the extras. . . . We were told we would have comfortable shelter for the children." Another extra was critical of Cimino himself: "He demands formality. Crew members call him 'Sir.' He is never seen making small-talk, and even during breaks and lunch he continues working." Actually, crew members never called him "Sir," and it is hard to be critical of a director who pushes himself harder than anyone else. "Overall, the extras have been made to know that they are merely atmosphere for the movie," but that, of course, is what extras always are. A handout ordered: "Please do not approach the actors or crew members"—standard procedure on big movies. The $30 a day the extras on *Heaven's Gate* were receiving now seemed rather a meager amount; the long drives to and from the set seemed less of an exciting adventure than they did at the beginning.

Not only was there a growing amount of hostility from the townspeople working on the movie, there was hostility from a more important area for the movie: the press back in Los Angeles. Ever protective—even paranoid—Cimino, who was contractually in total control of advertising and promotion, had taken an unusual decision: he had banned all journalists from coming to Montana. He refused to speak to the movie press and demanded a code of silence from cast and crew as well.

Normally, the unit publicist would organize and control a series of key interviews and background pieces during shooting to build anticipation for the movie, targeting the important industry papers like *Variety* and the *Hollywood Reporter*, as well as more traditional but no less important outlets like the *Los Angeles Times* and *Newsweek*. The pieces would be staggered over the course of the production, with another big push when the movie opened.

In the lusher days of the industry, press junkets were also organized for selected journalists to be flown out to the location, sometimes by private jet, where they were lavishly entertained and could see the filming and meet some of the cast—and certainly the director. Cimino allowed none of this; he built a giant wall around the film. Even the thousands of production stills taken during the filming were not distributed—according to Bach, Carelli and Cimino refused to show them to United Artists. What seemed protective began to be regarded by the press as hostile. Gossip from the set was eagerly sought, and despite the studio's denials, it was soon clear to the press that all was not well in Montana, and it was not going to get better.

On August 26, the *Los Angeles Times*, with not much information to be gleaned about the movie shooting in Montana, printed a hostile article about United Artists itself entitled "Shootout at the UA Corral." It was flattering about the old regime who had formed Orion and vicious about the new one under Andy Albeck—he was described as "an office boy." It portrayed the studio as being staffed with accountants who were contemptuous of artists (which, of course, was exactly what Cimino felt).

The floodgates opened with an article published on September 2. Les Gapay, once a staff writer on the *Wall Street Journal*, had moved to Montana to pursue a freelance career. He sniffed out that there must be a good story about *Heaven's Gate*, and he asked Ted Albert, the unit publicist, if he could write a piece. Albert refused. Then, in an example of journalism at its most resourceful, Gapay applied for a job as an extra and wrote his story from the inside, surreptitiously taking photographs.

He revealed pretty accurately how far the movie had gone over budget. Having talked to disgruntled extras, he told stories about how many of them had been injured, about how a crew member had told one carriage driver, "If people don't move out of the way, run them over," how gruesome the violence was, how Cimino moved at a snail's pace because of his nit-picking attention to detail.

This was not the vague gossip that had floated from Montana to Hollywood. Although Gapay's piece was not totally accurate, it was gleefully regarded as such. It was syndicated in other newspapers, including the

New York Times and *Post,* the *Chicago Tribune,* and the *Miami Herald.* The day after it appeared, *Time* did a piece on the movie called "The Making of Apocalypse Next." UA had to go on the defensive, as they were inundated by calls from journalists. Steven Bach was critical in his book about David Field's press quote, "I think Michael is making a masterpiece," but it's hard to know what else he could say. Nobody has ever thought that the movie industry is at the top of the truth-telling league, and there were enough stories about Cimino and United Artists' toxic relationship already—*Time* described it as "switchblades and garbage-can covers." All the studio could do was to keep smiling, however unconvincingly.

The appearance of the hostile press pieces coincided with the start of the last weeks of shooting, the most grueling on the whole picture. Cimino was going to shoot the climactic battle between the mercenaries and the immigrants, scheduled to take four weeks. In the script, it is about twenty pages long, but like the wedding sequence in *The Deer Hunter,* he had expanded it, and in his first cut of the film, it would last ninety minutes.

As usual, his attention to detail was costly. The expansive location had been re-turfed, and an irrigation system had been installed to keep the grass green—which was seen only briefly, as the mass of horses, carriages, and riders soon chewed it up. It was a complicated and labor-intensive sequence, covered by many cameras. Explosive squibs were attached to clothing and would detonate to simulate the hit of a bullet. After each take, new squibs had to be fitted. The wheels of carriages had to be rigged so they would fall off and the carriages would overturn at the right moment. Stunt men had to fall off horses repeatedly.

In fact, like all of Cimino's big sequences, it was meticulously and carefully planned. Of course it was dangerous—all sequences like that are—but Cimino had hired two expert horse wranglers whom he totally trusted, Allan Keller and Rudy Ugland, to lead the team. The locally recruited "Bohunk Cavalry" were immensely experienced horsemen. The stunts were coordinated by Buddy Van Horn, who had worked on *The Deer Hunter.* There was a squad of medics and nurses to cope with any injuries.

Despite the planning and the well-organized backup team, however, the shooting was punishing. One of the carriage drivers told me sardonically, "It wasn't like driving a Hummer." A lot of the time, the riders could not see where they were going because Fuller's earth was liberally used for explosions and dust clouds—it spreads higher than most natural soils, resulting in a blast that looks larger. Herb Lightman, editor of *American Cinematographer*, wrote about his experience of working as one of the many cameramen used in the sequence: "It has an epic sweep. There are hundreds of immigrants fleeing for safety with their wagons. During a take there is so much dust that I feel like I'm shooting in Braille. It gets in my eyes, nose, throat, lungs and several bodily orifices I never knew I even had. When 'Cut!' is called, we feel like real battle casualties." Lightman observed Cimino working: "A slight figure in this larger-than-life milieu, in his own quiet way he towers above everyone on the set. I find myself filled with respect and admiration (and, yes, affection) for this dogged artist."

Later, there were stories about the filming being chaotic and badly organized. There were rumors of many horses being killed and riders being seriously injured, but that was partly because it looked so realistic that it seemed that those things must actually have happened. The final toll was a few injuries, one horse accidentally killed, and an actor, Waldemar Kalinowski, whose leg was crushed when he tipped his carriage over and had to be hospitalized. A helicopter was flown quickly to the location, and Cimino supervised him being stretchered in. Kalinowski later sued the production and received an insurance settlement. With a certain amount of poetic justice, there was one more small injury: Les Gapay, the journalist turned extra, reported, "A horse steps on my foot and X-rays show that one toe has a crushed bone." However, compared to a stuntman almost being killed during a car-chase sequence in 1965's James Bond movie *Thunderball,* or Vic Morrow being decapitated by a helicopter on the set of *The Twilight Zone* in 1982, the team on *Heaven's Gate* handled the dangerous filming with meticulous care.

By then, everyone just wanted to get to the end. The morale of the crew had plummeted, and Cimino, normally brilliant at coping with stress, was clearly under strain and moved from being demanding of the crew to being bad-tempered with them as well. The British actor Nicholas Woodeson told me that filming the last sequence was like a grim journey that had to be endured: "What Napoleon's retreat from Moscow must have been like." Cimino finished shooting it at the end of September—two days early. The last sequence of the movie was filmed on October 2 in Butte, a complicated night sequence in which Sam Waterston, playing Canton, the head of the Stock Growers Association, recruits mercenaries. Cimino shot it uncharacteristically simply in one evening with just three camera setups. Then the crew went to the War Bonnet Inn for a hastily arranged wrap party.

Garry Wunderwald from the Montana Film Office told me, "I didn't know what to give Michael for some kind of remembrance. I went to the state livestock department and asked them to design a brand for his horses. We called it the MC Ranch. He was really touched, and when we got back to the Outlaw Inn, we decided to heat it up with a torch and imprint it in the bar."

Bryan Buchanan said that at the party "when everyone was hugging each other, I said something like, 'It was great working with you,' and Michael comes over and plants a kiss right on my lips and says, 'So were you.'"

As a leaving present—although they stayed friendly for many years—Cimino gave his driver, Van Robinson, a leather-bound copy of the script with Van's name embossed in gold. Patty Nelson told me that

Cimino's brand (Photograph courtesy Gary Wunderwald)

Cimino had been fretting for a month over what to give him. Then there were two final tasks for Robinson: he drove Joann Carelli's black Jeep to New York, and then he flew back to Montana and drove Cimino's one to Beverly Hills.

With filming over, there were two betrayals that Cimino could not forget. He demanded that United Artists censure Lee Katz and prohibit him from having "any and all contact with myself and Joann [during postproduction] as he is only a divisive influence." Then he fired Charlie Okun, the production manager who had been his friend for fifteen years, because he believed that he had worked secretly with Katz behind his and Carelli's backs. (Okun moved on from Cimino to Lawrence Kasdan, for whom he produced *The Accidental Tourist* and *Wyatt Earp*.) "I didn't get fired, I got whipped," he said. Unexpectedly, Cimino made one conciliatory gesture. Although it was probably more for form's sake than anything else, he wrote to David Field, thanking him for his "continued support and enthusiasm."

Carelli did not leave Kalispell without recriminations, and she fired one of her characteristic broadsides: "The longer you stay in a place like this, the more people seem to think you have a lot of money. After all,

The T-shirt (Photograph courtesy Bryan Buchanan)

you're from Hollywood, right? They really start to rip you off. It was like hold-up time without a gun." George Ostrom, in the *Kalispell Weekly News*, gave as good as he got: "Joann Carelli seems to be a woman with a wealth of dollars and narrow-minded opinions to match. Those of you who were around the filming may recall her as a sort of pain in the neck driving around in a black Jeep. Her remarks . . . are out and out, bald-faced lies, a fact that I doubt bothers her at all." Almost certainly it didn't.

With the cast and crew gone, Kalispell reverted to its sleepy self. The Outlaw Inn no longer had all its rooms occupied; the bars and restaurants now had space for the locals; the hunters were gearing up for the fall season. In the town, there was a surprising sight: people wearing bright yellow T-shirts with the words "I made it through Heaven's Gate" printed on the back.

CHAPTER 11

THE VIOLINIST ON ROLLER SKATES

ON SEPTEMBER 28, as the punishing battle sequence was being completed up at North Fork, something surprising happened: Joann Carelli got married. For a long time, nobody knew; many people never knew at all. Her new husband was David Mansfield, and he was twenty-three years old, more than a decade younger than her. He had been a crucial part of *Heaven's Gate* during shooting, and his later contribution would make an indelible mark on the final film.

One of the most beautiful scenes in the movie takes place in the immigrants' wooden roller-skating rink. A band is playing, and a small figure with curly dark hair—who the poet Allen Ginsberg described as having "the face of a Botticelli angel, a Florentine princeling"—does something astonishing: he steps down from the stage with his fiddle and plays it perfectly as he skates around the rink, his legs splaying outward then coming together as he goes faster and faster. This is Mansfield. As usual, there were many takes for the sequence, and I asked him if he had ever tripped up. "I didn't tend to fall," he said, shrugging. "I'd had a few skating lessons and, well, I knew how to play the fiddle."

David Mansfield playing the violin (Alamy)

He also knew how to play the viola, mandolin, mandocello, dobro, bass, classical guitar, steel-string guitar, and pedal-steel guitar expertly. He came from a musical family in New Jersey—his father was the first violinist of the New York Philharmonic. "I studied violin as a kid and started picking up other instruments," he told me. By the time he was sixteen, his band Quacky Duck and His Barnyard Friends were signed to Warner Bros. and released two albums. At seventeen, he was playing with Bonnie Raitt and Gram Parsons.

"In 1975, I met and played with Bobby Neuwirth, a friend of Bob Dylan's, at a gig at the Bitter End," he told me. "It was a bit of a free-for-all, with people turning up and getting on the stage. Dylan and Neuwirth had been hanging around the Village and coming up with wild ideas, and one of them was for the Rolling Thunder Review. When the tour came around, I was going to be in Neuwirth's band and Dylan was going to use the core band of people he used on his album *Desire*, but when we started rehearsing, everybody began playing on everything and we became one big repertory company."

Mansfield played on and off with Dylan for several years, and in 1978, he was asked to join his world tour. On September 30, they played

Madison Square Garden, and Carelli, taking a break from preproduction on *Heaven's Gate*, had tickets. She thought he was brilliant.

Back in Los Angeles, where Mansfield was living, they met. "She called me in because they were looking for people to be in the band," he said. Cimino and Carelli had a very specific conception of how to get the music they wanted for the immigrants' roller-skating rink sequences. She always had impeccable taste in music—she had found Stanley Myers, the composer of *The Deer Hunter* score—and was trying to "cast" the band. "Joann spearheaded the choice of musicians. She was definitely running things. She took us all to Michael, and he said yes or no." In the end, she found an extraordinary group of players, some of whom had played together before: Mansfield, his friend T Bone Burnett (who later went on to produce the Who and Elton John), Norton Buffalo, Stephen Bruton (part of Kris Kristofferson's band), Gerry McGee, Sean Hopper (later a member of Huey Lewis and the News), and Cleve Dupin. Normally the tracks would be prerecorded by professional session play- ers and then musicians would be hired to mime to the track, called a playback, but in this instance, the band actually played the music. Unusually, Carelli and Cimino also wanted them to act in the movie.

Mansfield told me, "Michael had had good luck with casting non-pros in acting roles, and he wanted to combine each one of the band members' parts with some small role in the film so they would seem woven into the town. I was the kid in the brothel, and T Bone worked in Jeff Bridges's bar. We would be seen poking through the tapestry of the film all the way through."

"All the way through," of course, meant staying in Montana for seven months. Mansfield had no idea it would work out that way: "Like many people, I was originally hired for a few weeks." When he arrived, he found the world of *Heaven's Gate* very strange. He knew nothing about movie sets or the rough-and-tumble life of location shooting. "I was shy, a bit of an introvert." He was different from the other crew members in many ways. For one thing, he was one of the youngest people in the crew. He did not have much interaction with Cimino and Carelli at the beginning, and he felt that "they were like the grown-ups." He was also very religious—Penny Shaw, who had the room next to him at the Outlaw Inn, told me that on Sundays he would stay in his room and listen to church songs.

But life in an isolated movie location can be friendly and inclusive. Mansfield, with his quiet charm, became one of the most popular members of the crew and was especially close to Jeff Bridges and John Hurt. And, of course, there was the music. "It was a big deal, the fact that the band really was a band, and we all became a very tight unit. We spent a lot of time in the bar, taking it over and playing," he said.

Carelli had found a piece of music by Doug Kershaw, an upbeat Cajun-style tune called "Mamou Two-Step," and the band did two arrangements, the first a fast one that Mansfield skated and played the fiddle to, the second a slow version that Kristofferson and Huppert danced to alone in the skating rink. There was a recording studio a couple of hours away in Missoula where they recorded the tracks, with Carelli producing.

By then, there was gossip circulating around the crew. There are always affairs on a movie set—known in the business as "locationships"—and it is hard to keep them secret. People began to have the feeling that Carelli and Mansfield had become involved. They were discreet about it: Bryan Buchanan told me, "I don't think anyone saw them together as a couple. It was just a gossipy thing." Among the crew, it was regarded as an unlikely pairing. He was gentle and shy. Carelli was neither of those things, and people who talked to me had some difficulty working out the dynamics of the relationship.

It was obvious that Cimino knew. Van Robinson told me, "David and Joann—it kind of flared up. Michael didn't say much about it. He just pressed on." Whatever his and Carelli's relationship had become, it was clearly a broad enough canvas to include other people around the edges. Even if he was exaggerating, Cimino talked often about his girlfriends. (Penny Shaw told me he had once said to her sadly, "One day there'll be somebody sitting next to me at dinner and I'll just ask them to marry me.") Whatever girlfriends he did or did not have, it also seems unlikely that he was the only man in Carelli's life, but whatever happened outside their "secret world" appeared not to affect their relationship at all. There was also some gossip about him and Isabelle Huppert. In his book, Steven Bach wrote that, because Cimino had been so adamant about casting her, David Field wondered if they were having an affair before filming started. In Kalispell, they spent a lot of

Cimino and Isabelle Huppert (Photograph courtesy Penny Shaw Sylvester)

time together, and it was clear that he had a crush on her, but nobody ever thought it went beyond that. David Mansfield wondered whether Cimino wanted to imply a closeness to Huppert simply for a little retaliation. For her part, Huppert was passionately loyal to Cimino all his life, and she had an enduring friendship with both him and Carelli.

Whatever Cimino knew about the relationship, he was unaware that Carelli and Mansfield had married. It was kept a secret from him as well as from most other people. Clearly, the problem was not the relationship but the marriage: it implied that someone had moved from the edge of Cimino and Carelli's canvas and was now in the middle of it.

Mansfield, of course, told his family, but according to him, Carelli made them promise not to reveal it. The only member of her family he met was her brother, Arthur (who had worked on *Heaven's Gate*). He never met any of the others, with whom he said she did not have a good relationship, and he has no idea whether they ever knew about the marriage. Both he and Patty Nelson remember Carelli's mother turning up at a *Heaven's Gate* screening—uninvited, Nelson believed—but Mansfield was not introduced to her.

Both Nelson and Penny Shaw, who were close to Mansfield, were aware of the marriage. When Shaw was helping Cimino edit the movie back in Los Angeles, she began to feel awkward that he did not know. She was talking on the phone to Nelson one evening: "I said, 'Somebody's got to tell him,' and Patty said, 'Well, you have to.'" She and Cimino were driving in his Jeep to Dan Tana's, one of his favorite restaurants, where they often had dinner, and she finally plucked up the courage. She told me, "I said, 'Michael, there's something I really feel you should know.' He said, 'What?' 'People know, and it's just not fair. Joann and David got married.' He got very angry with me. 'Don't be ridiculous. No, they didn't.' I said, 'Yes, they did.' He never mentioned it again."

CHAPTER 12

THE GATES OF HELL

AFTER FILMING FINISHED in Kalispell on October 2, Cimino did not return to Los Angeles until November 12, almost exactly the day United Artists had planned to open the movie. The 1.5 million feet of film had been transported back, and the editor, Tom Rolf, alongside Penny Shaw, put together a very rough assembly of the footage for Cimino to begin work on. If United Artists had been a conventional studio, it would have had editing suites on its lot. Luckily for Cimino, it did not, and space had been rented at MGM in Culver City. Even there, away from the prying eyes of United Artists, he did not take any chances.

Shaw said, "We had bars put on the cutting room windows, and then we had all the locks changed so that nobody could come in." (Cimino denied this.) "Michael said, 'I'm not showing them it until I'm ready.' He wasn't afraid of anybody. Sometimes a call would come in from somebody and he'd get on the phone and scream and yell. He'd slam it down and turn to me and just smile. Then we'd keep going."

As usual, Cimino was completely focused. Despite the mass of footage, with many takes of many scenes covered by many cameras, he was in total command of the material. He knew exactly what he had shot even though he had two hundred hours of it. It was still a daunting task. Shaw told me, "In the cutting room we would start at six o'clock in the morning because he'd say, 'Well, if we come in [early], then there'll be nobody around to bother us, no phone calls or anything.' Then we worked till ten P.M."

As he had all the way through shooting, he depended heavily on Shaw for both her support and her knowledge of the footage, which was almost as great as his. The actual editor was Tom Rolf, a Swedish American who had edited *Taxi Driver* for Scorsese four years before, but as editing went on, Cimino began to lose confidence in him. Shaw told me that he gave Rolf less and less editing to do and began taking away his equipment until finally there was just a chair in his office.

Inevitably, with the punishing hours in the editing suite, Shaw spent most of her time with Cimino. Although they worked six days a week, Cimino insisted she go riding with him (even though she didn't like it much) on Sundays in Saugus, north of the San Fernando Valley, where *Heaven's Gate*'s chief wrangler, Rudy Ugland, had a ranch. Shaw did not remember Joann Carelli being around much—she came back and forth from New York—and Cimino seemed rather lonely. He was thinking of buying a ranch house in Hidden Valley, and he took Shaw to see it. When they were looking around, he pointed his finger and said, "This could be your room." Fond as she was of him as a friend, it was hard to get close to him. At Christmas, he appeared to have no plans, and Shaw, who had a large and warm family—nine brothers and sisters from her actor father Robert Shaw's various relationships—suggested he come to Ireland and join them, but he declined.

Cimino and Carelli had worked out a postproduction schedule that would involve him delivering a movie of three hours (more than that would remove his right to final cut) on May 1, 1980. The finished version (after sound editing, effects, and music had been added) would be ready by October 25, with an opening planned for November 19. Because of the lead time needed to book theaters and organize publicity, this last date effectively became set in stone.

There was still the problem of the Harvard prologue and the yacht epilogue, neither of which had been shot yet. United Artists had cautiously agreed to Cimino filming them as long as a budget could be agreed on. No figures had been submitted yet, so the additional shooting was on hold. Bach and Field regarded it as a carrot to keep Cimino in check during editing, but the sequences were already beginning to look expensive. Harvard had refused permission to film there, and Cimino was talking about building a giant set of the college in Florida.

In truth, their carrot was rather a feeble one, because Field, and to some extent Bach, were themselves passionate about the prologue and epilogue. Whatever Field felt about Cimino personally, he believed that he was a great filmmaker and knew, as he always had, that those sequences would not only give the story a context, but would add a heart-breaking and elegiac resonance that would make the movie unforget-table. They finally got Albeck to agree to it—as long as the budget was no more than $3 million.

On March 11, Bach was given some shocking news: Albeck told him that Field had handed in his resignation and was going to 20th Century Fox. He had given no reason for his leaving, nor did Field ever discuss it with Bach. It was announced in the press as being for the usual boilerplate "personal reasons." Bach was not necessarily delighted by Field's depar-ture: in some ways, the head of production job-share had suited him. He was not a power-crazed Sammy Glick clawing his way to the top. He liked the pampered life of a Concorde-flying movie executive with an expense account. He was now going to become the one who would have to take full responsibility, be the sole Cimino-wrangler, and maybe have to stop giving the best "Yes" in the business.

Field told me why he had actually left: "Everyone thought it was because of *Heaven's Gate*. In fact, it was because I could not go on work-ing with Steven Bach." It was not an easy decision. Later he said, "I have one regret in my life, and that's that I left United Artists. I've fought myself for walking away in the middle."

Six days after Field's resignation, Cimino and Derek Kavanagh flew to England on March 17 to begin preparing the Harvard prologue, which Field had fought so hard for. The university was going to be re-created at Mansfield College, Oxford. They were also going to do some blue screen (a more convincing version of the old back-projection) shots of Kristof-ferson on his steam-yacht for the epilogue.

The relationship between Cimino and Kavanagh was still spiky, but they had been working together to see if the sequence could be made for the allotted $3 million. Another experienced production manager was hired—Denis O'Dell, who was an expert on shooting in England. He had often worked with the director Richard Lester, from *A Hard Day's Night* onward. Because of money, Cimino could bring only a few heads of department (production designer, costume designer, and cinematographer) and O'Dell found an English crew to work with them. Inevitably, Cimino disliked him. In the final credits, although the tongue-twisting names of the immigrants were all spelled correctly, he was listed as "Dennis O'Dell."

As the prologue was set twenty years before the main action in Wyoming, Kris Kristofferson shaved his beard to look as if he was twenty-one—not entirely convincingly, as he was forty-four. There were five parts to the shoot: the Pinewood yacht material; Kris Kristofferson running down a street; a celebratory marching band that he joins; the graduating students listening to valedictory speeches by John Hurt and Joseph Cotten, to be shot in the Sheldonian Theatre; and a complex set piece involving more than a hundred dancers waltzing to "The Blue Danube" around a giant tree in the quad of the college. As there was no tree there, it was planned to cut up an existing one into sections and bolt each one together from the bottom upward.

On March 18, Kavanagh and Cimino called Bach to tell him that the budget came to $5.2 million and involved thirteen shooting days plus rehearsals. Bach, with the backup of Andy Albeck, told them to come home immediately. The next day, a budget of just under $3 million was submitted. The shoot was on.

Cimino and Carelli hired the distinguished British choreographer Eleanor Fazan to supervise the dance sequence. They had known her for some time—she had been married to Stanley Myers, the composer Carelli had found for *The Deer Hunter*. Back in January, even though the prologue sequences were not necessarily going to happen, Cimino had begun preparing it, and Fazan was flown to Los Angeles. He explained to her what the subtext of the sequence was: the aristocratic characters played by Kris Kristofferson and John Hurt were at the end of an era and did not realize that their lives were about to change. They would face a different world in Montana, far away from their rich East Coast upbringing. Fazan told me, "Michael was fascinated by class. He loved it"—as he clearly had since his illusory Gold Coast youth in Westbury. Michael Stevenson, the British assistant director on the Oxford shoot, said, "Michael wanted real aristocrats to be in the carriages. The daughter of Lord and Lady Harmsworth was one of them. With her friends, we had that wonderful look."

Unlike real aristocrats, Kris Kristofferson did not know how to waltz, and Fazan gave him lessons in Los Angeles. Although Cimino was exacting, she loved working with him. "He was strange, but boyish," she said. "I really liked him. He was shy in many ways. I felt he always wanted to be friendly but wasn't quite sure how to do it. He wasn't the sort who would say, 'Sit down and have a cup of coffee and a gossip.'"

Fazan returned to England and worked for three months to find and rehearse the 160 dancers. Because of money, she was not allowed to use Equity (the UK actors' union) dancers and had the more difficult task of trying to find cheaper extras who could dance. When this proved challenging, she got in touch with ballroom dancing clubs and found them that way.

They rehearsed in London, and Cimino vetted them when he arrived in England. He was generally happy with her choices. "I think he trusted me," she said. However, as he had done with the immigrants in *Heaven's Gate*, he took hours moving them around into different groups, "painting" them onto the canvas of the scene. Fazan told me, "I warned the dancers, 'Be ready. He may decide he doesn't like your face and put you at the back. Just smile and say, "I'm working for a genius. If he wants me to go over there, then I'll go over there."'" In one of his unpredictable acts of generosity, Cimino had canvas chairs made for the lead dancers with their names on the back, but there was also some collateral damage. Carelli and Cimino did not like the musical director, Alfred Ralston, so he went. Cimino had asked Fazan and her assistant, Terry Gilbert, to waltz for him so he could see how it looked. He made them do it so many times that Gilbert finally said to him, "I'm not putting Eleanor through any more of this." He was relegated to the very back of the dancers. But generally, Cimino liked English crews. He felt they were more dedicated and hardworking. He was amused by the remains of the old class system, in which crew members tended to call their director "Guv'nor."

Cimino and Kavanagh's new budget called for a significant loss of shooting days. Now they would have one day to shoot each of the five parts of the prologue, with one day of rehearsal for them. For even a fast director, this would have been a tough call for huge sequences involving hundreds

The graduation waltz (Alamy)

of extras. In Kalispell, when pushed into a corner about the slowness of the shooting, he had told Bach and Dean Stolber that he knew perfectly well how to move more quickly. "Ask Clint," he said. Bach was outraged. "I find it incredibly sad, Michael, that you should try to win our confidence by rubbing our noses in your willingness to do in a moment for Mr. Eastwood what you have refused to do for us for three and a half months."

Now, in Oxford, he did do it for them. The shooting was meticulously planned and finished on time and on budget. More than that, the sequences—particularly Fazan's giant waltz sequence—were among the most stunning in the movie. Cimino always had a particular affection for those sequences. In 1983, three years after the shattering death of his movie, the National Film Theatre in London gave a one-off screening. He was there, and he asked Fazan to go with him. She told me that when they came out after, he asked her what she felt: "I said, 'It makes me want to dance again.' I thought he was going to cry." In 1990, when she was awarded a British Academy fellowship, he wrote a warm and gracious tribute that was read out: "My dear genius, I am both honored and favored by the gift of your friendship."

When he returned to Los Angeles, there was a more significant piece of collateral damage. Penny Shaw had stayed behind to continue editing, and she had hired an assistant to go to England and collate the dailies. Cimino was angry that the assistant ran up a large telephone bill, and he told Shaw to sack him. She told Cimino that the size of the phone bill was because he had made a long transatlantic call to her every night to discuss the footage, and she refused to let him go. "He stood behind me in the editing suite and was shaking with rage: 'Don't ever not do something I tell you to do,' he shouted," Shaw told me.

Anyone else would have been off the picture, but Shaw was too valuable: she was the only person who knew the footage as well as he did. However, their relationship was ruptured beyond repair. Other people would come into the editing room and say to her, "Michael wants you to . . ." and her position was made increasingly uncomfortable. Once, when she rejigged the schedule, she received a fiery memo from Carelli: "I will not tolerate any schedule changes without my approval. This has happened before and any further attempts to ignore my requests for approval can only indicate your desire to resign." Nonetheless, Shaw had gone through a lot with Cimino, and her commitment to the picture was total. She stayed on until it was finished. With Cimino, the lashing out and banishing of people he was close to seemed to be something he could not help doing. In an interview he gave in 1978, he said rather chillingly, "In every friendship there is the potential for destructiveness as well as nourishment."

Cimino's three-hour version was due to be shown on May 1 and would be the first time anyone at United Artists would see the edited movie. The English shoot meant that Cimino was behind in the cutting even though another editor, William Reynolds, a seasoned Hollywood hand who had worked on *The Sound of Music* and *The Sting*, had come on board. It was clear that they were not going to achieve the May 1 date. Because Bach was pressing him about progress, Cimino gave him a taster by showing the footage from the Oxford prologue. Bach thought it was stunning, but there was an underlying melancholy for him—if Cimino could shoot material that brilliant that quickly when he wanted to, why hadn't he done it Montana? When the screening finished, there was a worrying moment: Cimino intimated that the movie might be more than three hours long: "He said that he had not seen it himself from start to finish and had not timed it precisely."

On June 3, Bach sent him a memo demanding a date to see the movie. Cimino did not reply. (This is not as unusual as it might seem. Kubrick never showed Warner Bros. any footage from *The Shining* until the day before it opened.) Bach sent another memo, and finally Cimino agreed to a screening on June 26. It was shown at the main theater on the MGM lot, where security guards blocked the entrance until Andy Albeck, Lee Stolber, and Bach produced identification—"Mr. Cimino's orders." They sat down, and the movie began. They were still sitting five and a half hours later.

There was no question of where the money had gone—every dollar was on the screen—but Bach and the others were shattered. The movie may have looked stunning, but the effects were deafening and the dialogue under them was difficult to hear, which made the story confusing. Bach said, "The battle, the pandemonium, the chaos, the terrorized animals, the blood, the dust, the debris and explosives were relentless. The brain numbed." They all found it interminable. When I asked Penny Shaw how that long version differed from the final version, she simply said, "It was longer."

United Artists were horrified at the problem they had on their hands. It was now June 26, and it had taken Cimino seven months to edit the footage. They were locked into the November release date, which gave Cimino four months to re-edit it, as well as supervise the complicated and time-consuming sound editing and mixing.

Strangely, Cimino did not have to be persuaded very hard that the movie was way overlength. He agreed to deliver a shorter version in time for the November opening. He may have calculated that if he showed Bach and United Artists a ridiculously long cut, they would be delighted to accept a final version at almost any length less than five and a half hours. As Pauline Kael said perceptively in her 1985 *New Yorker* review of Bach's book, "In all probability Michael Cimino could read Steven Bach a lot better than Bach could read Cimino."

To speed things up, another editor, Jerry Greenberg, was hired to specifically work on the climactic battle sequence. Cimino had worked with him in his advertising days in New York and knew he was brilliant at action sequences—he cut the famous car chase in William Friedkin's *The French Connection*. Even though there were now three editors working on the picture, Cimino was still in total control, working sixteen-hour days alongside them. Now, as he often did when it suited him, he became more elusive than ever. Carelli had always been the conduit to him—United Artists did not even have his phone number—but now, according to Bach, she became a barrier. Bach said, "She politely (or not) explained that Michael was in the editing room, at the lab, in the screening room, indisposed, unavailable."

On July 15, Bach told Carelli he was removing her from the picture. He reported that she told him, "I can't tell you what a relief this is. I'm tired of being the fall guy, having the fights, making everybody mad at me because they can't find Michael to get mad at." Carelli denied to me that she had been sacked off the movie, and even if she was, it was a pointless act. Whether or not she had an official producing role, she would still be, as she always had been, Cimino's gatekeeper. In any case, she continued to work on the picture, sorting out the publicity and the music.

Cimino had originally wanted John Williams, the composer of both *Star Wars* and *Jaws*. At that point, he was looking for a big symphonic score of the traditional Western kind, like those for *The Big Country* or *The Magnificent Seven*. Carelli, although she never directly gave him advice, counterintuitively thought that it should have a smaller score just because it was such a big picture. In the end, John Williams was asked to run the Boston Pops and pulled out.

Cimino asked Carelli to look for other composers. After considering John Barry, who had done the *James Bond* movies, the Italian composer Ennio Morricone, who had scored all of Sergio Leone's movies, including *The Good, The Bad, and the Ugly*, came in for a meeting while they were shooting in England. Carelli told me that he was extraordinarily rude: while she was sitting with him waiting for Cimino, he pretended to be asleep but came to life as soon as Cimino appeared. They decided against Morricone. In the meantime, with no clear direction for the music, Carelli suggested that prospective composers should listen to immigrant folk songs to get a feel for the movie.

In fact, David Mansfield had already been doing it: many of the actors who played immigrants had been hired because they were first- or second-generation Americans, and during shooting, Mansfield heard them sing folk songs they had learned from their parents or grandparents. He told me, "I started making some recordings myself in my home studio. I thought there might be some interest in using them in some form or fashion. I wasn't pitching myself to do the score. I was way too intimidated to think like that." As "The Blue Danube" waltz had been such an important part of the prologue, Carelli also asked him to do various arrangements of it, some fast, some slow, but she did not say how they might be used.

"I played some tracks for Joann, and she took mixes of them," Mansfield said. "Then she gave them to Michael to listen to."

The usual way directors work with composers is called "spotting"—a very exact process that involves deciding on which specific frame a music cue starts and on which frame it ends. The composer will then write music to exactly that length and record it to a time-coded print of the picture. Cimino, intuitive enough never to follow the norm, did it differently. "He started laying the tracks over some of the film like temp tracks," Mansfield told me. "It was a gradual process. He was fooling around with the demos. He got excited, and when he used up the maybe four tunes I'd given him, he asked for more. It was like I was recording a library of music for him." Gradually, without any formal declaration, it became clear that Mansfield was composing the score for *Heaven's Gate*.

When Steven Bach asked Carelli who was doing the music, she said, "David Mansfield. You know him. He plays John DeCory in the movie."

"That little *kid*?" he asked.

"He's no little kid. He just looks like a little kid. Who do you think arranged all that roller-skating music and found the antique instruments and taught those guys to play them? He used to be in Bob Dylan's band. I discovered him." She did not mention to Bach that they were married.

Hiring Mansfield was not nepotism on Carelli's part. With her finely tuned eye for talent, she used him not because he was her husband but because she recognized how brilliant he was. She was proved right: even people who hated the movie when it was released—which was almost everybody—were stunned by the beauty of the music. When the soundtrack album was reissued in 1999, *Rolling Stone* called it "vindication in vinyl" for the movie.

However, as usual with Cimino, there was a credit issue. On promo posters for the soundtrack album (United Artists had pressed an

The pre-release poster with Cimino's music
credit (Author's collection)

ambitious half a million copies) Mansfield is not mentioned, nor is his
name on the front cover of the LP. When advance posters for the movie
itself were printed, they read, "Music by Michael Cimino and David
Mansfield." On later versions, the credit was only for Mansfield. When
I asked him why this had happened, he said he did not really know but
thought Carelli might have changed the posters because, although never
one to downplay Cimino's contributions, even she felt that it would be
overdoing it for him to have so many different credits on the movie.

However, it still rankles Carelli. She told me that Cimino was brilliant at music and that he really did all of it: Mansfield just arranged
it. She herself took a credit as the album's producer and bought the

publishing rights to the music (which she still owns) and, according to Bach, leased them back to the movie.

By October, Cimino and his team of editors had reduced the running time to three hours and forty minutes. He would not cut it further. Bach was shown various sequences, but neither he, nor anyone else at United Artists, was ever shown the entire movie before the New York premiere on November 18. Strangely, Bach did not insist on seeing it beforehand, but even if he had, there was nothing that could be done: they had run out of time—the opening was only a month away. UA were essentially stuck with whatever Cimino wanted to give them.

Even though they could have forced him to do so, he resisted having a preview of the movie. He said that Universal had insisted on one for *The Deer Hunter* and it simply proved that he had been right all along about its length. Because he was still working on the movie, it would have been hard to organize a preview, but not impossible if Cimino had been prepared to show a rough version of the movie. There was a precedent for that: Coppola submitted an unfinished version of *Apocalypse Now* to the Cannes Film Festival in May 1979, billing as a "Work in Progress." Even though it was somewhat different to the eventual release cut, it shared the top award, the Palme d'Or. For *Heaven's Gate*, a preview would have been the only opportunity to gauge an unbiased audience reaction—after the devastating reviews and damaging publicity when it opened, everyone had been prewarned it was going to be terrible, and most of them thought that it was.

ON NOVEMBER 18, CIMINO flew in from Los Angeles, bringing the print of the movie that would be shown at the premiere in New York. He had been working on it until the last minute. The posters outside the theater had been supervised by Carelli and Cimino and showed a haunting picture of Kris Kristofferson standing in the Heaven's Gate skating rink in silhouette, backlit by a shaft of light streaming in through the window behind him. Cimino had also been in the picture, standing to the left of Kristofferson, but his figure had been removed to create the striking image—the only time he would ever be airbrushed out of any aspect of *Heaven's Gate*. The tag line read, "What one loves about life are the things that fade."

The premiere began in the time-honored fashion of Old Holly-wood: red carpets, backed-up lines of black limos, and an eager, jostling crowd waiting to see the stars. Forty years after its publication, the spirit of *The Day of the Locust* was still alive. The author Don Winslow was hired to be an usher at the screening. He said, "You know that tired saying, 'you could cut the tension with a knife'? There hasn't been a blade forged that could cut this tension. . . . We were actually undertakers at a very expensive funeral. . . . I left the theater [after the movie started], went into the lobby, and saw a man standing alone, his face in his hands, mumbling, 'What am I going to do? What am I going to do?' I found out later it was the director, Michael Cimino."

Isabelle Huppert remembered half the audience leaving at the intermission—"We felt as if we were criminals." After three hours and forty minutes of the film, there were only a few pockets of polite applause—Jeff Bridges remembered a graveyard-slow clapping of hands—and as the eight minutes of credits rolled, people were rushing for the exits. The attendance at the lavish party at the Four Seasons was so sparse that when a well-known New York party-crasher arrived, nobody bothered to kick him out. Everyone hated the film.

The next morning, the reviews were probably the most devastating ever published for a movie. The media, antagonistic to Cimino since his hostile attitude to them in Kalispell and after, turned on him in a vicious attack. Vincent Canby's review in the *New York Times* was the most destructive: "*Heaven's Gate* fails so completely that you might suspect that Mr. Cimino sold his soul to the Devil to obtain the success of *The Deer Hunter* and the Devil has just come around to collect. . . . Watching the movie is like a forced, four-hour walking tour of one's own living room. [It] is something quite rare in movies these days—an unqualified disaster." Roger Ebert wrote, "It is the most scandalous cinematic waste I have ever seen. . . . This is one of the ugliest films I have ever seen"; *Variety*: "The balance of director Michael Cimino's film is so confusing . . . and ponderous that it fails to work at almost every level." Pauline Kael later wrote that the press had always been "waiting to ambush Cimino." Kris Kristofferson said, "It was like you had a beloved child of yours murdered and then the murder blamed on you." Cimino was so unpopular that it was reported that cheers rang out in the Polo Lounge at the Beverly Hills Hotel as producers heard about the reviews.

It's possible that they might have been marginally less terrible if Cimino had addressed the problems that a preview might have highlighted. With the advent of Dolby technology, for example, sound effects had become pinpoint sharp and could be manipulated easily at different levels. The first scenes shot in Wallace were particularly problematic. It was those sequences that set up the plot—what precisely Kristofferson and John Hurt were doing there, how the plan to kill the immigrants was going to be implemented—but the sound mix of the train noise, the carriages, the horses, the muttering of the crowds was so rich and detailed that it drowned out the crucial dialogue. The cinematographer, Vilmos Zsigmond, and Cimino had also decided to tint the film with a kind of yellow glow that seemed intended to have the look of an animated antique etching. To many, it seemed as if the picture was shrouded in nicotine smoke.

However, making a few simple changes probably would not have mattered—the list of things that critics hated was simply too enormous. They leapt gleefully on every tiny detail—many of them petty and irrelevant. Canby commented, "The situation is not helped by the fact that the university looks not like Harvard but like Oxford, where it was actually filmed." In fact, few movies are shot in actual locations: in Warren Beatty's *Reds*, Lancaster House in London did not look much like the Winter Palace in St. Petersburg but, like Harvard, it was a convincing substitute. There was also bemusement about why a Frenchwoman, Isabelle Huppert, would be in Wyoming in 1890, a curious objection given that the movie was filled with immigrants from many European countries.

As they did for *The Deer Hunter*, critics fell on its historical "inaccuracy." The characters played by Kristofferson, Hurt, Bridges, and others were based on real people but somewhat fictionalized; the climactic battle was larger and more dramatic than it had been in reality. Though Cimino never purported to be making a documentary, many critics denied him the right, afforded willingly to other directors, to artistic license. Since the birth of the industry, historical inaccuracies have been rife in movies. Few critics berated David Lean for the multitude of inaccuracies in *Lawrence of Arabia* or Ridley Scott for playing fast and loose with Roman history in *Gladiator*.

The next day, with the uniformly terrible reviews already in the morning papers, Cimino, Carelli, Kristofferson, Huppert, Bridges, and Mansfield flew to Toronto for the second premiere. Next they would fly on to Los Angeles for the third. But before the Los Angeles screening, Cimino did something very uncharacteristic: despite the fact that the Toronto screening had gone rather better than the New York one, he lost the ferocious certainty he had about himself and his work: he asked United Artists to withdraw *Heaven's Gate* from theaters for it to be recut. This was something unprecedented in the movie industry. Although other movies had been cut after release—Stanley Kubrick quietly removed twenty minutes from *The Shining* three weeks after it had opened in the US, and the movie's run continued unbroken, but in its shorter form. No movie had actually been pulled so quickly.

Before the withdrawal was announced, United Artist canceled the Los Angeles premiere, which was to have been held in the largest of the Plitt Theatres in Century City Plaza on November 20. The night before, 1,200 telegrams were sent to the guests, a herculean task before email. Patty Nelson, Cimino's secretary, told me, "I can't even describe what happened. It was horrendous." The telegrams read, *At Michael Cimino's request, United Artists is canceling the screening of* Heaven's Gate. . . . *You will receive another invitation when we are able to reschedule it.* There never was another one. The Plitt remained dark after the aborted premiere. A few years later, the large auditorium was demolished and reconfigured as several smaller theaters—a chilling metaphor for what would happen to the movie business after the catastrophe of *Heaven's Gate*.

On November 24, a full-page ad in the form of a letter—the wording pre-agreed with UA—from Cimino to Andy Albeck was printed in *Variety* and the *Hollywood Reporter*. Cimino seemed to have forgotten his mantra "Never complain, never explain": *Dear Andy . . . It is painfully obvious to me that the pressures of the schedule and the missing crucial step of public previews clouded my perception of the film. . . . I am asking you to withdraw the film from distribution temporarily to allow me to present to the public a film finished with the same care and thoughtfulness with which we began it.* The next day, Cimino moved back into the cutting room.

The withdrawal and recutting were, according to Bach, completely Cimino's idea. It was not a good one. His uncompromising instincts—or at least those parts of his instinct structure that had to do with achieving his goals—failed him, but it was understandable: the shocking and unprecedented events of the previous few days might have sent any director into a panic. What is less understandable is why United Artists agreed to it, and Bach gave no reason why they did. Canceling the theaters that the movie had been booked into, going back into the cutting room, and paying for another expensive ad campaign was going to cost them additional millions.

More than that, there was not much basis to believe that a shorter version of the movie released six months later would fare any better. Of course, United Artists could not predict the future, but they did not seem to be able to read the present either. The length had certainly been one of the issues with critics, but they had so many other objections as well that pleasing them would be almost impossible. Was Vincent Canby really going to reverse his devastating judgment? United Artists knew the material very well by this time—they had seen the five-and-a-half hour as well as the release version, and they knew what footage was there. The movie was what it was: all that could be achieved was that it would be more or less the same—only shorter.

If Cimino and United Artists had gritted their teeth, refused to complain or explain, and simply stood by their movie, it would still have been a massive flop, but they would at least have had the dignity of their conviction. The reception had been devastating and embarrassing, but generally, Hollywood has a high embarrassment threshold. Certainly, they were going to lose a lot of money, but everyone knew how risky the movie business was, and they were protected by being part of a large and secure conglomerate, Transamerica.

The stock market could be sensitive to the share price of studios and their unpredictable results. In 1977, Columbia held a sneak preview of their upcoming movie *Close Encounters of the Third Kind* in Dallas. A journalist conned his way in and reported in *New York* magazine, "The picture will be a colossal flop." The studio's share price instantly fell by 20 percent. In fact, he was wrong. The movie was a giant and instant hit, and the share price bounced back. Transamerica and United Artists fared much better. Three days after the movie's opening, Aljean Harmetz, in the *Los Angeles Times*, reported, "The possible $50M loss involved in *Heaven's Gate* hardly caused a ripple in TransAmerica stock which went down 3/8th of a point today." It swiftly recovered.

With its horrifying reviews and financial loss, the movie would always have been part of Hollywood legend, but with the news of the withdrawal and the recutting, it became a laughingstock as well—the movie had cost $40 million to make, taken six months to shoot, a year to edit, and now the filmmakers themselves seemed to be agreeing with the terrible reviews.

The jokes began quickly. In Johnny Hart's *B.C.* comic strip, a man goes into a library and asks, "Do you have a book on how to make a bomb?" He is handed a copy of the *Heaven's Gate*'s screenplay. Later, its very title became a gift for cheap gags about other flops: as Watergate begat Contragate and Irangate, thus Cimino's film begat Heavensgate and later, Warrensgate (Beatty's *Ishtar*) and Kevinsgate (Costner's *Waterworld*). Cimino's movie became the poster child for failure.

Bad though they were, the reviews had been tucked away on the arts pages, but now the story escalated: the movie moved to the news pages. On December 1, both *Time* magazine and *Newsweek* ran stories—"How to Play Hollywood Hara-Kiri" and "Hollywood Turkey," respectively. Ten days after his review, Vincent Canby was calling it "the Phenomenon not the movie." Even Kalispell had its revenge: "Was *Heaven's Gate* the Worst Movie Ever Filmed in a National Park?"—beating 1954's *Cattle Queen of Montana* to the top spot. Critics who had liked *The Deer Hunter* were now having second thoughts. Stanley Kauffmann in 1978: "Cimino has a true filmmaker's instinct." In 1980: "On the basis of *The Deer Hunter*, there was no reason to believe that Cimino could make an organically sound film."

Cimino, back in Los Angeles in his cutting room with the bars and changed locks, managed to insulate himself from the hostility. His secretary, Patty Nelson, told me, "Michael was just not talking about it and refused to read anything about it. He just kept going."

Within a month of the New York premiere, he had cut an hour out of his movie. No individual scenes were removed, just made shorter, a narration was added to help the story, and some of the violence was toned down. Cimino implied later that this 160-minute version was a "butchered" cut, but the decision-making process was entirely his, and United Artists had no real involvement other than to agree with his wish to recut and relaunch in the first place. This time there were sneak previews, but there was not much sneak about them. Even though the viewers did not know what movie they were going to see, the moment the opening credits rolled, they realized that this was a movie they already knew a lot about. However, the reaction was marginally better: "It was clear that if the audience didn't love the picture, they didn't hate it either," Bach wrote. There was only one group of people who did love it, who whooped and hollered when it was screened for them: the citizens of Kalispell, for whom Cimino organized a special screening when the short version was released.

Despite United Artists falling in with Cimino's wish to withdraw the movie, his abrasive behavior to them did not change. He fired off a memo asking when his contractual payment of $45,000, due on the completion of the film, was going to be paid; he complained about UA's "petty harassment" of Carelli; he said he would do no publicity in the run-up to the movie's release and would not necessarily agree to do any at the time it opened. In the end, he ignored UA's planned series of interviews and organized some of his own, which was embarrassing to them and counterproductive to the movie.

The Kalispell screening ticket
(Author's collection)

In the few he did, he reverted to his never-complain-never-explain stance, and he was reflective and dignified in the face of hostile and sometimes ridiculous questions. The day before the movie reopened, he talked to Gene Shalit on NBC. "The ballpark figure was $35 million. . . . A hundred American families making $25,000 could live on that for fourteen years. Is it obscene to spend that much money for a single movie?" the film critic asked him.

Cimino replied quietly and not unreasonably, "Is it obscene to spend $30 or $40 million on a blatantly commercial effort whose sole purpose is to make more money?" The year before, United Artists had released the James Bond movie *Moonraker*, which had a budget of $34 million. There had been no mention of poor American families.

Two months before the Shalit interview, there had been an article in *Rolling Stone* in which Carelli was quoted as saying, "Michael was a little crazy up there in Montana. We should have said, 'No, Michael, no. You cannot build this town larger than you said you would.' . . . I should have walked off." If anyone else other than her had made a statement like that, Cimino would have banished them forever. When Shalit asked him about the quote, he admitted he should have listened to her: "I should have paid more attention to my producer, Joann Carelli. Sometimes the most rational voice is the one you don't hear."

Then, and at no point in the future, did he refuse to take the blame: "I would respond to *Heaven's Gate* in the same way that Jack Kennedy responded to the Bay of Pigs. I take full responsibility. I think if you're a boxer and you step into the ring, you can't complain about getting hit." He did not deny it was painful, however: "At least in the old days, when they lashed you to a post and whipped you, they stopped once you passed out."

The movie opened in 810 theaters across the country on April 21 with a new poster campaign: the stark black-and-white image of Kristofferson had been replaced by a dreamy picture of Isabelle Huppert in his arms, looking up at him lovingly alongside a waving American flag. It bore a disconcerting resemblance to the poster of 1976's *A Star Is Born*, on which Barbra Streisand also looked up lovingly at Kristofferson. The enigmatic tag line "The things one loves about life are the things that fade" was replaced by the possibly more commercial, more romantic but not

The image from the second release
poster (Alamy)

very accurate, "The only thing greater than their passion for America . . .
was their passion for each other." The new tag line might have been more
about Cimino than the movie: Carelli told me that the only constant for
Cimino was his love of America, right back to the Indian story.

The movie failed miserably. A sales executive from United Artists
said, "It's as if somebody called every house in the country and said there
will be a curse on your family if you go see this picture." The reviews were
hardly any better than they had been the first time around. Vincent Canby:
" 'Heaven's Gate' looks like a fat man who's been on a crash diet. Though
it's thinner, it's not appreciably different." Stanley Kauffmann: "A long
bore has been converted into a tolerable non-success." Only one journalist
was brave enough to admit he loved the short version—Kevin Thomas in
the *Los Angeles Times*. He wrote, "In its new two-and-a-half-hour version,
Michael Cimino's *Heaven's Gate* is an experience that leaves you feeling
you have witnessed a true screen epic. . . . Now it is time to sit back and
enjoy all that Michael Cimino has wrought." However, in a rare moment
of critical vulnerability, he said, "I don't think in twenty years of movie
reviewing I've ever been so totally alone."

Andy Albeck made one last attempt to salvage their leaky vessel. He and Bach fought hard to have *Heaven's Gate* entered for the Cannes Film Festival in early May—the French critics tended to be more welcoming to auteurs. Bach had screened the movie for the festival's president, Gilles Jacob, who did not like it much but agreed to put it into competition because it would be a newsworthy event. Cimino and Norbert Auerbach, United Artists' head of international distribution, went together and gave a polite press conference. The movie did not fare particularly well—there had been a little booing at the screening—but Cimino was courteously received. However, as the festival got underway, a bigger story than the disaster of his movie surfaced: Transamerica was going to sell United Artists to Kirk Kerkorian, who owned MGM.

The received wisdom, then and now, pinpointed Cimino as the culprit, the man who single-handedly "bankrupted a studio." In fact, it was just as inaccurate as the belief—invented by an early biographer—that George Washington cut down a cherry tree. Bach was not slow in corroborating the Cimino myth: the subtitle of his book included the phrase "The Film that Sank United Artists."

However it came about, the sale was shocking to Hollywood. When Transamerica bought UA in 1967, it had remained an autonomous business run by its existing management with no interference in its decision-making process. Now the studio, one of the oldest and most prestigious in the business, was going to be emasculated and subsumed into another studio, which was owned not by a canny mogul like Darryl Zanuck or Jack Warner, who understood the almost unfathomable equation of the movie business, but by Kerkorian, a secretive billionaire who was more interested in building a hotel empire in Las Vegas than in filmmaking. To an industry that values tradition, it was like the willful destruction of an ancient monument, and it was Cimino who had done the bulldozing. Could one man alone really destroy a part of Hollywood history? People believed the answer was yes.

Inevitably, the heads began to roll: Andy Albeck was the first to be fired (he and his wife later started a Christmas tree farm in New Jersey), and Norbert Auerbach took over his job. Steven Bach would follow later and then leave the business. Auerbach's tenure in the top job did not last long, and he left too.

In truth, there were many factors involved in the sale of United Artists, and few of them had much to do with Cimino. In 1981, the year the recut version of *Heaven's Gate* was released, the movies green-lit by Andy Albeck, Steven Bach, and David Field—the team that had taken over from the Krim/Benjamin regime in 1979—began to come through, and most of them did not perform well financially or critically. Even movie buffs would have some difficulty recalling them—*Deadly Blessing*; *Cutter's Way*; *Those Lips, Those Eyes*; and the improbable Ringo Starr prehistoric comedy *Caveman*. There was a modest financial success with the Meryl Streep movie *The French Lieutenant's Woman,* and a major critical success with Scorsese's *Raging Bull,* even though it did not go into profit for many years. Only the James Bond movie *For Your Eyes Only* was a huge money-maker—$195 million—but that came from the old regime.

Despite the lackluster slate of films and the early write-off of *Heaven's Gate*'s $44 million loss, the studio still made a respectable profit of $22 million. United Artists was not bankrupt, or even heading in that direction. "With a nip of reorganization here and a tuck of new management there, no studio ever quite seems to go over the edge," Aljean Harmetz said in the *Los Angeles Times.* In fact, United Artists did not slow down after the debacle—they were still spending huge sums on acquisitions: $500,000 for the movie rights to Tom Wolfe's *The Right Stuff,* and $250,000 for Truman Capote's *Handcarved Coffins.* The most staggering buy was $2.5 million for Gay Talese's giant nonfiction history of America's sex life, *Thy Neighbor's Wife.* It was widely regarded as unfilmable, and, indeed, it never was. Nor was the Capote book. *The Right Stuff* was eventually made, but by another studio.

The studio could have weathered the Cimino storm, but there were other factors over which they had no control. Transamerica had always been the parent company of a random group of businesses that included UA and Budget Car Hire. Now they were beginning to divest themselves of the companies that did not relate to their core product divisions—insurance and investment. Then there was the money: United Artists had been bought for $180 million twelve years before; now Transamerica sold it to Kerkorian for an astonishing $383 million. There was really no downside for them. Even Bach, contradicting his book's Film-that-Sank-a-Studio subtitle said, "At that price, 'Who *wouldn't* sell?'"

Outside the industry, *Heaven's Gate* seemed a small footnote to the sale. In a story about it, the *New York Times* mentioned the movie but said that United Artists had not been looking to sell—Kerkorian had initiated the talks with them. The news agency UPI reported the sale price but made no mention of the movie at all.

What could be laid at Cimino's door was that United Artists had somewhat lost their appetite for filmmaking because of him. However, the wider damage to Cimino's reputation had been done—the industry believed that he was totally to blame for a bankruptcy that did not actually happen. It still does. In 2016, the website *Screen Rant* included *Heaven's Gate* in a list of movies that "bankrupted their studio." Even one of the industry's papers of record, the *Hollywood Reporter*, noted in 2020 that the movie, "earned a place of infamy for bankrupting United Artists." Curiously, in 1991, the company that did really go bankrupt was Orion—the spin-off company that was formed by the hugely successful management team of Krim and Benjamin, who ran United Artists before Albeck, Field, and Bach took over.

In one of Cimino's favorite Westerns, John Ford's *The Man Who Shot Liberty Valance*, a journalist says, "This is the West, sir. When the legend becomes fact, print the legend"—and that was exactly what happened.

IN THE YEARS after its infamous release, the legacy of *Heaven's Gate* would never leave two of the most controversial figures in its making—David Field and Steven Bach. When Bach was writing his book, *Final Cut*, which was published in 1985, Robert Wunsch, a UA colleague, called Field and said that Bach would like him to help with the project. Field asked him why Bach was not calling himself. Wunsch replied that he was "frightened that you'd shout at him."

Cimino was understandably angry about the book. He said, "It should be classified as fiction. He's made money off my blood, my work." After it was published, he called Field and said that they should sue Bach. Field told him it would generate more publicity for the book but suggested they write a *New Yorker* piece together. He added, "You'll have to accept the fact that I'll disagree with everything you say." That was the last time he spoke to Cimino.

In 2004, an unflattering documentary about the making of *Heaven's Gate* was made, based in part on the Bach book. Maybe as a small act of revenge for being fired by Cimino from the movie, Willem Dafoe was the narrator. After twenty-five years, Bach had not lost his vitriol about Cimino. When asked if he had any animosity toward him or the movie, he replied, "It would be like wishing ill of a corpse." David Field, for the first time, agreed to be interviewed, and he told the story of Bach's backstabbing over the casting of Isabelle Huppert. When he saw the film at a screening, that part had been cut out, and he was certain Bach had had a hand in it. Surprisingly, at the screening, he saw Joann Carelli watching it with a woman friend. He had not seen her in twenty-five years, and on the spur of the moment, decided to go and talk to her. When she saw him, she left the theater as quickly as she could, but her friend came up to Field and said, "Why can't you do the decent thing and leave her alone?"

Bach left the movie business and moved to Germany, where he wrote a well-received biography of Marlene Dietrich. Field found himself there and called Bach to suggest dinner. They had not talked for more than twenty years. He told me that Bach was so shocked he began to stutter. They did meet, and finally Field asked him about the betrayal over Huppert that had stayed with him all those years—the betrayal that he believed had removed all of United Artists' power over Cimino. Bach looked him in the eye and said that he had no recollection of it. They never spoke again. Bach died in 2009. Field continued to be a successful producer and screenwriter after leaving United Artists. He still writes poetry.

PART III

1981–1996

CHAPTER 13

FOOTLOOSE IN HOLLYWOOD

HOWEVER THEY RECONFIGURED their relationship after Joann Carelli's marriage to David Mansfield, she and Cimino were as close as ever despite the problems they had had on *Heaven's Gate*. A crew member told me that at the end of shooting, "You knew that all was not entirely well between them." While most of Carelli's things stayed at Cimino's house in the hills, she and Mansfield lived in his small rental on Laurel Canyon before moving to somewhere larger in the flats of Beverly Hills. When they were in New York, they stayed with David Nagata, Carelli and Cimino's friend from their advertising days. Eventually they moved back east permanently—she had always disliked Los Angeles—buying the next-door apartment to Cimino's on the twenty-second floor of the United Nations Plaza, which Truman Capote had owned.

In Los Angeles, the movie business did not welcome Cimino back. Cary Woods, who worked with his agent, Stan Kamen, told me, "He was poison." Carelli told me that many people felt he put a brave face on the disaster of *Heaven's Gate* and the seemingly irreparable damage to his reputation. His secretary, Patty Nelson, said that his attitude was, "'This is all nonsense'—and that was that." Carelli told me that she did not find it painful herself—the pain was seeing how Cimino was almost destroyed by it, whatever he told others.

Hollywood is an unforgiving town, and Cimino suffered the humiliations that all out-of-favor directors and actors do: vanishing development deals and canceled meetings; small but significant discourtesies like turndowns from smart restaurants that would once have been happy to find a table on a fully booked evening; unreturned phone calls (he later said, "The telephone is the sharpest sword in Hollywood."). It was hard to know who to trust, particularly when some in the usually collegiate movie community were unsupportive. Martin Scorsese said, "*Heaven's Gate* undercut us all. I knew at the time that something had died." Jerome Hellman, who had produced *Midnight Cowboy* and *Coming Home* and was always auteur-friendly, said, "If you look at the cost overruns and films out of control being made by guys with two credits like Cimino, you begin to see how they built a disaster in there." Coppola said, "There was a kind of coup d'etat that happened after *Heaven's Gate*." For someone as proud and uncompromising as Cimino, he became strangely vulnerable.

Cimino had hired Van Harrison, his driver when he was shooting in Montana, to look after the land he had bought up there. Harrison told me, "One time he asked me to show him some accounting, and he questioned it. I got a little angry and I said, 'Now wait a minute, Michael. What are you saying here?' He said, 'Oh no, Van, I didn't mean anything. You've got to understand—I'm not around people I can trust very often.'"

In 1981, *Heaven's Gate* was not the only reason why the Hollywood pyramid was beginning to look shaky, but nonetheless, it was positioned at the top. A new era had been invented: the first person to give it a name was Michael Dempsey in *American Film* magazine in September of that year—"Post-Cimino Hollywood." He imagined the studios' thinking: "A rogue movie overruns its budget by a factor of three thanks to a pretentious director who's got a head like the Goodyear blimp just because he lucked into a few Oscars. . . . A forlorn cry rings through the town, 'We had it made until that artiste, that *genius*, ruined it for everybody.'"

Actually, Cimino's name in the title of Dempsey's piece could have been replaced by several others, but it was somehow easier to throw it all on one man and one movie. Francis Ford Coppola was also critical of Cimino, but nobody mentioned his film of that year, *One from the*

Heart, which was an equal catastrophe. Its budget rose from $15 million to $26 million, and it made even less than the micro-gross of *Heaven's Gate*—$700,000. One of its major expenses was building a Las Vegas airport set, complete with a jet. If Cimino's movie was the *Titanic*, there were ample *Lusitanias*. But their captains, like Coppola, tended to be more popular figures than the spiky and antisocial Cimino. In contrast to Cimino's hostile attitude to the press, Coppola had an expansive charm—he would invite journalists to visit his sets, cook them an elaborate spaghetti dinner himself, and serve wine from his own vineyard.

In fact, whether the blame could be laid at *Heaven's Gate* or not, all auteur directors were equally at risk by this time. Cimino and his movie were the culmination of a gradual trend that had gathered speed throughout the 1970s: the studios began to mistrust those directors. Although they had seemed to hold the world in their hands at the start of the decade, they had begun to lose their luster. A studio executive told me, "In the '70s, we were freewheeling. In the 1980s, we were freefalling." There was a distinct chill in the air. Peter Bart, *Variety*'s longtime editor, said, "At the beginning of the decade you had a group of young directors who wanted to be on schedule and on budget. They were grateful for being allowed to make movies. By the end of the end of the decade they had become the big exploiters of the system."

The problem with those directors was that their first low-budget hits, which had so delighted the studios, tended to be followed by more expensive ones that were less successful and not as good. The studios had hoped there was a magic formula that could be replicated, but there is no such thing as logical magic, and the new directors seemed unable to find it again either. After *Easy Rider*, Dennis Hopper made *The Last Movie*—a metaphysical Western about a film crew making a metaphysical Western in Peru—at triple the budget. It lasted two weeks at one New York theater and has hardly been seen since. After *The Last Picture Show* ($1.3 million budget, grossing $29 million), Peter Bogdanovich made *At Long Last Love* ($5.25 million, $2.5 million), a frothy Cole Porter musical starring Burt Reynolds and Cybill Shepherd, neither of whom could sing or dance, and it was a critical disaster. After the unexpected gold mine of *M*A*S*H* ($3 million, $86 million) in 1970, Robert Altman followed it with a string of underperforming movies like *Quintet*, starring Paul Newman in a snowbound dystopia that *Variety* described as "Robert Altman's latest impenetrable exercise in self-indulgence" ($9 million, $1 million).

The punishment was swift as the movie industry began to backtrack. At the 1981 Oscars, Scorsese's *Raging Bull*—an acknowledged masterpiece then and now—was the favorite to win Best Picture, but the award went to Robert Redford's directorial debut, *Ordinary People*. It defined the "old" Hollywood: a redemptive family drama starring Donald Sutherland and Mary Tyler Moore that was so defiantly old-fashioned it could have been made in the 1950s with Gregory Peck and Jennifer Jones.

The auteur directors continued to work—their talent was not in question—but it was harder to find financing to make their personal projects. Robert Altman said, "The pictures that they [the studios] have to make . . . are not the kind of pictures I want to make. And the pictures that I want to make they don't want to make." He and the others discovered that those directors whose films were unsuccessful were not lauded for their impressive attempt to attain the highest artistic achievement and failing; instead, they were despised for arrogantly daring to fly too close to the sun.

Among his later projects, Peter Bogdanovich directed one episode of the TV series *The Wonderful World of Disney* and was sacked off the Richard Pryor/Gene Wilder potboiler *Another You*. William Friedkin directed *Putting It Together*, a promo documentary about the making of a Barbra Streisand album. Robert Altman began making microbudget movies like *Come Back to the 5 & Dime, Jimmy Dean, Jimmy Dean* in 1982, which cost $850,000.

The only one of them who seemed to avoid the cull was Scorsese. He continued to make more or less personal projects that normally didn't make much money but were almost always critics' favorites and nominated for awards—Best Director for *The Last Temptation of Christ* in 1989, and *Goodfellas* the following year. For studios, it was worth keeping a hand in the prestige drawer.

Writers were affected as well. Carole Eastman (under her alias of Adrien Joyce) had written the seminal *Five Easy Pieces* with Jack Nicholson in 1970 that had the quintessential storyline for the new cinema: piano prodigy escapes both his intellectual family and himself by working in the blue-collar oil fields of California. Apart from the Mike Nichols 1975 misfire *The Fortune,* her only subsequent credit was not until 1992's critically lambasted dog comedy *Man Trouble,* a sad example of the lost magic formula—it reunited the *Five Easy Pieces* team of her, actor Jack Nicolson, and director Bob Rafelson, but to disastrous effect.

Robert Towne, who had "polished" *Bonnie and Clyde* and written the influential *Chinatown* in 1974 and *Shampoo* the following year, was one of the most revered auteur-writers of the decade. His passion project on which he had worked for years, *Greystoke*—what would now be called an "origin story" about Tarzan—was made in 1984 but rewritten. Towne replaced his credit with a pseudonym—P. H. Vazak, the name of his dog. By the 1990s, he was working on Tom Cruise action movies like *Days of Thunder* and *Mission Impossible.* A producer told him, "Here are six big action sequences. Can you write a movie connecting them?"

Hollywood has always existed on a mixture of caution and recklessness. Now caution came to the fore. Instincts were no longer followed; chances were no longer taken. Moviemaking has always been a high-wire act, and for that you need to be fearless. Instead of deciding on films by the kind of informed gut feeling that the best studio bosses had often possessed, they were run through economic models and shown to focus groups as if they were launching a new brand of toothpaste.

There was another change. Peter Biskind recalled a conversation between Richard Schickel, *Time* magazine's film critic, and Pauline Kael. She said to him, "Remember how it was in the '60s and '70s? Movies seemed to matter." I think what Kael meant was that there were simply fewer movies in the '80s that you might fall out with a friend over. Movies like *The Deer Hunter* and *Last Tango in Paris* divided people—they had a distinctive tang, an aftertaste, that most of the '80s movies did not. There were some exceptions, like David Lynch's *Blue Velvet,* but they felt like one-offs.

Now the studios often relied on directors like Sydney Pollack or Alan Pakula, who were better behaved and bought into the system in a way that directors like Hal Ashby or Robert Altman did not. They were the equivalent of the classy and trustworthy directors of the old Hollywood, like William Wyler, John Ford, or George Cukor, consummate craftsmen and expert storytellers with movies like *Out of Africa* and *Presumed Innocent*. There were still director-writers who worked on "personal" projects, like Lawrence Kasdan with *The Big Chill* in 1983, or Barry Levinson's *Avalon* in 1990, but, good though they were, the movies now seem a little colorless—auteur-lite.

The reliable directors of the '80s were making movies that were custom-built for success (even though inevitably some flopped). The more iconoclastic of the directors who had started in the '70s had had a different mindset: they were prepared to take a chance on failure, to grandly go down in flames. Robert Altman must have known that it would take a miracle for 1977's aggressively uncommercial *3 Women* to find an audience. It was an impenetrable mood-piece starring Sissy Spacek and Shelley Duvall, which was inspired by a dream Altman had in which he was directing a film starring the two actresses. So, too, Scorsese's *The Last Temptation of Christ* in 1988. Could he have believed that a film in which Jesus is not the Messiah, has sex with Mary Magdalene, and, Mormon-like, has two wives and many children after his resurrection could work in Middle America?

The business had changed. Even though they did not have Cimino to blame, some studios seemed to have lost the appetite for making films, just as United Artists had. Columbia was sold to the Coca-Cola Corporation in 1982, and Universal was bought by the liquor conglomerate Seagram's in 1995. The problem with selling to corporations that were not in the movie business was that the studio executives had to answer to bosses who knew nothing about it. While Hollywood had always been about the bottom line, the decisions had been made by people who at least loved movies and understood the bizarre alchemical process of making them. The corporations that bought the studios were used to dealing with physical products, and they did not understand ones that did not sit in a warehouse and have a tangible value. This product was colors that flickered on a screen.

As the studios began to lose their nerve, the agents moved in. Michael Ovitz and others left William Morris in 1975 and created a different kind of agency called Creative Artists Agency (CAA). By the 1980s, they had become not only the most powerful agency, but the most omniscient presence in Hollywood. Ovitz, visionary but unpopular, began to position his agency as a kind of studio. In the past, the talent—writers, directors, and stars—were under contract, and they could be assigned to any project the studio wanted. That model was long gone, and the now-unattached stars and directors could pick and choose. Scripts were developed in the hope that the studio could attach the talent that would get the movie green-lit. Now CAA, with an extraordinary number of star clients, did it for them by "packaging." The package often comprised the writer, the director, and the stars, all represented by the agency, and it was offered to the studios at an enormous price on a take-it-or-leave-it basis. In a town where status is the defining currency, the directors and stars seemed willing to ignore the rather demeaning undertones of being "packaged" because CAA took commission not out of their salaries but from the budget of the film itself. Everyone benefited—except the studios.

In an uncertain time, many of the packages were simply too attractive, if not good, to turn down—expensive takeout rather than home cooking. Universal bought *Legal Eagles* from CAA in 1986. Ivan Reitman, coming off the giant hit *Ghostbusters*, was the director; Robert Redford and Debra Winger were the stars. It hardly mattered what it was about (rival lawyers, as it happens). In fact, so cynical was the package that the part Winger played had been written for a man and it was simply rewritten for a woman because she liked the idea. The budget was $40 million, and it was a significant disappointment. Unlike *Heaven's Gate*, the only money you saw on the screen was in the actors' faces.

In the 1980s, Michael Cimino was never included in a package. He was no longer a star director, and never would be again. Just as *Heaven's Gate* had become a symbol of all failed films, so Cimino became a symbol of all failed directors. In the years after the fall, he kept a dignified silence. However, even though he chose to fly under the industry radar, his legend was always way above it. He became an almost mythical figure—a kind of Hollywood boogeyman who could strike fear into children, or at least the children of movie executives.

JUST BEFORE SHE and Cimino left for England to shoot the Harvard prologue, Carelli saw a CBS documentary called *VisionQuest*. She always had a smart eye for material and knew instinctively the kind of story that

Cimino would respond to. VisionQuest was the name of an unorthodox social program to rehabilitate delinquent teenagers by sending them on a wagon train across the Rockies. Unlikely as it seems, the name was used by Plains Indians to refer to moving through "a rite of passage into adulthood"—exactly the subject of *Conquering Horse*, Cimino's early script. The documentary followed one of those wagon trains on a 1,600-mile odyssey from Arizona to Colorado and focused on some of the ninety-six delinquents and their problems with theft, prostitution, and drug abuse.

As Carelli knew he would, Cimino loved it, and now, languishing in his eponymous era, began to work on it as soon as the recut *Heaven's Gate* opened and closed.

There was also another project that came to him, but not through any recognized studio channels: two unknown Russian producers allegedly bankrolled by one of Italy's most famous producers, Carlo Ponti, told him that they owned a Russian screenplay about the life of Fyodor Dostoyevsky (rumored to have been written by the novelist Aleksandr Solzhenitsyn) and asked him to rewrite and direct it. Cimino was immensely literate and had once thought of doing a movie of *Crime and Punishment*.

As Cimino often did, he looked for a writing partner (whether he acknowledged them or not), and he came up with an off-the-wall but inspired idea: Raymond Carver, famous for his series of spare and brilliant short stories in *The New Yorker*. He and his partner (later wife) Tess Gallagher, an acclaimed poet in her own right, flew from their home in Washington State to Los Angeles to meet Cimino and Carelli, who showed them *Heaven's Gate*.

I talked to Tess Gallagher, as fearsomely protective of Carver as Carelli is of Cimino, in Ireland, where she spends part of the year. She remembered them feeling like strangers in the strange land of Hollywood. "We were poets," she told me. "We were short story writers. We weren't used to working with anyone else. We could feel the invasive quality of his world." When one of them wrote a story or poem, it got published, but they discovered that screenwriting was a much more nebulous profession.

However, they were excited at first: "We got kind of high about it. Hey, look at us, we're going to Hollywood." And of course, there was the money—one of the reasons that serious writers, from William Faulkner to Joseph Heller, are often drawn to work there. "I know there was enough for Ray to buy a Mercedes. We called it the car that the movies bought."

Carver and Gallagher were very impressed by *Heaven's Gate*, but there was one particular detail that made Carver want to work with Cimino: in a spacious interior scene that was full of people moving around and talking, Carver spotted a small window at the edge of the screen looking out onto the street where a man was juggling. Gallagher told me, "Ray was saying, 'OK, OK, you've got all this big bombast stuff. You've got calamity, you've got crowds, you've got dancing, you've got horses, but look at that juggler over there—that small thing happening in the background. . . .' That represented the artist for Ray." Later, Carver wrote a poem called "The Juggler at Heaven's Gate—for Michael Cimino"—"*The eye keeps going to that juggler. That tiny spectacle.*"

Initially, Cimino asked him to work on the Dostoyevsky script, but Carver found it "ponderous, boring, and inconsistent with everything I knew about his life. 'Is there a storyline here?' I asked. 'Does it have a dramatic narrative?'" Cimino knew how to appeal to a poet: "He said, 'I think there's a spiritual dimension to it.' I was impressed. I could go on that." Gallagher did the research, and she and Carver began to write a completely new script together. Two months later, they delivered a 220-page script. Carver was nervous what Cimino's reaction would be, but "he called at once to tell me he was immensely happy with the result." However, he told him that Carlo Ponti had left Los Angeles, dropped out of sight, and was making no effort to produce the script. Carver was surprised that "Cimino has simply put the 220-page screenplay aside and moved on to other projects"—the usual modus operandi of a director, but not necessarily of a poet. One of the other projects was *VisionQuest*, and he asked Carver to co-write the script with him.

The script was given the elliptical title of *Purple Lake*—not a place but a reference to the nail-polish color of one of the girls on the wagon train. Now, they found that working more closely with Cimino was not like the relatively simple process of rewriting a script on their own. They discovered one of the major downsides of screenwriting: "It was work for hire, and I don't like that. I don't like to have a boss," Carver said.

Gallagher was particularly unhappy. She told me, "I would have liked to connect with Michael more. I thought he was a jitterbug kind of guy. It wasn't that he didn't try. He was full of human tensions. I seemed to be a kind of secretary. It was demeaning," particularly, she said, as most of the scriptwriting was done by her rather than by Carver.

When they finished a draft of the script, Cimino came up to see them in Port Angeles in Washington, where they were living. He asked Carver to go on a trip upstate to Bellingham, where he had shot some of *The Deer Hunter*. Gallagher said, "He wanted to leave me behind. It was supposed to be a guy-bonding experience. That was against our relationship. We were always together. It was beyond tactless. It revealed how little Michael understood Ray and me."

However, there were parts of Cimino that they responded to. Gallagher told me, "I did like him in that way one likes someone out there striving and fighting his windmills alongside you, no matter how fate disposed of his ambition. Ray survived alcoholism—he knew what it was like to have a life and then find it shattered. We hoped that what we were doing would be good for Michael too."

The script they wrote was partly based on the documentary, but some significant things were added. The program is run by a woman instead of man, and the script starts in a sleazy bar in Mexico, where she goes to persuade her washed-up, alcoholic ex-husband to help her with the wagon train. The story takes on a redemptive quality as the trip turns out to be as much for his rehabilitation as for the troubled teenagers. In the documentary, they are heading for Colorado, but the writers made a spectacular change: halfway through the trip, they alter direction and head for New York. The movie ends with the wagon train, pursued by police cars, going through the Holland Tunnel and entering Manhattan—just the kind of bravura (and expensive) set piece that Cimino was brilliant at.

Despite how commercial the script was—much more so than the Dostoyevsky one—it did not happen either. Gallagher told me, "When we had it all finished, we had a rendezvous with a room full of people—a lot of we-know-what-we're-doing people. They wanted the kids tougher and meaner. We called the guys 'Writer-Killers'—you could never satisfy them. We didn't know we were wasting our time."

Carver and Gallagher never saw Cimino again, but there was a strange postscript to their relationship with him. They wanted to publish the Dostoyevsky script, but they had a problem. Gallagher said, "The news came that the two Russians in Italy were saying that they owned it. I had to hire a lawyer in Rome to fight the suit. These process servers turned up at the house to see Ray, but by this time he had passed on. I said, 'Raymond Carver has relocated.' They asked where they could find him and I gave them the address of the place where he was—the cemetery."

When Carver died in 1988, Gallagher was surprised to get a call from Cimino. "He said, 'Tess, I'm so sorry you had to lose Ray.' We had a little chat. I thought it was lovely of him. He said, 'If there's ever anything I can do for you, will you promise to call me?' Not all of Ray's so-called friends were as gracious as that."

The fact that those two projects did not get off the ground (as so many of his later projects did not either) does not single out Cimino from other directors. Many had projects that for whatever reason—normally budget, casting, or the ubiquitous "creative differences"—never got made: Kubrick's *Napoleon* project, which had Jack Nicolson attached; Martin Scorsese's *Gershwin*; or Paul Verhoeven's seemingly commercial *The Crusades*, which was to star Arnold Schwarzenegger at the height of his career.

There was no doubt that Cimino was a pariah in the early '80s, but there are certain upsides for studios when they hire one: after whatever kind of fall those directors have had, they tend to be desperate for a job and therefore cheaper, more malleable, and better behaved. In the fall of 1982, Cimino was offered a movie, one that, unusually, was almost certain to happen because Paramount were fast-tracking it and had to start shooting before the spring of 1983, when a Screen Actors Guild strike was threatened.

It was a musical called *Footloose* and was the first screenplay by a young lyricist, Dean Pitchford, who had won an Oscar for the title song of Alan Parker's movie *Fame* in 1980. It was about a rebellious teen-age kid, Ren (eventually played by Kevin Bacon after Tom Cruise and Rob Lowe were considered), who moves from Chicago to a small town in Utah where dancing—and by implication fornication—has been banned for years by the town council. He falls in love with the pastor's daughter, secretly teaches the local teenagers to dance, and eventually wins over the town.

Musicals had fallen out of fashion since the disastrous failures in the late '60s and early '70s of *Hello, Dolly!*, the Julie Andrews vehicle *Darling Lili*, and the reviled musical remake of *Lost Horizon*. However, *Fame* (teenagers studying at New York's School of Performing Arts) had been successful, and *Flashdance* (female steelworker dreams of being a dancer) was in development. They, and *Footloose*, were what Pitchford called "Popsicle Movies"—designed to appeal to a younger and hipper audience who were now watching MTV, which had started broadcasting in 1981.

Pitchford lives in the Hollywood Hills in a house with gold discs on the wall and cushions embroidered with the logos of the musicals he has written. He told me that he had first offered the script to his friend Craig Zadan (later to produce *Chicago* and *Hairspray*) in 1980. He was a development executive at United Artists—coincidentally one of Steven Bach's last hires. "Craig said, 'This is very exciting, but I'm not going to show it to UA. We're about to open a movie called *Heaven's Gate*, and we're all terrified what's going to happen,'" Pitchford told me. When Zadan was fired after its opening, he took the script with him and went into partnership with Dan Melnick, who sold *Footloose* to Paramount. They offered the script to Herbert Ross, who had been a Broadway dancer and later choreographed *Funny Girl* before directing its sequel, *Funny Lady*, and *The Goodbye Girl*. Paramount would not meet his price, and he left the project.

Although Dan Melnick had worked at both Columbia and 20th Century Fox, he was happier being a maverick independent producer who liked to break the rules. He had a radical idea—Cimino. Pitchford told me, "Dan was a provocateur who decided he could single-handedly resurrect Cimino's career and give him a chance at redemption." He had done this before: after Sam Peckinpah had made the disastrous Charlton Heston Western *Major Dundee* in 1965 and was sacked off Steve McQueen's *The Cincinnati Kid* a week into shooting, Melnick offered him a project quite unlike anything he had done before—a gentle character piece for television, *Noon Wine*, based on a Katherine Anne Porter novella, starring Jason Robards and Olivia de Haviland. It resuscitated his career: his next movie was *The Wild Bunch*.

Herbert Ross was Hollywood dance royalty, an ex-choreographer turned director, and had been an obvious choice for *Footloose*, but Melnick had an instinct for musicals—he had been married to Richard Rodgers's daughter—and Cimino was not actually such a counterintuitive choice: he had studied ballet and had meticulously supervised the kinetic choreography in his early commercials as well as the brilliant waltz sequence in the prologue of *Heaven's Gate*. He once said in an interview, "I really love music and dancing. To me it's a great pleasure to be on a set with dancers and music and a camera all around." Melnick was perfectly realistic about him. In a statement that could equally have applied to Peckinpah, he said, "It's fair to say he has difficulty with authority figures, but that doesn't diminish his talent." He hired Cimino believing that he had the attitude of a pariah director: "Cimino was anxious to prove to the world and himself that he could do it." Melnick kept him on a short leash. The budget was a low $7.5 million, and cost overages were to be deducted from Cimino's salary.

As it turned out, his pariah qualities were in short supply. Almost immediately there was predictable writer trouble. Pitchford had not met Cimino before he got the job, and Melnick left them alone: "Dan's attitude was, 'We'll let you guys bond. Just do your own thing.'" Inevitably, Cimino's thing was not Pitchford's thing. "Cimino insisted that the movie should be harder, grittier, and dirtier. He was all about the working-class roots of the Kevin Bacon character. He was obsessed by the neighborhood in Chicago where the boy would have come from. He kept saying, 'That's too light, that's too much fun.'"

They met only a few times. "We talked in the office first, but most of it was done on the phone. Didn't even know where he lived. Never went there. Bikes took pages to him," Pitchford said. He did not bond with Cimino: "He was very cool. I would have thought he'd be grateful for this chance. There was real condescension. He knew I was gay, and I thought he felt it was beneath him to deal with a gay man because his movies were so macho."

The main bone of contention was the start of the movie. In the original script, the movie began with the boy and his mother arriving in Utah. Pitchford told me, "Cimino said, 'We are now going to build up the opening,' an opening he had conjured out of nowhere. 'There's going to be a farewell party in Chicago, and you're going to get a whiff of the world he's leaving.' With every conversation we have, the party is getting bigger. I thought, 'Oh my God, he wants it to be the wedding in *The Deer Hunter*.'"

Pitchford's friend and producer, Craig Zadan, thought that Cimino was trying to sabotage him, then come in as the savior of the screenplay and offer to rewrite it. Cimino did exactly that, asking Melnick for $250,000 to write a new script. Melnick said no, and after three months on the picture, Cimino was fired. "I get along with gangsters, kings, and dictators. I guess I can't deal with middle management. It's my downfall," Cimino said ruefully.

In the end, they agreed to pay Herbert Ross's asking price, and shooting began four months later with the original Pitchford script. With its zippy MTV vibe and iconic soundtrack of songs, including "Holding Out for a Hero" and "Let's Hear It for the Boy," *Footloose* grossed $80 million. Melnick said, "It might have been a good film if Cimino had directed, but it wasn't the film we came to the party with."

Cimino's uncompromising position may have been foolish, but it was impressive that he was still unwilling to do work that he did not believe in or could make his own. In the obituary he wrote of Cimino in *Variety* in 2016, Owen Gleiberman said, "Cimino didn't want to be a hired hand, a cog in someone else's moviemaking machinery." However, most of the projects he was offered after *Footloose* were essentially cog movies.

IN NOVEMBER 1982, WHILE Cimino was working on *Footloose*, Joann Carelli and David Mansfield had a daughter they named Calantha, the Greek word for "lovely flower." Cimino's secretary, Patty Nelson, told me, "Michael was very proud of Joann, that she was out of bed the same day. I said, 'Michael—that's what normally happens,' but he was so impressed. He was like a proud husband and father."

Nelson, too, had a baby in 1984, and Cimino seemed rather perplexed. "He said, 'Wow—how did that happen?' I was still working a week before my daughter was born. Michael kept saying, 'Patty—so how long are you going to be out?' After Joann jumped out of bed so quickly, he obviously thought that maybe I have the baby on Saturday and come in early Monday morning. Joann was very nice. She came to my house after my daughter was born and brought some little presents." In the end, Nelson never went back. She had worked for Cimino for ten years, but he resented losing people he trusted. They never spoke again.

By then, Calantha was two, and proud though he seemed to be of her, Cimino, of course, was not actually her father or Carelli's husband—David Mansfield was. Mansfield told me, "I felt people were thinking, 'Does Joann have a houseboy?' We went round in a threesome. There were these adjoining apartments in New York and adjoining homes in the Hamptons. Joann liked cooking, and Michael was always in and out. She ate, lived, and breathed Michael. She was always at his beck and call." Francis Grumman, Cimino's friend from his advertising days, told me, "Mansfield never took Joann away."

At the same time, Mansfield's career was not going well either. He told me, "After the critical bombs quieted, I was going round Los Angeles looking for an agent, and I had one agent tell me I would have been better off having no credit at all on *Heaven's Gate*."

There had been strains in the relationship from the beginning. Mansfield had always been religious and took marriage very seriously; he found it hurtful that Carelli seemed unwilling to make it public. Steven Bach, in *Final Cut,* gave an exhaustive run-down of what had happened to the dramatis personae of *Heaven's Gate* subsequently and simply said, "Joann Carelli became the mother of a daughter by composer David Mansfield," with no mention of the fact that they were also married.

Even though he was Calantha's father and Carelli's husband, Mansfield felt diminished by the fact that Cimino clearly felt that there was no impediment to his very special and exclusive relationship with her. Together, the three of them formed a misshapen triangle, but there was a curious closeness between them all, a kind of codependency. Mansfield felt a tentative warmth toward Cimino: "As we worked over the years and got a little closer, there were aspects of mentorship in it, but it never really turned into a close relationship of equals." As he felt while he was working on *Heaven's Gate*, Cimino and Carelli, both nearly twenty years older than him, were still the grown-ups.

The marriage did not survive, and Mansfield and Carelli divorced in 1986. He made every attempt to be an exemplary divorced father. He saw a lot of Calantha and gave her piano lessons, but he found Cimino's appropriation of her as his daughter immensely painful. In 1996, he married the director Maggie Greenwald and had two more daughters.

What was curious was that, just as Mansfield had been no impediment to Cimino's relationship with Carelli, their parting did not prevent Cimino from continuing to work with Mansfield for the next four years. Of course, Mansfield was a hugely talented composer, but there were some equally talented *Heaven's Gate* alumni. The cinematographer, Vilmos Zsigmond, and the production designer, Tambi Larsen, made as indelible a contribution to the movie as Mansfield, but Cimino never worked with either of them again.

After his last collaboration with Cimino—1990's *Desperate Hours*—Mansfield continued to compose film music and has had an extraordinary career as a musician, working with Johnny Cash, Van Morrison, Elvis Costello, and others. He and Carelli have not been in touch for many years.

CHAPTER 14

CHASING THE SUN

AFTER CIMINO LEFT *Footloose* in January 1983, he tried to get *The Fountainhead* off the ground again without success, even though there was briefly the possibility of Barbra Streisand playing the powerful heroine, Dominique Francon (he hinted that there was an affair—"We had to keep our relationship secret."). A movie he had been involved with since 1975—*The Yellow Jersey*, about the Tour de France—fell to pieces even though Dustin Hoffman was attached.

In the summer of 1983, a movie was in preproduction at MGM: *The Pope of Greenwich Village*, about two cousins who get involved in a robbery—a project that is instructive in showing the chaotic and random path a movie can take in order to get into production. In 1981, Al Pacino and James Caan were cast as the cousins, with Ulu Grosbard directing. Caan dropped out because he was not going to be paid as much as Pacino. Ted Kotcheff was then going to direct but was replaced by Francis Ford Coppola. The title was changed to *The Village* and then changed back. Mickey Rourke had replaced Caan; Pacino dropped out, and Eric Roberts came in. Then Coppola left, and Ron Maxwell came on before getting dismissed a few weeks before filming.

There are various different stories about Cimino's involvement in the movie. Allegedly, after Maxwell's departure, he was hired and then fired as he had been on *Footloose*, but Carelli denied to me that he had ever been approached or had any involvement whatsoever. However, the film critic and friend of Cimino, F. X. Feeney, told me that he believed Cimino had directed a few days of uncredited reshoots after production had finished. Ironically, it was distributed by MGM/UA—the name of the new company formed after United Artists was bought by MGM.

Peter Bart, who later became editor in chief of *Variety*, was then senior vice-president for production at MGM/UA. He was in a position to know the real story, which shows an unexpectedly gracious side to Cimino. In Bart's book *Fade Out*, he said that Freddie Fields, the president of MGM, told him he wanted Cimino to direct the movie after Ron Maxwell left. He liked the project but wanted to come to New York to look at the budget and schedule before committing. A worried Bart asked Fields if Carelli would be involved—"The sheer mention of her name still produced tremors among surviving UA personnel." Fields said probably not.

Cimino arrived in New York and stayed at Fields's apartment. He met the cast and crew and was, Bart said, "meticulously polite, even deferential. . . . He was the Italian prince, mixing smoothly, easily, among the great unwashed." After a few days, he decided to turn down the project because he felt both the budget and the eight-week schedule were unworkable.

It was now a week before shooting, and Fields immediately offered the movie to Stuart Rosenberg, a workmanlike director whose only real success had been Paul Newman's *Cool Hand Luke* in 1967. He came over to Fields's apartment in a torrential rainstorm and rang the doorbell. To his amazement, "Standing there, smiling warmly, was none other than Michael Cimino. . . . [He] helped Rosenberg with his bags and offered him a towel to dry off," Bart reported. Cimino explained that although he was not going to do the movie, he was happy to help him. "During the course of the next six hours, Cimino went through his extraordinarily copious notes, which he had inscribed in miniscule handwriting on every page of the script." Fields told Rosenberg that Cimino's work had been invaluable—"He's been a terrific consultant." When the new director began shooting, he realized that Cimino had been completely right about the budget and schedule. The movie flopped badly.

The movie that did happen for Cimino was *Year of the Dragon*, also for MGM, based on an undistinguished novel by Robert Daley about a fight to the death between a maverick New York cop and a Chinese gang lord. Dino De Laurentiis, the Italian producer and a consummate dealmaker, had bought the rights to the book in 1983. He was a colorful character, even by Hollywood standards. He never bothered to learn much English and had rather a grand manner—he was driven around in a white Rolls-Royce—but possessed a great deal of charm. He employed an Italian couple, one of whom was his personal barber and the other his personal espresso maker.

His producing career had started in 1941, and his numerous credits ranged from early Federico Fellini movies to Jane Fonda's *Barbarella* in 1968. He moved to Los Angeles in the early '70s and brought with him the heady aroma of international finance from unspecified sources. He began to produce an impressively eclectic series of pictures, ranging from Milos Forman's prestigious *Ragtime* to Ingmar Bergman's arty *The Serpent's Egg* to the disreputable but much more profitable *Death Wish* starring Charles Bronson.

Early in 1984, De Laurentiis offered *Year of the Dragon* to Cimino. Unlike most other people in the industry, he had a certain amount of sympathy for him: he felt United Artists was to blame for *Heaven's Gate* by not controlling the production better. With forty years' experience, he had no fear of difficult directors.

De Laurentiis laid down his ground rules: "I called Cimino and told him, 'Michael, let's be absolutely clear. The studios have made you a whipping boy. You insist on the final cut and the last word on everything. . . . I'm ready to have you make a film—a project that will clean up your image and put you back on your feet. But . . . forget the final cut.'" Cimino agreed, but with one face-saving stipulation: he asked De Laurentiis to include a provision for final cut in his contract, but he agreed to a secret side-letter stating that whatever the contract said, the producer actually had final cut.

They both agreed that the existing script should be shelved. Joann Carelli had shown Cimino a script she admired by Oliver Stone called *Platoon*, which the writer could not get off the ground. He had won an Oscar for the screenplay of *Midnight Express* in 1978 and wrote Brian De Palma's

Scarface in 1983. Cimino loved *Platoon* and asked Stone to co-write *Year of the Dragon* with him. Stone was disenchanted with Hollywood and was reluctant to take on the project. Cimino came up with a smart idea: he suggested that Stone take a smaller writing fee from De Laurentiis on the condition that De Laurentiis financed *Platoon,* with Cimino producing. De Laurentiis agreed, and Stone signed on. De Laurentiis was no more reliable than anyone else in Hollywood—he never did the movie. It was made by another studio in 1986, with thanks to Cimino in the credits, and won Stone Best Picture and Best Director Oscars.

Stone got on very well with Cimino, though he described him as "the most Napoleonic director I ever worked with." He said, "Michael would talk it and I would write it. I enjoyed the research enormously." Cimino would later call him "one of the greatest writing talents in movies." (He tended to be more complimentary about his co-writers if they were famous: Raymond Carver, Stone, and later Gore Vidal and Robert Bolt.) "Oliver Stone and I were together twenty-four-seven. We went every night to Chinatown and got to know one of the gangs, the Shadow Chasers." Cimino felt he had an affinity with the Chinese: "They're the most wonderful people to work with. I'm at home with them, they're fun," and then added a characteristic Cimino aside: "I've had several Chinese girlfriends—they were exquisite, beautiful."

It was impossible to film *Year of the Dragon* in the real New York Chinatown, so he built it on the huge backlot of De Laurentiis's new studio in Wilmington, North Carolina. He and his production designer, Wolf Kroeger (who had designed the amazing ramshackle set of Sweethaven Village for Altman's *Popeye*), were meticulous. Cimino and Kroeger took plaster casts of the actual pavements so their set would have the right chipped curbs, and they re-created the 14 percent gradient of Mott Street. "People think that cities are all horizontals and verticals," Cimino said. "Lampposts and signs are often at an angle. Most studio builds are pool table flat. New York is a rocky little island." They re-created the street in such extraordinary detail that even Stanley Kubrick, an expert in building elaborate sets himself, thought it had to be the real Chinatown.

Shooting started on October 27, 1984. Cimino cast Mickey Rourke, who had had a small part in *Heaven's Gate,* and John Lone as the protagonists. A model, Ariane, played the Chinese American TV reporter who

The Chinatown set (Alamy)

becomes involved with Rourke. (Carelli told me that they wanted Joan Chen to play the part, but she was unavailable.) Francis Grumman, the cameraman with whom Cimino had worked on commercials in the late '60s, was doing some second-unit shooting. I asked him if he thought Cimino had changed his directing style after the painful experience of *Heaven's Gate*. "He was the Michael I knew. Everything he had gone through was not apparent to me. If there was anything, it might have been that he was a little subdued," he told me.

However, subdued or not, he finished the movie on time, stuck to the very reasonable budget of $24 million, and had a good relationship with De Laurentiis. The movie opened wide on August 14, 1985, and immediately ran into the kind of storm that Cimino had gotten used to: again, he was accused of racism. On September 3, a lawsuit was filed against the filmmakers by the Federation of Chinese Organizations of America, citing defamation and seeking $100 million in damages, and the swiftly formed Coalition Against *Year of the Dragon* picketed movie theaters. Cimino said, "When I did *Thunderbolt*, they said I was homophobic. When I did *Deer Hunter*, they said I was a right-wing fascist.

When I did *Heaven's Gate,* they said I was a left-wing Marxist. When I did this movie, they called me a racist. Well, which is it? Can I be all of those things?" Three weeks after the movie opened, a disclaimer was added to the credits: "The film does not intend to demean or ignore the many positive features of Asian-Americans. . . ."

The reviews were mixed. Pauline Kael called it "hysterical, rabble-rousing pulp, the kind that goes over well with subliterate audiences." Sheila Benson, who had hated his previous films, said in the *Los Angeles Times,* "From the first second of 'Year of the Dragon,' it is clear that Michael Cimino is one of the great, operatic film makers." In the end, the movie did respectable business but not much more, bringing in only $18 million in the US. It eventually went into profit when foreign grosses and DVD revenue were added.

The movie's operatic qualities are its best ones. It has the kind of stunning set pieces that Cimino did brilliantly—a chase through a parade in Chinatown, a shootout in a crowded restaurant, the duel between Rourke and Lone on a deserted bridge at night—but there are many unconvincing aspects. Rourke—too young for the role and grayed up—has a curious time-warp quality (did New York cops wear trilbys in the '80s?) that seems to have strayed in from the era of Jack Webb's *Dragnet.* His girlfriend, played by Ariane, is not only wooden and unconvincing as a TV reporter, but has an improbable lifestyle—the credits list nine dress designers specifically for her—and resides in a stunning apartment with a sunken bath in the living room and incredible views of the Brooklyn and Manhattan Bridges over the East River that even Katie Couric might have had difficulty affording.

Whatever the faults of the movie, De Laurentiis had done Cimino an enormous favor: he had made him a viable choice as a director again. Six months after *Year of the Dragon's* opening, a newly formed company called Gladden Entertainment offered him another movie—Mario Puzo's *The Sicilian,* an offshoot of *The Godfather,* about Michael Corleone's exile in Sicily and his friendship with the (real) rebel leader Salvatore Giuliano.

One of the partners in the company was the ex–head of production at Columbia, David Begelman, who had been discovered forging checks there. He was never charged and did not even suffer much disgrace: he was suspended for a while, but when the CEO of the studio refused to reinstate him, the shareholders—so impressed by Begelman's track record—had the CEO fired instead, and Begelman returned. In 1982, Bruce McNall asked him to join Gladden.

McNall was exactly the kind of attractive high roller who gets fast-tracked into the movie business. In a Santa Monica diner, he talked to me about the ups and downs of his colorful career, including his four-year spell in jail, starting in 1993, for defrauding six banks. He had made his initial fortune dealing in antiquarian coins and later bought the Los Angeles Kings hockey team.

At Gladden, he and Begelman had some modest successes, including *The Fabulous Baker Boys* and *Weekend at Bernie's*, when, at the beginning of 1985, Bert Fields, one of Hollywood's most famous lawyers, offered them the rights to the Puzo book for a nonnegotiable $2 million. "We bought the book because Michael Corleone was the main character," McNall told me. However, there was a problem: when Paramount acquired the rights to Puzo's *The Godfather*, they also purchased the rights to the characters—not unusual in a movie deal. While Gladden owned the story of the new book, they did not own Michael Corleone, and he could not appear in the movie.

They initially hired Steve Shagan to write the movie—he had been nominated for an Oscar for the Jack Lemmon picture *Save the Tiger* in 1973—and began to look around for a director, preferably an Italian American. Coppola, Scorsese, and De Palma all turned it down. McNall told me, "Then we thought of Cimino. We checked him out with Dino, who said he had been good on *Year of the Dragon*. At our first meeting he was charming, smart, and impressive. He had a good vision, but early on he started to complain about Begelman."

The budget was $17 million, including Cimino's salary of $2.5 million and Begelman's $1 million. Cimino insisted on final cut, and, as Gladden believed he had it on his previous picture, they gave it to him up to a length of 120 minutes. It was only much later that they learned about Dino De Laurentiis's secret side-letter. Cimino also wanted to be the producer alongside Carelli, but her title was not agreed on until well into production.

Cimino did not like the script. The original writer, Steve Shagan, met Cimino only twice. He said, "I could tell right away he had his own agenda. I found him remote and insulated. I think I got him a little upset. He was so serious that I said, 'Michael, this is a screenplay, but that's it. None of us have given the world penicillin.'"

Cimino wanted Gore Vidal to work on the script. Vidal was always keen to take movie money (he would be paid $250,000 for *The Sicilian*) and was not choosy about the projects he took on. In 1979, he was quite happy to write the quasi-porn movie *Caligula*. Cimino sent him the Shagan script and asked what he thought it needed. Vidal replied, "It needs a trip to Lourdes."

On *The Deer Hunter*, Michael Deeley had assigned Katy Haber to be Cimino's assistant during postproduction. She was a bright and sassy Englishwoman who had had a long personal and professional relationship with Sam Peckinpah. Carelli called her and asked her to work on *The Sicilian*. "Michael wanted me to go and help Gore with the script in Ravello [where he lived]. All through preproduction, Michael and I were joined at the hip. We had a great time," she told me when we spoke. However, as soon as the cast and crew arrived in Palermo, he distanced himself from her. She said that "as a macho guy, he didn't want the Italian crew to see him being dependent on a woman."

The early casting process was reasonably amicable. They offered Marlon Brando $5 million for three weeks of work playing (another) Mafia don, but he turned it down. A young John Turturro played Giuliano's cousin, who, Judas-like, betrays him. However, from the start, Cimino and Begelman fought over the casting of the rebel leader, Salvatore Giuliano, who was now, without Michael Corleone in the movie, the main part.

At first, Cimino wanted Daniel Day-Lewis to play him, but he was almost unknown in America. In the end, he went for the better-known French actor Christopher Lambert, who had played Tarzan in *Greystoke* in 1984. Inexplicably, Begelman believed that it would be confusing to have a Frenchman playing an Italian, even though the movie had American and British actors playing them, but in the end Cimino got his way, and Lambert, as well as a voice coach, was hired. McNall told me, "Michael was very convincing. We all thought he knew what was best."

Michael Stevenson, the British assistant director, was in Italy with him. They had worked together on *Heaven's Gate* and *Year of the Dragon* and had become close friends, which was not always the case with the spiky Cimino. He always liked to hint enigmatically that he had Mafia connections ("I never met a hit man I didn't like"), and Stevenson told me, "Michael had letters in Italian from John Gotti and also the Magaddino family and Joe Bananas [the nickname for Joseph Bonanno]. They were to be given to the dons in each area of Sicily and said that Michael could film anywhere he wanted. He and I were invited to Joe Bananas's daughter's wedding before we started shooting."

Filming began in Palermo on July 14, 1986. Cimino had assembled the team he wanted: Wolf Kroeger, the production designer on *Year of the Dragon*; assistant directors Brian Cook and Michael Stevenson; and his trusted horse wrangler, Rudy Ugland. Cimino was not so happy about the people in the production office, most of whom had been put there by Gladden. He was at odds with them from the start and told Begelman, "This is an A crew working with a B production team."

Whether or not he actually had the letters from John Gotti and the others, the movie soon ran into problems caused by the unions, which were Mafia-controlled. Cimino dismissed an Italian assistant director and brought in Michael Stevenson, which caused all the others to resign. The transport union went on strike, but Bruce McNall, with his network of colorful contacts, got a Sicilian coin-collecting friend to sort it out—they got them back to work by giving them all small parts in the movie.

Despite Cimino's war with the production department, he got on with everyone else, and the shoot went smoothly despite far-off locations, long, hot days, and his time-consuming and meticulous eye for detail. Bill Krohn, the LA correspondent of *Cahiers du Cinéma*, asked if he could come and see some of the filming and was surprised to get a terse telegram from Carelli simply reading, "Come to Palermo."

In a long article about the movie, Krohn described the dedication of the cast and crew, as well as observing Cimino—wearing a black T-shirt with "GHOST" emblazoned on the front—at work: "The inside of the house has been dressed by the art department but Michael has a number of adjustments to make. A pillow is added to the bed, cloth-wrapped cheeses are arranged on the table. An assistant is sent to pick wildflowers to substitute for the flowers already there. A portrait of Marx is hung. A red flag is propped in the corner. I ask if he always dresses the set himself: 'You always end up doing it yourself.'" The actors, as usual, were impressed with him. Krohn quoted Christopher Lambert as saying, "Michael is a very passionate person who thinks nothing of going to the extreme, going to the point where the edge becomes so dangerous that if you go beyond it you fall. He is giving so much that you want to give the same back."

Always keen on aristocrats, Krohn reported that Cimino explained to him that, "In Sicilian aristocracy a Count is often of a higher order than a Prince," and proudly reeled off the guest list for a lunch he was having: Marquesa di Villa Urupi, Conte Giuseppe Tasca, the Prince and Princess Pepito, Barone Francesco Agnello, and more.

Whichever grand Italians he took pleasure in meeting, he still had to deal with the Americans. Of all the Gladden people, Cimino disliked David Begelman the most. When the executive arrived in Italy for a visit, Cimino simply vanished and never saw him, instructing Katy Haber to keep Begelman away from him at all times. However, he bombarded Begelman with memos. Unlike his utter disinterest in the budget of *Heaven's Gate*, he had a forensic command of *The Sicilian*'s. In one of many memos to Begelman, he wrote, "I was told that Sicily was 30% to 50% cheaper than the US and that $8.5M in Sicily represented anywhere from $12M to $16M US. In fact, Sicily is proving to be more expensive. In addition the dollar has declined by almost 15% since December." In another memo: "I cut 12,500 extra man days to 7500, reduced the music budget by $50,000 and effected a $24,000 reduction in the wardrobe figure."

Haber told me that he wrote these detailed memos in his spidery handwriting—some of them six pages long—late at night after an eighteen-hour day and asked her to type them up. There is almost no detail of the production and budget that they do not cover: he demanded to see the petty cash statements; he asked why a crew member was allowed to fly first-class. Begelman seemed unwilling to do much: he replied disingenuously, "Please try to use your considerable talents for cooperation to avoid these points of irritation and confusion."

Carelli's position was, as always, uppermost in Cimino's mind. Despite the fact that, according to Michael Stevenson and Katy Haber, she was not seen much in Sicily, he was writing to Bruce McNall a month before the end of production to tell him, "I am greatly annoyed and disappointed that there seems to be no resolution to the producer credit situation." The eventual credits read "Produced by Michael Cimino and Joann Carelli."

Shooting ended in the last week of September. Cimino's rigorous attention to the budget had paid off: he was a couple of days over schedule and there was a small overage, but not even Begelman or McNall blamed this on him. He returned to Los Angeles on the twenty-eighth to begin editing in cutting rooms that had been rented on the Warner Bros. lot.

The editorial staff were Françoise Bonnot and her assistant, Lizi Gelber. Bonnot was a distinguished Frenchwoman who had worked with Roman Polanski and Costa-Gavras, and had done *Year of the Dragon* with Cimino; Gelber had been part of the editorial team on Sergio Leone's *Once Upon a Time in America* in 1984. They had both been in Sicily during the filming, but Gelber told me that they had seen little of Cimino. In the usual way, they had been collating the dailies and putting together a rough assembly of the material, but Cimino was working long days on the movie and, as is common with many directors, did not have time to look at the footage. Anyway, with his exacting eye for detail, he always remembered exactly what he had shot. More than that, having worked with her before, he trusted Bonnot.

Now, in Los Angeles, they were all working closely together to Cimino's rigorous schedule—they often worked a hundred hours a week, and always for seven days. As before, nobody else was allowed into the cutting rooms. "Because he hated Begelman, I was told never to communicate with him or Gladden's postproduction supervisor," Gelber said. Carelli was mostly in New York, but David Mansfield was there a lot of the time because he was composing the music. Occasionally they would come in together, bringing their daughter, Calantha, who was now four. "I was a little scared of Joann," Gelber told me, and added, "Michael wasn't a pussycat either, but together. . . ."

The editing went well—"Michael was open and generous with Françoise and I during the cutting"—and they often drank champagne at the end of the day. Nonetheless, Gelber felt that there was a great deal of anger under the surface: "Once I was with him in his black Jeep and I asked, 'What is this compartment for?' He said, 'It's for a shotgun—the world is full of vermin.'" Anyone from Gladden and most journalists were in that category.

In March 1987, after six months of editing, Cimino had a 143-minute version that he was very happy with. However, he had final cut only up to 120 minutes. This was not dissimilar to the situation on both *The Deer Hunter* and *Heaven's Gate*, and the fact that it played out quite differently was indicative of Cimino's diminished power. He knew there would be problems if he showed Begelman only the long version, so he asked Gelber to prepare a short one as well. He told her to simply cut out all the action sequences—which were spectacular and showed where the money had gone—and string together all the remaining dialogue sequences so the movie would be 120 minutes of talk. A lavish wedding scene that was supposed to be interrupted by a violent attack cut directly to a hospital, where guests were being treated for injuries suffered at an attack that hadn't occurred on-screen.

I asked Gelber whether she was surprised to be asked to do this. She said, "It was no more surprising than anything else Michael did." There was no pretense that it actually had to work. Begelman was outraged by the quality of the 120-minute cut: he considered it to be a "bad joke." The problem was that the final-cut provision in a director's contract is inalienable—the producer has no legal right to change what is delivered. Cimino was essentially saying: accept the longer cut or you have to release the short version.

Pushed up against the wall, Gladden did something that seemed not only foolish but illegal: ignoring Cimino's contractual right to final cut, they decided to get someone else to recut the picture. They did not reveal who it was. In fact, it was an unlikely savior for an action movie—the director Stanley Donen, who had made *Singin' in the Rain* and *Seven Brides for Seven Brothers*. He was prepared to do it as a favor for Begelman as long as it was kept secret—it was considered bad form for one director to recut another's work. At the end of May, Cimino filed a lawsuit to protect what he saw as his legal rights.

In a classic example of a Hollywood lawyer's multitasking, Gladden hired Bert Fields, who was on the opposite side of the fence from them when he negotiated the sale of the movie rights to the original Mario Puzo book. There was a month-long Directors Guild hearing that looked as if it would go Cimino's way—the Guild were never sympathetic to any weakening of their members' power. However, Cimino had made a fatal error on which the case eventually turned: it was proved that he had neither been involved in nor even seen the 120-minute version that purported to be his "final cut." He had simply given Lizi Gelber instructions.

John Dellaverson, one of Bert Fields's team, told me that in his testimony, Cimino had been "emotional, theatrical, and flamboyant." He remembered him even crying at one point. Fields argued that there should be an obligation for a director to prepare his final cut "in good faith," and the arbitrator agreed: "[Cimino's] inattention is a far cry from the attention, care and review that . . . directors normally accord to the versions they submit as their final cuts." Cimino lost the case. Lizi Gelber told me, "One evening, when we were clearing out the cutting room, I found him sitting dejectedly in there. He said, 'I'm really unlucky. Other directors do their films and there are never any problems for them.'"

There was a second legal case. After arbitration, the Writers Guild, whose behind-closed-door decisions were often extraordinarily opaque, gave sole screenplay credit to the original writer, Steve Shagan, even though he freely admitted, "I didn't recognize much of what was on-screen." Gore Vidal sued the Writers Guild, the first writer in forty-seven years to take them on in federal court. He had always been happy to fight quixotic battles with the establishment, and he was delighted to be the only writer ever to spend a great deal of money to get his name on, not off, a movie that was an embarrassing critical and financial disaster. His attorney was the ubiquitous Bert Fields, changing sides yet again. In the end, Vidal lost his case: Shagan's credit remained.

There was always good copy to be written at Cimino's expense, and the court cases were too public to stay under the radar. In September, the *Los Angeles Times* ran a piece entitled, "How Do You Market 'Sicilian'? Carefully," and then a later one, "The Real Body Count of Michael Cimino's 'Sicilian.'" In the article, Bert Fields was quoted as saying, "Trouble has never sold a movie," and it certainly did not sell this one.

The Sicilian was released on October 23 in Stanley Donen's cut. Bruce McNall admitted to me, "We could never get the short version to work. We knew it was a turkey, but we had to release it." The reviews were terrible—the *Los Angeles Times*: "Fuzzy and inert"; *Daily*

Variety: "Flat, unexciting and unconvincing"; the *Hollywood Reporter*: "A catastrophe"—and the box office was disappointing: $5.5 million. Unlike the reviews for *Heaven's Gate*, these ones were not totally unfair. The film looks beautiful, and the set pieces are spectacular, but the script is pretentious and awkward—brilliant though he was, Vidal was seldom better than a hack screenwriter—with lines like "Alexander [the Great]? He wasn't a Sicilian like you or me. There's no fire in our heaven to fall."

Despite the reviews, Cimino had the perfect get-out-of-jail-free card: like Orson Welles's *The Magnificent Ambersons*, or the Judy Garland *A Star Is Born*, his movie had been butchered by philistines. Who knew what treasures might be found in his long version? (In fact, not many: Cimino's original cut was given a small release in Europe, where the reviews were not much better.)

His reputation had already been wounded by *Heaven's Gate*, but the reception of *The Sicilian* was actually not much more damaging to him than the duds other well-known directors had made, like Sidney Lumet's *Garbo Talks* in 1984 or Alan Pakula's scarcely released *Dream Lover* of 1986. *The Sicilian* was simply the kind of flop that happened regularly, the expected dent in a gambling studio's run of luck, rather than an unprecedented and noteworthy one like *Heaven's Gate*. In fact, by the time Cimino had delivered the two contentious cuts of his movie to Begelman in the spring of 1987, he had started work on another project and was preparing it for a September start.

An Irish screenwriter, Eoghan Harris, had written a script about Michael Collins, who fought a long and bloody battle to liberate Southern Ireland from British rule in the early 1920s. Marlon Brando had seen it and sent it to Barry Spikings, who had left EMI and formed a new company, Nelson Entertainment, which was funded by Columbia. Spikings, the only *Deer Hunter* producer who had not fallen out with Cimino, offered him the project. In April, Cimino and Carelli flew to London and opened an office in Sloane Square, where they were to begin casting and crewing up. Calantha, now nearly five, was put into preschool.

Michael Collins, although more of a politician than a gangster, was not dissimilar to *The Sicilian*'s Salvatore Giuliano. He was still a very contentious figure in Ireland, and as the movie was being prepared, the Troubles between the North and the South had become particularly violent again. "Any film had to be sensitive . . . it could not look like a nationalist movie without inflaming unionist fears," Eoghan Harris told me.

Harris was the writer who had described to me how Carelli "interpreted" for Cimino when they first met in Paris. "My relations with Michael Cimino were acrimonious from start to finish," he said. "He told me my idea of Collins was wrong, that he was not a revolutionary turned peacemaker, but more like a gangster who would reach out for the throats of those who opposed him. At this point Cimino reached out, wrapped his two hands around the bottle of wine in the ice bucket, and began to throttle it. I felt he was a danger to the film, editorially and politically. Accordingly, I gave some critical comments to the English newspapers, which ended with me being stood down from the screenplay."

Cimino asked Robert Bolt, who had scripted *Lawrence of Arabia* and *Doctor Zhivago* for David Lean, to write a new screenplay. Sarah Miles, Bolt's wife, remembered, "Michael Cimino made a quaint entrance into our lives in tight trousers and high-heeled cowboy boots. He was to be Robert's latest taskmaster."

Bolt had had a serious and debilitating stroke in 1979, and although his mind was not impaired, his speech was almost incomprehensible. Carelli told me that Cimino was sensitive to his problems, and although other people found it difficult, he learned to understand Bolt quickly and they got on very well. The movie was now called *Blest Souls*, but Bolt had only three months to write the script if production was to start in September.

Cimino had brought Michael Stevenson on board, and they scouted for locations in Edinburgh and Liverpool. Carelli's smart eye for casting had found Sean Bean and Tilda Swinton to play the leads—both relatively unknown then—and she told me that Bono wanted to do the music. On August 1, Cimino shot some rehearsal footage with Bean and Swinton at Burghley House in Lincolnshire, but by August 18, the project had been "temporarily postponed"—usually Hollywood-speak for "canceled forever." Nelson had spent $2 million on preproduction. (The Liam Neeson version of the Michael Collins story, made in 1996, was a completely different project.)

Carelli said, "One day, the Columbia production team call Michael in London and tell him to come to California. He gets on a plane. Meanwhile, a company producer goes to the team office in London and says to them: 'This is ancient history! Finished!' The reason they gave: at the Atlanta headquarters of Coca-Cola [who had bought Columbia in 1982] some Irishmen had threatened to blow it up if they shot a film about Michael Collins. I said to myself, 'Rubbish! How dumb! Who would believe that?'" Carelli told me that Cimino was very upset that some of the crew thought he had known about the cancellation in advance and had fled back to Los Angeles. In fact, it was a complete surprise to him, she told me.

Everybody I talked to seemed rather hazy about the real reason—even Barry Spikings, who had been instrumental in the cancellation. Carelli and Michael Stevenson both told me they had no real idea. In the *Hollywood Reporter*, an unnamed Nelson representative gave the usual boilerplate reasons: "script dissatisfaction" and "weather problems," but not political pressure. Carelli told me that everyone was very happy with the script, and it seems unlikely that anyone could have been worried about the weather in England and Ireland in August. Everybody had always been happy to blame Cimino for all manner of problems on other movies; but on this one there was never any implication that it was anything to do with him.

In fact, Barry Spikings instantly offered Cimino another project. By September 4, less than three weeks after the collapse of the Michael Collins project, Cimino was setting up an office in Los Angeles for *Santa Ana Wind*, a romantic drama by a maverick screenwriter called Floyd Mutrux. The *Los Angeles Times* reported that "a tight-lipped rep in Cimino's office" said that it was "about the San Fernando Valley and the friendship between two guys." When I asked Carelli why Cimino would take on another Nelson project after he had been treated so badly by them, she told me that they had dangled a carrot in front of him by saying that they were going to store the *Blest Souls* sets in readiness for a later start date (although there is no evidence that they actually did). Spikings also told him that, because it was a small character piece, he could "slip it in" quickly.

On January 26, it was abandoned. A Nelson spokesman used the curious phrase, saying that the cancellation occurred "in the normal course of business"—as if canceling a movie was somehow more normal than actually making it. In fact, Nelson was in trouble: several banks had cut their borrowing power after they defaulted on some loan agreements and they had laid off twenty employees. Cimino had found that it was hard enough getting projects off the ground with proper studios, but working with shakily financed independent production companies took uncertainty to a whole new level.

Although Dino De Laurentiis's company DEG had financial problems as well, he had been much more prolific than Gladden or Nelson—since he moved to the US in the mid-'70s, he had been involved in an astonishing forty movies. His business had gone bankrupt in 1987, but with his unique mixture of charm, toughness, pragmatism, and—most importantly—seemingly magical access to finance, he was still a figure who inspired confidence. He bounced back almost instantly and formed a new company. Now he offered Cimino its first production. In the spring of 1990, a year after *Santa Ana Wind* had imploded, he began preproduction on *Desperate Hours*, the story of a violent escaped criminal who invades the house of a family with many problems of their own.

The project had a track record of success: written as a novel by Joseph Hayes in 1954, it was quickly turned into a Broadway play starring Paul Newman as the criminal and then a 1955 William Wyler movie with Humphrey Bogart. De Laurentiis had acquired the rights for a remake to star Mickey Rourke. The screenwriting team of Lawrence Konner and Mark Rosenthal, who had written the *Romancing the Stone* sequel, *Jewel of the Nile*, in 1985, updated it. At the start, they were working with a young director, Christopher Cain, who left the project and was briefly replaced by William Friedkin. Then Rourke suggested Cimino.

When I met Mark Rosenthal in Santa Barbara, he described what happened (although he admitted that he might be "retrofitting my animus into this."): "We're told Chris Cain is fired. My guess is that Dino was having trouble getting big stars to work with a director with only a few credits. Then we hear about Michael Cimino getting it.

"Before we went in to meet him, there were already rumors that we might not be around much longer. We think, if we're friendly and open, he'll like us. I remember Cimino being smaller and slighter than I imagined, less Italian, but in Dino-world, being any kind of Italian meant something. As the meeting went on and we're looking through the script, I felt he was just pecking at various things. It was a long meeting, and he never even did the fake schmoozing that directors do.

At the end of it there was sadness—we knew we weren't going to be part of this. And we never got called again." By the time the movie started production in Utah on October 27, the *Los Angeles Times* reported that Cimino was shooting his own script.

Comparing the Konner/Rosenthal script with the finished film, it is clear that Cimino did make many changes (although the inevitable Writers Guild arbitration did not allow him a credit). As always, Cimino needed the project to be his own. Mickey Rourke's long monologue (Rosenthal called it "an aria"), in which he deconstructs the family's bourgeois and contemptible lifestyle, was reduced to a few lines; the dowdy lawyer who helps Rourke escape becomes a glamorous siren, played by Kelly Lynch; the invaded house is ridiculously grand, and the father—meant to be a cynical chaser of the American dream in his late thirties—is played by an improbable Anthony Hopkins.

The sad thing is how little the movie *was* his own. All of the projects and movies Cimino worked on after *Heaven's Gate*—although they were essentially works for hire—had some personal resonance for him, even *Footloose*, which played to his love of music and dance. Carelli had no doubt that *Desperate Hours* was beneath him, and she told me that she didn't understand why he wanted to do it at all. Richard Brooks, the director of Truman Capote's *In Cold Blood* and the Diane Keaton movie *Looking for Mr. Goodbar*, told him pragmatically, "You need the job."

Also, De Laurentiis had been loyal to Cimino, and there was always the possibility of other projects. He did not have final cut on the picture. After poor previews, a few scenes were removed, one of which was Cimino's favorite: an intense confrontation between the lawyer and a woman detective in a huge, empty football field that De Laurentiis felt had a worrying (to him) lesbian subtext. For once, Cimino's relationship with the actors was problematic, and there were difficulties with the performances—"Mickey's been shot in the head with Brando. This whole 'I don't have to know my fucking lines' thing. Tony Hopkins wanted to kill him," Cimino said. As a whole, the movie is oddly soulless and unconvincing, both underpowered and overblown at the same time.

One of the reasons people liked working with De Laurentiis was that he was always generous: he took a two-page ad in the *Hollywood Reporter* congratulating Cimino for completing principal photography

Cimino and Kelly Lynch on the set (Alamy)

five days ahead of schedule, calling the movie—in a typical piece of Dino-bombast—"a picture of shattering importance." However, when it opened in October 1990, the reviews were as terrible as the box office returns—$2.7 million on a budget of $18 million.

In 1995, Cimino directed his seventh and last feature film. An ex-musician from the Bay Area, Charles Leavitt, had written a spec screenplay called *Sunchaser*, about a delinquent Native American teenager with terminal cancer who takes his arrogant oncologist hostage and forces him to drive through Arizona to a mystical mountain where he believes a shaman can heal him.

It had been bought by New Regency, a company run by the kind of colorful figure who quickly finds a home in the movie business: an Israeli billionaire called Arnon Milchan, who allegedly had worked for Mossad and had been an arms dealer (his unauthorized biography is called *Confidential: The Life of Secret Agent Turned Hollywood Tycoon Arnon Milchan*). He had already produced *Once Upon a Time in America* and *Pretty Woman*.

Both Diane Keaton and Mel Gibson had been attached as directors but had dropped out, and Milchan offered it to Cimino. Of all the projects he had worked on since *Heaven's Gate, Sunchaser* had the most personal resonance for him. "When I was very young, I was lucky enough to spend some time . . . with the tribe of Dakota Indians," he said. "I immersed myself so heavily in their culture that, in a way, it became my religion—a religion based on a very simple idea: a stone, a cloud, a rock, everything is spirit, is life. *Sunchaser* allowed me to return to this." The movie had echoes of one of his first screenplays, *Conquering Horse*, about a young Sioux boy's rite of passage, but there were also similarities to the project he had written with Raymond Carver, *Purple Lake*, in which a group of troubled teenagers go on a redemptive wagon train.

When he started work on the picture in the spring of 1995, he took the logical next step in how he dealt with screenwriters: there was not even the usual dismissive meeting—he never met Charles Leavitt at all before he began to do his own work on the script. Despite Cimino afterward going to Writers Guild arbitration to get credit and again failing, Leavitt told me that only about 15 percent of it was changed, but it was enough to alter the tone: the boy, played by Jon Seda, is the healthiest-looking terminal cancer patient since Ali MacGraw in *Love Story*; a scene that took place in a poor Mexican church in Leavitt's script becomes an improbable—for Arizona—all-singing Black Gospel gathering; Anne Bancroft gives an embarrassing cameo as an aging hippie; the long-haired shaman at the end, in Leavitt's view, "looked like Fabio."

However, in many ways it is the most interesting of Cimino's last movies, with its underlying mysticism and feel for landscape. Jon Seda, healthy though he looks, is powerful as the inarticulate and angry teenager, and the characters are set against the mountains of Arizona, shot with all of Cimino's pictorial brilliance. There was one particular way in which he made the movie his own: just as he had changed the name of Giuliano's girlfriend in *The Sicilian* to Joann Carelli's Italian name Giovanna, he changed the name of the oncologist's daughter from Sarah to Calantha.

Although he was not granted final cut, the producers did not interfere with the editing. Pablo Ferro, his mentor from his commercials days in New York, recommended Joe D'Augustine after Cimino fired the original editor. He remembered vividly their first meeting: "It was kind of eerie. I was led into this dark editing room with black velvet curtains, and there was this guy hunched over. They bring me into his chamber,

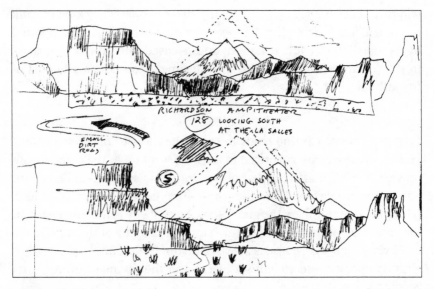

Location sketch by Cimino (Courtesy Joe D'Augustine)

as if he was the pope. Everyone was speaking in hushed tones. He had something covering his face, a handkerchief."

After a shaky start, D'Augustine began to like working with Cimino. "The guy was crazy," he told me, "but he was a genius. I wanted to be his friend. When we were thinking of composers, I brought in Jack Nitzsche [who had scored *One Flew Over the Cuckoo's Nest* in 1975], and they didn't get along. I said, 'He's a troubled guy,' and Michael said, 'Well, so am I!'"

D'Augustine liked Cimino's idiosyncratic approach: "We're sitting there watching the movie, looking for places to add sound effects. We get to the scene where the kid is on the phone, calling 911, shouting, 'There's a guy here with a gun.' I said, 'Do you want to put in their side of the conversation?' Michael says, 'I don't know what they'd say,' and then he picks up the phone and dials 911. He says, 'There's a man here with a gun, a very large one,' and then he hands the phone to the sound guy so he can write down what they say."

Although Milchan left them alone to edit, D'Augustine felt that Cimino was very dismissive of him, which impacted on the movie. He told me, "They turned on him brutally, those people. They kind of sunk the movie just to spite him." Indeed, it failed miserably. Unsupported by its distributor, badly reviewed, and released only in a few theaters in the southwest, it grossed an infinitesimal $30,000 on a budget of $31 million.

THE FOCUS ON Cimino tends to be on the disaster of *Heaven's Gate*, and many people are surprised to learn he went on to make four more movies. The film after it, *Year of the Dragon*, is still remembered and has many supporters. The other three have generally been forgotten. (Hollywood remembers the giant flops, but nobody is that interested in the run-of-the-mill ones—there are simply too many of them.) Despite its flaws, *Year of the Dragon* is at least a distinctively Cimino-esque film, with its operatic and violent set pieces and the theme of immigrants versus the law.

He tended to be scrupulous about scripts, and he had written or co-written his first four films. The last three—despite quixotically fighting for credit—were mostly the work of others. Only *Sunchaser* has some merit as a screenplay, but at that stage in his career, he admitted, "I made what was available."

What is interesting is why Cimino could not make these movies work. There was nothing wrong with their subjects—they were perfectly serviceable projects that could have been successful. William Wyler had made a good version of *(The) Desperate Hours* in 1955; *The Sicilian* was based on a giant best-seller by a famous author.

I think it had to do with control. His default position was that—in an Ayn Rand line he used in the screenplay of her novel *The Fountainhead*—"No creator was prompted by a desire to please his brothers." In his first four films, he had no desire to do that (except maybe to please Clint Eastwood) and managed to get away with it. Now, he was in a different position: he had to be subservient to those "brothers," and they had no fraternal feeling toward him. Carelli said that it was like taking Picasso and tying his hands behind his back.

Other great directors had the same problem. After three brilliant and successful movies, *North by Northwest*, *Psycho*, and *The Birds*,

Hitchcock had two high-profile failures—*Marnie* (1964) and *Torn Curtain* (1966)—and was nervous. In 1966, the always persuasive Lew Wasserman at Universal pushed him to take on a very commercial project: *Topaz*, a spy thriller based on a best-selling book by Leon Uris, the author of *Exodus*. Hitchcock thought the project was "inadequate," and it was a miserable experience, devoid of his usual wit and style. It was a disaster.

However, there were other auteur directors who could bite the bullet and throw themselves into a movie even if it was not material they would have chosen. Orson Welles took a trashy pulp thriller, 1958's *Touch of Evil*, and—even after its inevitable recutting by the producer—subversively turned in something close to a masterpiece. Martin Scorsese, who tended to come up with projects himself or with his inner circle of friends like Robert De Niro and Paul Schrader (who wrote *Taxi Driver*), was offered *The Color of Money* in 1986 by Disney, one of the most interfering of all the studios. It was a conventional underling-takes-on-champion story—*Rocky* set in the world of pool halls—and Paul Newman was already attached as the star. With bravura technical skill (particularly making one pool ball heading toward another as exciting as a car chase), he managed to almost turn it into a proper Scorsese film—and an enormous hit.

However, being workmanlike and pragmatic did not play to Cimino's strengths. He seemed unable to operate without the heady oxygen of total control—the absence of vertigo that he had felt on *The Deer Hunter* and *Heaven's Gate*—and now his sure and confidant touch wavered. He was working with new collaborators who were highly regarded in the industry but somehow lacked the magic that Tambi Larsen had brought to the production design of *Heaven's Gate* (he had retired) or Vilmos Zsigmond to the extraordinary cinematography of that and *The Deer Hunter* (Cimino had fallen out with him because Zsigmond felt he had taken too much credit).

More than that, Carelli, with her enabling belief in his genius, was less involved. She was credited with co-producing *The Sicilian*, but nobody I talked to saw her around much. The casting of the last three films lacked her magical instincts. Cimino would never have let his guard down to admit that there were any small flaws in his earlier films (or maybe he just thought there were none), but for the first time, he expressed dissatisfaction with his work. On *The Sicilian*: "I made a huge casting mistake with Christopher Lambert . . . he couldn't do it." On *Desperate Hours*: "The worst thing was that he [Mickey Rourke] was the one that ruined it. It wasn't a performance." One reviewer said that the movie felt as if it was directed by "a robot." Ironically, the last three movies might have worked better if they had been made by a less talented and more pragmatic director who believed in the material more—a robot, but programmed in a different way.

One of the other things that was different about Cimino's last three films was his treatment of masculinity. All his movies were an examination of it in some way or other—an attempt to understand the different ways it takes to become a man. The insecure greenhorn Jeff Bridges versus his confidently masculine mentor, Clint Eastwood; the strength of Robert De Niro coming to terms with the war while Christopher Walken descends into madness when he can't; Kris Kristofferson's passion for the cause that ultimately destroys him, and the craven Christopher Walken, who is murdering the immigrants for money.

In those films, the characters are utterly convincing, and their dilemmas appear to be deeply felt by Cimino. In the last three movies, the masculinity of the characters seems a posture—Christopher Lambert as that stock character of the noble peasant leader, the mannered Mickey Rourke as the violent criminal, and Woody Harrelson as the arrogant doctor—as if their macho-ness has been sprayed on. Whatever Cimino was going through, it was as if he had lost faith in the power of masculinity.

Sunchaser was Cimino's last feature. It was 1996. He was fifty-seven, and his career was essentially over. Joe D'Augustine, the film's editor, added a poignant footnote to his time with Cimino on the movie: "I thought he was an unhappy man. Pablo Ferro told me that Michael called him one day and said, 'I don't want to be Michael Cimino anymore.'"

PART FOUR

1996–2016

CHAPTER 15

SHADOW CONVERSATIONS

"THE ENTRANCE GATES, a few centimeters thick, are made of old maple wood," Cimino said. "I know one thing for sure: it was me that put them up." There were two sets of them, one at the street end and the other up the hill and around the curve where the house was. The gates were rarely open. They did not need to be: after *Sunchaser* in 1996, almost nobody was invited there. Mickey Rourke, who was in three of Cimino's films and considered himself a close friend, never visited the house. "Not even once!" Rourke said in an aggrieved tone.

Cimino had never been very social in a city where there was a general assumption that all larger-than-life Italian American directors, like Francis Ford Coppola and Martin Scorsese, must be throwing big pasta parties fueled by gallons of red wine from their personal vineyards in Napa Valley. In the early years, the years before *Heaven's Gate*, people like the producer Irwin Winkler and his wife, Margo, went there for small dinners cooked by Carelli, but now she spent the majority of her time in New York or their neighboring houses on the beach at East Hampton. Cimino was often there, too, but in Los Angeles his choice was to be more or less alone for the last twenty years of his life.

He was widely reported to be a recluse. The *Los Angeles Times* reported, "He lives in Beverly Hills, but it might as well be Kathmandu,"

His agent, Mike Wise—the days of the higher-profile ones like Stan Kamen were gone—called him "The Howard Hughes of Hollywood." However, "recluse" has an ambiguous meaning in Hollywood. It could be someone like Hughes, so terrified of germs that he never left his room, or it could be someone like Cimino, who simply did not go to industry screenings, award ceremonies, or networking parties, all essential parts of the Hollywood director job description. More than that, he sought no publicity—an eccentricity by Hollywood standards. "I don't need a publicist," he said. "I need a good offensive line, 350-pound guys in front of me."

He was rumored to have been spotted occasionally at rather unlikely places—Coogie's, an old-fashioned diner in Santa Monica, or Duke's Coffee Shop on the Sunset Strip, not the kind of establishments that feature in the *Hollywood Reporter*'s "Power Lunch" column, which reports which important industry people have been seen together in which chic restaurants around town. He seemed to some people to have become as elusive, mysterious, and unsettling a person as *To Kill a Mockingbird*'s Boo Radley.

It would be untrue to say that nobody at all was invited to the house, even though it contradicts the appealing "recluse" story that plays so neatly into the Cimino myth. However, finding more than a couple of friends who had thrashed those metaphorical 350-pound guys and broken through the gates of his home proved difficult. The nature of friendship for Cimino was ambiguous all his life. I asked everybody I interviewed the same question: "In the years you worked with Cimino, did you regard yourself as a friend or a collaborator?" Almost nobody said friend.

Yet there were people to whom he showed a certain cautious warmth, people who felt close to him for as long as he permitted it. F. X. Feeney, a highly respected film journalist who died in 2020, told me, "He needed people, but at the same time, he needed distance from people." There were four or five he saw quite often in the last twenty years of his life, and he met each one in a regular, but separate, restaurant. The one thing they had in common was that they did not know who the other friends were, and none of them ever met Carelli. One of them, Stefan Wenta, told me that he had no idea who she even was.

F. X. Feeney met Cimino through Jerry Harvey, who ran the Z Channel, the cult but influential channel dedicated to cinema art. He was instrumental in discovering lost movies (he found a missing John Ford one, *Up the River*, which starred a young Spencer Tracy and Humphrey Bogart, unseen since 1930) and restoring the reputation of forgotten directors from Hollywood's past. He also pioneered the concept of broadcasting a "Director's Cut." Cimino had benefitted from the channel when Allan Carr had organized a showing of *The Deer Hunter* on it before its release. Now Harvey came to Cimino's rescue again.

Feeney had written a mildly dismissive piece about the short version of *Heaven's Gate* in *LA Weekly*. He let me read his unpublished memoir, *Z Lives*, in which he described what happened afterward: "One daybreak he [Harvey] woke me by phone and skipped hello. 'Boy are you wrong about *Heaven's Gate*. . . . You haven't seen the director's cut.' I said, 'It doesn't exist.' He told me, 'Wrong again!'" Everybody believed that all known prints had been destroyed and the original negative had been chopped up to make the short version, the only one to still exist. Following a prompt from David Chasman, in charge of United Artists' UK operation, Harvey had tracked down the one intact print, which was sitting in a British warehouse.

Showing *The Deer Hunter* had been different: an exciting, exclusive sneak preview of a hot new movie. *Heaven's Gate* could not have been colder, and it was a characteristically defiant act on Harvey's part to show the 219-minute version that almost everyone other than him had hated. The Z Channel had ninety thousand subscribers, but, of course, they were committed movie obsessives and not the general public. When Feeney published an ecstatically revised opinion of the film in *LA Weekly*, he felt that he "might as well be talking about a dead horse at the bottom of a mine shaft." A year later, the Z Channel magazine sadly reported that even though the broadcast "was an unqualified success of an unprecedented event, the film virtually hasn't been seen anywhere else in the United States since." Nonetheless, Harvey's quixotic act had lit some kind of spark.

Feeney did not actually meet Cimino until Jerry Harvey's wedding in 1986. Cimino was the best man and wore John Lone's white suit from *Year of the Dragon*, a movie Harvey loved. Cimino was initially wary of Feeney because he was a critic. When I met him at the place he always saw Cimino, Coogie's, the diner in Santa Monica, he told me that Cimino had said to him, "I don't want to get too close. You and I are like Kirk Douglas and Woody Strode in *Spartacus*. We might have to face each other in the ring one day."

Their friendship developed after a tragic event: in April 1988, Jerry Harvey, brilliant but troubled, shot his wife and then turned the gun on himself. Without him, the Z Channel floundered. Its last broadcast was in June 1989, the movie John Ford's *My Darling Clementine*. Feeney co-produced a 2004 documentary called *Z Channel: A Magnificent Obsession*, in which many of Harvey's friends and people he had worked with were interviewed. Feeney felt it was important for Cimino to be one of them, but he declined to be included.

Cimino and Feeney already had a link when they met—they had both grown up in Westbury, Long Island—and they considered collaborating on a screenplay. "For a couple of years, I would drive up to his house nearly every morning. Show up at nine A.M. and he's already six hours into his workday. He burns with plans, projects, a rage to create," Feeney told me. He became probably the closest person to Cimino in Los Angeles in those years. "You're the only person in the world when he's with you," Feeney said. "That may have been an unconscious kind of compartmentalizing. There was a circle of people he felt comfortable with one-on-one. If you were comfortable saying nothing with him, he got along with you too."

In his own way, Feeney was as passionately protective of Cimino as Carelli (who he never met in thirty years of friendship with Cimino). Profiling him, he wrote, "People often ask me what Michael's house is like. I protect his privacy by putting it in general terms. He surrounds himself with beauty, simplicity, rugged landscape and clean light. . . . He's situated his home at an altitude where there are more coyotes than cops." I found it a touching notion that giving a more specific description of the house might somehow breach his privacy.

Feeney saw him often, sometimes as much as three times a week, either at Coogie's or at his house, where, Feeney told me, Cimino was always alone. He became his amanuensis—Cimino likened their relationship to that of Maxwell Perkins and Thomas Wolfe—advising on and editing whatever writing project he was working on. Feeney adored Cimino, but his best friend, the actress and director Irene Miracle, told me that the director was not always as generous in return. Feeney had helped edit his novel *Big Jane*, but Cimino told him that he would not be acknowledging his work because it would be "too awkward" for him.

Feeney's loyalty was such that, after the cut version of *The Sicilian* had been such a disaster in the US in 1987, he spent his own money to fly to Paris and see the longer, European version, to which he gave the only ecstatic review the movie ever had. Feeney called the Stanley Donen cut "a masterpiece of executive sabotage" and Cimino's long cut "a work of genius."

Feeney loved the unpopular *Sunchaser* as well, but it was the cause of a rift between them in 1996. In order to generate some publicity for the movie, Cimino asked Feeney if he could persuade *People* magazine to run a story. Cimino had one stipulation: he knew that the disaster of *Heaven's Gate* would be mentioned—it always was—but he asked that it be put in not at the start of the piece but somewhere in the middle. Without Feeney's knowledge, *People* edited his article and referred to the movie as a "debacle" in the first sentence.

Cimino was incandescent with rage. Feeney told me that he called him and shouted, "You're an informer. It's like you work for the Nazis. What is it? You charm everybody and then suddenly you stab them in the back. Maybe we can't be friends after lying. I'm going to let go of this friendship." They did not speak for eighteen months, and then out of the blue, Cimino called: "I was really unjust to you. I have forgiveness to ask. I reacted because I was drinking. I was doing all sorts of terrible things, and I just had to blame somebody." Feeney instantly forgave him, and their relationship resumed.

It was hard for Cimino to express what he needed from friends. Feeney told me, "I think he was a guy like John Ford, who kind of had his nose to the glass looking in on amazing family gatherings but could not get there himself on a certain level. I would sometimes call him on his birthday and he'd say, 'Thank you for remembering.' If I was crazy busy and did not have time to meet him, he would reach out to me on the day and say, 'Have you gotten free?' Then, of course, I'd say. 'Yes, I'm free.'"

Like everything else in his life, Cimino kept his friendships in special compartments that never overlapped, and he revealed different sides of himself to each person. There was no common denominator to the people he liked, and for most of them, even though they took great pleasure in knowing him, there was an element of mystery about why he had chosen them in particular, an uncertainty about what exactly he was looking for from the friendship.

Cimino's relationship with a woman called Cindy Lee Duck was different from the others, not least because she was twenty-five years younger than him. I had found a small reference to her in an article about Cimino, and I wrote to her. I had a reply thirty seconds after I sent my email. Most people I got in touch with regarding Cimino took a long time to reply, and some did not reply at all. Duck, by contrast, began to pursue me in a succession of emails. Why hadn't she heard from me? When was I coming to LA? When would we meet?

She is a multitasker of the kind that thrives in Hollywood: she had once been an actress but was now looking to raise $100 million of movie finance from financiers in the Middle East. On the side, she worked for a bail bond company, and it was their truck she arrived in when we met. We went to the restaurant she and Cimino frequented (Caffe Roma on Canon Drive), and the first thing she said was that I didn't need to talk to anyone else, that she was his only real friend. They had met briefly in 1985, when she visited Mickey Rourke on the set of *Year of the Dragon*, but it was only ten years later that they became close. She was promoting a trendy nightclub called the Doheny Room and getting her celebrity friends to go there because, as she told me, "There is nobody in my Rolodex who isn't super-famous." One night, Cimino was there. He had a problem with the check and Duck sorted it out. In gratitude, he asked her to lunch.

They began to see a lot of each other, but not in a romantic way, even though she felt he was very interested in women. (He told a journalist in 2000, "My personal life is work, sex, and cars. . . . I have three or four different people. I like to spread it around.") Their relationship had a certain teenage intimacy to it. He told her about girls he was seeing ("I could always tell when he had got laid"), and she relied on him for advice about her life. They discussed diets ("All he ate was fruit and nuts and lettuce") and he liked to try on her jeans to see how much weight he had lost. There were even sleepovers: "I could call him at two A.M. and he'd say, 'Come right over,' and I'd sleep on his couch. There was never anyone else there."

Cimino was fond enough of her to give her presents—a set of pearl rosary beads, an autographed script of *The Deer Hunter*, and a silver buckle that Rudy Ugland, his friend who was the horse wrangler on *Heaven's Gate*, had given him, engraved with the words "Rudy's Ranch: Top Hand Award won by Michael Cimino."

Like the other friends, she never met Carelli, but unlike all of them, he introduced her to Calantha, who spent a lot of time with him in LA. One night, when Calantha was eighteen, Cimino suggested that Duck take her for her first visit to a nightclub, but he wanted to make sure that "her virtue" was protected. He talked proudly to her—and everyone else—of Calantha and her college achievements: "She's brilliant. She's amazing. Her major is Mandarin Chinese. She surfs. She plays the electric guitar like Keith Richards. She's a champion jumper, unbelievable on a horse." He always referred to her as his daughter, although Duck guessed that this was not true.

He told Duck that, as the proud father, he was going with Carelli to Calantha's college graduation. After he returned, he did not tell her that they had run into David Mansfield, her real father. Mansfield told me that they seemed "surprised" that he would be at his daughter's gradua-

Cimino's silver buckle (Photograph courtesy Cindy Lee Duck)

tion. It was an awkward meeting. Cimino lacked the social skills to ease a difficult situation and just looked uncomfortable. It was the last time that Mansfield ever saw him.

Cimino had a very different relationship with Roanna Martin-Trigona, a woman he met at a dinner in New York in 1995. Unlike Cindy Lee Duck, she found him attractive. Martin-Trigona told me, "We had an instant chemistry. Every woman should know Michael in the way that I did. He was crazy, but it was worth it. We called each other all the time. We read lots of poetry together, lots of Russian literature. He sent me a draft of his last novel, *Sailing to Byzantium*. It was magnificent. Then he rewrote it and asked me to destroy my copy. He said, 'I want to hear every page going into the incinerator.'"

As it turned out, they never got involved romantically: "There were pictures of Joann and the child all over his apartment. . . . I said, 'Michael, this is not exactly a turn-on.'"

Even though he saw only a small group of people regularly, he was not unapproachable to strangers. Shanda Lear, daughter of Bill Lear, who pioneered his own brand of jet as well as the eight-track cassette system, told me that she had gone to her hairdresser—"The guy that Warren Beatty based his *Shampoo* character on"—and was waiting to get her hair cut. "Another lady was with this guy who was kibitzing the hairdresser, telling him, 'Do this, Do that.' I'm standing next to him and say, 'Wow—you really know what you're talking about.' He said, 'Yeah, this is my ex-wife, and she's just getting back into circulation and I'm helping her look the best she can,' And I say, 'Gee, that's really nice of you.' He says, 'Well, that's what I do, I help people.' I said, 'Maybe you can help me with a guy I'm in love with.' He gave me some advice, and afterward, I called him and said, 'My God, what you advised was absolutely fantastic. What do you do?' He said, 'I'm a movie director,' and then he invited me to dinner with Maureen O'Hara." Cimino did not tell Lear that whoever the woman he was helping at the hairdresser's was, it could not be his ex-wife, because he did not have one.

They kept in touch for a while. The last time Lear saw him was when she invited him to an Easter lunch she gave at her home in Newport Beach. "There were lots of children there, and I said, 'Michael, you should go and pick up some Easter eggs.' He laughed and said, 'Shanda, I'm a Hollywood movie director. We don't pick up Easter eggs.'"

Jim Hemphill, a programming consultant to the American Cinematheque in Los Angeles, recalled a bizarre chance meeting with Cimino in a Chinese restaurant in 2015. One night he received a text from a friend who said, "I think Cimino is sitting behind me at Chi Dynasty. Get over here!" Hemphill said, "That initiated my encounter with the man who made the movie that meant more to me than almost any other. Cimino was always at the top of my list of directors I wanted to meet, yet I always assumed this was a pipe dream, given his Salinger-esque retreat from the public."

Hemphill and his friend spent an hour drinking to pluck up the courage to approach him and then "we walked over to Cimino's table: 'Excuse me, are you Michael Cimino?' 'Who wants to know?' was the gruff reply." They told him they were filmmakers, and he said, "Have a seat, boys." They spoke for hours. "He talked about moviemaking with more youthful enthusiasm than anyone I've ever heard, including Tarantino. I think he was genuinely touched by the fact that Chris and I had devoted so much of our lives to studying what he did." Hemphill asked Cimino if he could interview him onstage if they could organize a screening of *Heaven's Gate*. "He told me, 'No way. Never in America.'"

Although Cimino never talked much about the hurt he felt over his destroyed reputation in the US, he could not help letting it slip out sometimes. His friend Stefan Wenta, a Polish choreographer who had been principal dancer of the Warsaw Opera, told me, "He was simmering in his bitterness, but all the time still hoping. It was heartbreaking for me at the end of his life."

Cimino's bitterness was mostly directed toward his fellow directors, who he felt had not given him any support after *Heaven's Gate*. He said contemptuously that Francis Ford Coppola was "dried up." Terrence Malick: "He should be writing poetry instead of making movies." About Scorsese: "Don't put me in the same bag as him. He's one of those Xerox guys. I guess he must think the faster he speaks, the less people will question what he's saying." He even fired a shot at somebody he had enjoyed working with: "Oliver [Stone] thinks he's the greatest thing since chopped liver." He was even scathing about what movie people did outside Hollywood. An interviewer in 2002 reported, "Mr. Cimino rants that the nouveau Hamptoners, including the Ron Perelmans and the Steven Spielbergs, are ruining East Hampton," although he and Carelli were hardly *vieux* Hamptoners themselves.

By that stage, he felt that he had nothing left to lose. The industry had turned on him, and he had realized that any finance for his movies would come only from Europe, especially France, where he was becoming a revered figure. After three flops, nobody in America was interested. Carelli told me that they had discussed a project with two Hollywood producers who agreed to back it. Afterward, Cimino told her that he felt the meeting had gone well, but she—ever realistic—told him that they would never see them again, and they didn't. However, the problem with European finance was not only that it was equally hard to access, but if you did, you were never sure exactly what its provenance was and what strings might be attached. They were now dealing with the kind of financiers who, Carelli told me, had their attaché cases locked to their wrists with a chain.

After *Sunchaser* in 1996, the house in the hills became a place that was only for his work, which, in the absence of any directing offers, was now writing scripts and novels. Cimino was extraordinarily prolific, Carelli told me. It was hard to keep track of the mass of pages because sometimes he did screenplay versions of novels or novel versions of screenplays, and he kept altering the titles on the many different drafts of each. The projects had a scattershot quality to them, as if he was searching for a genre in which he felt comfortable.

F. X. Feeney helped him with a script called *Heaven Is a Sometime Thing*, which told the story of a waitress who has an affair with a brilliant golfer. He becomes so successful that he is taken up by high society and becomes estranged from his working-class girlfriend when he meets an heiress. In some ways, Feeney told me, it was similar to the triangle of Montgomery Clift, Shelley Winters, and Elizabeth Taylor in *A Place in the Sun*. *Sailing to Byzantium*, or *A Hundred Oceans*, the novel that he asked Roanna Martin-Trigona to incinerate, was about a dying tycoon reflecting on his life. A few years before Cimino died in 2016, he wrote a script called *Cream Rises*, the story of two girls disconnected from reality in Los Angeles who lead an aimless life of drinking and shopping. He wanted Taylor Swift to play one of the leads. Another project was called *One Arm*, about a boxer who loses his arm in a car accident.

There was one script that was different. Unlike most of the others, it was a project that was quintessentially Cimino, a huge, sprawling epic on an enormous scale based on *Man's Fate*, a French novel (*La condition humaine*) written by André Malraux in 1933 that had won the Prix Goncourt. Malraux was an intellectual and politician, revered in France but much less known in America. Like *Doctor Zhivago*, it tells the story of a group of characters caught up in a revolution, in this case the Shanghai massacre in which Chiang Kai-shek violently suppressed the Chinese Communist Party in 1927.

The book was not unknown in Hollywood, but nobody had managed to get it off the ground. It had been a passion project of Fred Zinnemann's and was a week away from production in 1969 when the new president of MGM, James Aubrey, canceled it. David Niven, Peter Finch, and Liv Ullmann were to star. Ten years later, the Greek director Costa-Gavras tried to make it, and in the 1990s, Bernardo Bertolucci considered directing it but decided to make a different project set in China, *The Last Emperor*.

Malraux's literary executor, his daughter Florence, had disliked many of the scripts written and guarded the movie rights zealously. When Carelli and Cimino approached her, she was unwilling to grant them an option, so Cimino did something that demonstrated his passion for the book: he said he would write the script anyway and took the chance that if Malraux's daughter did not like it, she would prevent him from making the movie.

In the end, she did like it, but there were many other hurdles for him to overcome, in particular the financing. The fact that it was such a good fit for him meant that he might make a movie with the sweep and passion of *The Deer Hunter*, but with its high budget, it also sounded to many people like *Heaven's Gate* in China. It did not generate much enthusiasm in Hollywood. Martha De Laurentiis, Dino's wife and producing partner, said, "If you edit it down, it could be a very tight, beautiful sensational movie, but violent, and ultimately a subject matter that I don't think America is that interested in."

However, Cimino was not deterred ("The screenplay, I think, is the best one I've ever done"), and he and Carelli looked to Europe, as they knew they would have to. The budget was estimated at $25 million, a conservative figure given that *Heaven's Gate* had cost more than $40 million twenty years before and his attention to expensive detail was going to be no less than it had been on the earlier movie: a location is described in the script in his usual precise way: *When we look out of the window of the hotel, we see a lamppost at 70 degrees to the west.*

He was planning to shoot on location in China, an ambitious plan given that almost no Western movies had ever been shot there. He said that he had the support of the Chinese government, but agreements to film in Far Eastern countries were notoriously unreliable then—the cooperation of the Thai army had been withdrawn with no notice when he was filming *The Deer Hunter.* More than that, *Man's Fate* took place during a politically contentious moment in China's history, and even though the government would have demanded script approval before filming, it could perfectly well change its mind afterward.

His first three movies had gone into production very quickly, but Cimino was realistic about how the industry had changed. He said that a long and tortuous search for finance could mean that "it takes ten years, and it can be impossible to keep a crew and actors together." Martin Scorsese, a much surer bet than Cimino, took thirty years to get his passion project, Shūsaku Endō's *Silence*, financed, and over the years various casts, including Daniel Day-Lewis and Benicio Del Toro, dropped out because of production delays before it finally started shooting in 2014. Cimino only ever managed to secure half the finance, and the cast he talked of in 2001—Johnny Depp, Uma Thurman, and John Malkovich—could not be contracted until the other half of the budget was found—and it never was. He made various location trips to Shanghai and Beijing over the years and was still talking about the project until he died in 2016.

In the end, none of his scripts were made, nor were the novels published in the United States. However, two of his books were translated in France: the novel *Big Jane* in 2001 and a short memoir, *Conversations en miroir* (Cimino's English title was *Shadow Conversations*) in 2004. Quite unlike anything that he ever wrote, it was an alternately bleak, reflective, and unfathomable work in which truth and fantasy are mixed up so

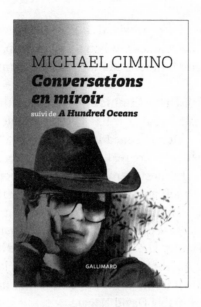

confusingly that it is impossible to tell one from the other. Somewhere between Fellini's surreal spin on his life as a director in *8½* and Billy Wilder's *Sunset Boulevard*, he describes the life of someone who may or not be Michael Cimino, a construct both opaque and revealing.

While it reads like an unedited, free-form stream of consciousness, as if, like Jack Kerouac writing *On the Road*, Cimino had put a large roll of paper in the typewriter and poured the words out in one go, F. X. Feeney told me that it was actually rather carefully edited. If the memoir is dream-like and contradictory, Cimino, the least improvisatory and most precise of writers, intended it to be that way.

The beginning of the memoir sets the tone: "I am a myth. I seldom smile these days. The swimming pool is empty. It has been for fifteen years." Real characters weave in and out, some named, most not. "My best and sole remaining friend told me that Orson Welles said that if you sit down in Hollywood at the age of twenty you will be sixty-five when you stand up," which must be F. X. Feeney, who quoted the same line to me. "Roanna" is mentioned, as is "Rose," about whom he says, "The most beautiful girl that I ever fell in love with was from Texas"—presumably Rosie Vela, the Galveston-born actress and model who played Kris Krist-offerson's Harvard girlfriend in *Heaven's Gate*. Other characters seem more fictional, like a toxic girlfriend called Mandy, who does not appear to even know his email address. When they break up, she asks what it is, and he writes, "The Myth tells Mandy, 'michaelcimino@nevercallme-again.com.'"

Cimino—or at least the Cimino he describes in the memoir—thinks constantly about death, what he calls "The Great Gate." He mentions six different suicides, which seems a lot in a forty-five-page manuscript. While four of the suicides are real, the others seem less so. After musing about the death of Ernest Hemingway, he mentions the British actor George Sanders, who left a note that read, "Dear World, I'm leaving you because I'm bored." Cimino writes, "We can die in an intelligent way like George Sanders or we can die stupidly." He remembers that the gun with which Jerry Harvey shot himself and his wife had been a present from Sam Peckinpah. He talks of the suicide of a Japanese American friend who had grown up in an internment camp in California. He is unnamed, but presumably David Nagata.

The other suicides, the ones that seem less real, are described in a curiously detached manner. He describes being called one night by someone who says that an old friend of theirs is "in a nasty state and is talking about topping himself." Cimino drove over and noted, "One myth is going to see another myth who is in the process of sinking a kitchen knife into his chest."

The memoir is full of Cimino's usual unreliable embellishments—"I was born on the Gold Coast"—but the way he describes his state of mind often seems poignant and truthful. Nostalgic for his less-complicated life in New York in the 1960s, he writes, "Thomas Wolfe cast a spell on us. We *should* be able to go home. I remember nothing other than laughing, dancing, stunning girls, beautiful sunny days and business. I want to go back."

He is scathingly honest—or at least playing the part of someone who is scathingly honest—about his health and his drinking: "I haven't eaten in two days, I'm starting to flirt with anorexia again. I am taking more medication than ever." He often said he was allergic to alcohol, and many people believed that he did not drink (but he also said he was allergic to the sun even though he drove a convertible). He describes the aftermath of a dental operation in which he is pumped full of Demerol,

Cimino in Venice, 2001
(Shutterstock)

drinks four vodkas, and drives to the supermarket to buy Tylenol: he crashes the car and is arrested. Van Robinson, his driver from *Heaven's Gate*, whom he had stayed friendly with, told me, "He had some run-ins with alcohol," and Cimino asked if Robinson would drive him around after he had lost his license.

Despite the despair he describes, he typically showed other sides of himself to his friends in the last twenty years of his life. Most of them told me that he seemed very happy most of the time, that they would spend warm and funny evenings with him. But clearly, even if the memoir is no more than a myth mythologizing, he was going through painful changes that distorted his perception of himself: he writes, "When the melody stopped one gloomy day, I rang Van and said, 'I've hit rock bottom. I think I'm dead and someone has come back in my place. I don't recognize this person.'" While he may have been speaking metaphorically, there were many people in Hollywood who did not recognize him either.

CHAPTER 16

THE WOMAN FROM
TORRANCE

THROUGHOUT CIMINO'S CAREER, journalists commented in some detail on his appearance. Directors are not movie stars, whose livelihoods depend on what they look like. Generally they tend to be rather anonymous, with the possible exception of Hitchcock, who let his manner, voice, and bulk become part of his myth. Nobody comments much on how Ron Howard or Ridley Scott look and dress. It was different with Cimino.

"Michael Cimino . . . is small, has dark curly hair and sad brown eyes. He looks more like a garage mechanic than a director," one interviewer noted. Another said, "Mr. Cimino is dressed in jeans and Western boots. Although it is cold in the room, his shirt is unbuttoned to reveal, California style, his bare chest." *Vanity Fair* commented that he was chubby and "looked like an Italian Garry Shandling and carried all the baggage of a small man." Cimino presented himself in many different ways, and those descriptions seem to be of three different people.

Because he revealed so little about himself in interviews—and what he did reveal was often contradictory—it was as if an elaborate physical description of him was needed to add some color to a washed-out portrait.

He was not unaware of this: he reported that a friend said to him, "Your problem, Michael, is that no one knows anything about you and they get worked up about it."

The early descriptions of him were not particularly offensive, but in the last twenty years of his life, that changed. Although he was interviewed only rarely in those years, he had not become a forgotten figure. The disaster of *Heaven's Gate* and the man who was given the blame for it were ingrained in the memory of Hollywood—he was still a source of fascination to the media, particularly his appearance. Whereas once he had been standard-issue Italian American macho—like Stallone or Pacino—he now gradually began to take on an androgynous appearance. He stopped resembling any kind of garage mechanic or any known version of Michael Cimino.

Interviewers clearly felt that there were no boundaries around the questions they could ask Cimino, that no aspect of his private life was off-limits. It would be unlikely that an interviewer would have asked Lana Turner if she had had a facelift or question director John Ford about what medical condition it was that made him need to wear an eye patch. With him, the questions were cruel and invasive, as if, after his downfall, he deserved no respect. It was open season on Cimino.

A 2002 interview for *Vanity Fair* was given the snide title of "Michael Cimino's Final Cut." The writer reported that he felt he had to ask Cimino about the change in his appearance. In 2015, the Hollywood *Reporter* quoted him as saying "many false things [have been] written about me by people who don't know me." As a response, the journalist said, "Well, let's set the record straight on one of those things . . . which is that you were transitioning between genders."

The descriptions of him were generally nasty, like "late-stage Bette Davis." Another journalist (using language then common) reported, "Even in Los Angeles, where nip-and-tuck surgery is a given, . . . word has channeled through agents' offices and industry hangouts that the macho director . . . is a pre-op transsexual." Another writer said that he "looks like a cross between a cowboy hipster and your great-aunt Bessie. . . . His hair is grayish red and eggbeater-bouffant even when pulled back in a ponytail. . . . His hands and arms are delicate and hairless. He smells girlishly good."

Cimino, age seventy-two, in
Novello, 2011 (Alamy)

There was no question that his new appearance was extreme, but it was no more extreme than many others in Hollywood. The difference was this: generally facial surgery is intended to make you look like the same person, but younger and better. What was curious about the work Cimino had done was that it seemed intended to deny his past self—he was simply unrecognizable. His old chunkiness was gone. He was waif-thin; the skin on his face had been pulled back and was unnaturally smooth, giving him a feminine appearance. His face appeared to be sculpted, with high cheekbones and full lips. It was hard to tell what his eyes looked like, as he always wore big sunglasses. He did not look old, but he did not exactly look young either, as if he was avoiding committing himself to any specific place on the age or gender continuum.

Some people suggested that he had had gender-affirmation surgery, or was planning to. Others believed him to be a cross-dresser, but nobody had seen him dressed as a woman themselves. They tended to know somebody who knew somebody who thought they had seen him dressed that way. One person had heard that Cimino had been seen "going into an airplane restroom as a man and coming out as a woman." Someone else reported a rumor that he had been seen wearing a dress while looking at the lions' enclosure at London Zoo—just the kind of bizarre stories that always came with the Cimino territory.

In June 1997, Army Archerd, the legendary *Variety* gossip columnist, called Cimino's lawyer, Eric Weissmann, asking him to confirm a story: he was now a trans woman and had asked that his membership of the Directors Guild be in the name of "Michelle Cimino." Weissmann spoke to Cimino, who denied it completely. That did not stop Archerd from publishing the rumor, ostensibly to deny that it was true.

Cimino was hardly the only person in Hollywood to refute salacious stories about themselves that had an element of truth. He must have known that people were going to disbelieve what he said about his appearance, as they had disbelieved that he was thirteen years younger than he actually was or that he had served in Vietnam. It suited him to have a swirl of truths and untruths circulating around him: it meant that nobody could pin him down and reveal the real Michael Cimino, whoever that was.

Sometimes he had a sense of humor about the stories. When F. X. Feeney asked what he had done with his hair, he said, "I don't know. It's like I fell asleep in the barber's chair. What can I tell you?" Gore Vidal called Cimino and said that he had heard he had become a woman. He replied, "If I thought it would do any good, I would." He said to an interviewer, "Can you imagine cutting your prick off? . . . I can't stand mutilation. I mean, tattoos!" He was asked if he had cheek implants: "This is my cheekbone. Feel it! Tell me if that's an implant." The interviewer conceded that it felt like bone. Cimino blamed the stories on a disgruntled ex-girlfriend.

However, he did not always follow his mantra of "Never explain, never complain." He was sometimes angry about the rumors. "If you can't stop somebody from working and making movies that you hate, what's the next best thing? Destroy them. It's personal assassination." He said bitterly that he had become "a fount of fodder."

Although it was no clearer to his friends what was happening to him, they had a view. Kris Kristofferson was asked about the rumors: "We had dinner to see if I could recognize him." Was he wearing a dress?

"No—which was comforting." F. X. Feeney said, "You are talking about an internationally renowned perfectionist. If he can't come out looking like Catherine Deneuve, forget it." Cindy Lee Duck told me that he was definitely not transitioning. "It was just an extreme facelift," she said. "I teased him about it. He liked my honesty."

What is surprising is that a more "sensational" story (at least by *National Enquirer* standards) was treated in quite a different way. The Wachowski sisters, Lana and Lilly, who had written and directed the three *Matrix* movies, both had gender-affirmation surgery in 2008 and 2016, respectively. While this was noted by the press, there were no unpleasant descriptions of their altered appearances or prurient stories about them, and the sisters were generally treated with a respect that was not accorded Cimino. Part of that may have been because people had become more understanding of gender issues by that point, with the success of the TV series *Transparent* in 2014 and the publicity surrounding Caitlyn Jenner, but in fact, the comments about Cimino continued up to his death and beyond. A cynical Hollywood observer might say that respect for the Wachowskis was because the *Matrix* movies grossed $1.6 billion worldwide, and there was every reason to believe that they could do it again. (A fourth *Matrix* movie began shooting in 2020.) Nobody believed that Cimino would ever make another successful film.

The fact that Cimino denied that there was any truth to the stories about him did not mean he was in denial to himself. He knew what he was doing, and the gradual reevaluation of his identity turned out to be a brave journey, through which he was helped by a woman with whom he had an extraordinary relationship.

After Cimino died, the Forest Lawn cemetery set up a memorial page online on which people were invited to add tributes. There were just four of them, three from people I knew about: a joint message from Joann Carelli and Calantha Mansfield, and ones from Francis Grumman and Roanna Martin-Trigona. The last one was from someone I had never heard of: Valerie Driscoll. She wrote, "Every day I think I'll hear his unmistakable voice on the other end of the phone. We had become friends through my retail business in Torrance over 12 years ago and I must say that he became my BEST friend. I love him so much and miss his intelligence and humor."

Nobody I spoke to had any idea who Driscoll was, but that was not surprising in Cimino's tightly compartmentalized world. However, it seemed incongruous that he would have had any kind of friend—best or not—who ran a "retail business" and with whom he spent time in the unlikely setting of Torrance, an anonymous suburb of Los Angeles near the noisy airport, the uninspiring place from which Mark Wahlberg was desperate to escape in *Boogie Nights*. It was a long way in every sense from Cimino's sophisticated and wealthy Hollywood world.

Driscoll's retail business turned out to be a wig shop called Hair to Wear, which had closed in 1996 when she left Torrance. It took a long time to track her down, and when I emailed, her reply read, "I must say your message was somewhat of a shock to me. I knew I was his 'secret friend' but for you to discover my identity . . . I am crying again. I miss him so much. He was my best friend and I am trying to be angry that he left me so I can get my act together."

She lives in Yucca Valley, much less affluent than nearby Palm Springs. Two hours from Los Angeles, past miles of otherworldly wind farms, the town is one long, dusty main street called Palms Highway, which heads eastward to nowhere in particular in the desert. It has a 1950s feel, like the depressed Texas town in *The Last Picture Show*—boarded-up stores and baking, empty streets.

I met her at Gadi's, a local bar that was already filling up with early-afternoon drinkers when I got there. She had brought with her two presents that she wanted me to have: a small French landscape that Cimino had bought for her, and something that had great sentimental value for her—a pair of black, patent-leather Chanel stilettos that he had given her. She told me that I would feel his spirit in both gifts.

She was in her early seventies, quiet and demure in a way that belied the colorful life that she described to me: "I grew up in Palos Verdes. I went to beauty school and became a hairstylist. I sold cars in the afternoons and did hair in the morning. It was fun. I really loved wigs. I'd done them for my dolls when I was a child." Now, in Yucca Valley, she was temporarily working as a pizza delivery driver, but she told me about some of her earlier professions. She had been a store owner, real estate flipper, commodities trader, cosmetologist, cocktail waitress, and masseuse, as well as some others: "Back when I was svelte and sexy, I hosted S-and-M parties as a paid dominatrix. Even though that beauty is gone, I can still muster up." She showed me photographs of her younger self in that role, blonde and glamorous, clad in black leather.

She had moved to Torrance in the early 1990s. She told me, "I went to work for a store called Del Amo Fashion Wigs, and I noticed cross-dressers coming in there a little bit, but I didn't know what they were called. I didn't know there was a whole community. The first one was a guy who drove up on a motorcycle. I got a little nervous because he gets off and he's wearing black leather. I'm like, 'Oh my God, what's going to happen now?' Even though he had lots of hair, he goes, 'I want to try on a woman's wig.'" Driscoll found herself drawn to her new clients: she understood what it felt like to be an outsider and wanted to help them negotiate the problematic worlds they moved between.

"After about a year at Del Amo, I said to my boss, 'I noticed these people coming in, the guys who are very shy. Would it be OK if I opened my own store and took care of them?' It was easier at my store. I could stand there and say, 'OK, look, this color won't go with your skin tone.' We could talk about it without having to be hiding behind a curtain. One of the reasons I was popular was that I never discussed other clients. I respected them all. I *never* judged any of my beautiful cross-dresser clients and friends."

A year or so after she opened her salon, she met Cimino. "I received a phone call from someone called 'Nikki,' who wanted a makeover session. He was very quiet, very nice—he hardly said a word. We weren't immediate friends; he was just a good customer. Nikki would send me cutouts from fashion magazines of hairstyles he liked. It was then my position to tell him which would work for him. I never imposed my curiosity about who he was. It was only after many months of visiting my shop we finally exchanged phone numbers. I only discovered his true identity many years later. At the time, he told me that he was a caregiver to an elderly couple in Beverly Hills and lived in their guesthouse. He said that the car he sometimes drove, a sporty Mercedes, was borrowed from them. His own car was a black '89 Mustang, which he customized with my suggestions because I wrote for a classic car magazine." Val suspected that Cimino's story about himself was probably not true, but she was used to her clients needing to be secretive about their identities.

I asked her what drew them together. "We each knew things that helped each other," she said. "I think she grew to like me due to my strength and independence as a woman. I was drawn to her softness, sweetness, and uncharacteristic naivety." Their relationship grew to be a mixture of the practical and the spiritual: "We had a real connection. She visited me in dreams. Sometimes we communicated telepathically. We had so much in common. We had both seen UFOs. I have never met anyone so brilliant. I think about our conversations all the time. She was really intelligent, and I'm not stupid, so we got along that way intellectually. We talked about very personal things, and I knew everything about her, except for exactly who she was. I once asked if she had always known she was different, and she said yes.

"I talked about my family a lot. She hated them and finally said to me, 'I don't want to talk about them anymore.' It probably reminded her of her own family for some reason. She mentioned two brothers who she didn't get along with. She didn't like her dad, and I don't think her mom was too much in her life either. I knew there were two women in her life, but she never told me anything about them, neither the mother nor the daughter. She didn't want me in that part of her life. She wanted a whole new life with me without that."

Driscoll felt she had given Cimino the confidence to change, to act on what he had grown to want: "As time passed, I began to notice subtle changes to her face, and soon his masculine features softened. I don't know at what point he decided he was done with being a guy. I just don't know. Michael became Nikki." Their makeover sessions continued until she gave up her shop in 1996 and moved to the Palm Springs area, where she ran a massage and spa business until it closed in 2005. After she left Torrance, their relationship continued mostly on the telephone—"Hundreds of calls," she told me. They would occasionally meet halfway at a hotel, but they saw each other less and less. "As she grew older, my magic wand did not work so well. Our last couple of makeover sessions didn't end with the exciting transformation it had before. We both realized the glamour days were over," she said.

After knowing each other for more than fifteen years, Val began to feel he was pushing her away. "She found another person to do her makeovers, and I became quite useless, I suppose. Disposable. She stopped calling me. I think she was questioning herself, what she was doing. 'So now what? Should I just go back to being Michael?' I missed her so much I couldn't help but search for her. I was bad—I had her cell phone number, and I used that to find out who she was." Driscoll's discovery did not go down well with Cimino. "I said, 'I know who you are,' and she was so angry with me. Our relationship changed completely. It continued somewhat, but became strained. I didn't feel like she was open anymore. That was really the end. I wish she had understood that my love for her never changed, no matter who she was as a man. The thing I remember best is Nikki driving away one night in the Mercedes sports car and waving through the window. I thought she was the most beautiful woman I ever saw."

CHAPTER 17

PHOENIX

WHATEVER THE COMPLEXITIES of Cimino's private life in the last twenty years of his life, there was a surprising shift of opinion about his public one. After years in the wilderness, critics, particularly in Europe, began to reconsider his career and his stature as a director. Over time, *Heaven's Gate* began to be looked on as a masterpiece, but it took more than two decades.

There are few movies that have been so completely reevaluated as Cimino's. There are films about which opinion has changed because they seem more relevant today than when they came out—1998's *The Truman Show*, for example, which depicted a world obsessed by reality television. There are films that were misunderstood and badly reviewed at the time, like Kubrick's *2001: A Space Odyssey*, which went on to be successes. Others were flops even though they were not badly reviewed—*It's a Wonderful Life* in 1946 or *Blade Runner* in 1982—and although they had their champions, they did not find a larger audience till much later.

Heaven's Gate was very different. There were no champions. Critics did not misunderstand the film, they just hated it. There was certainly no audience for it, but because it was withdrawn so quickly, it was not given the chance to find one.

The start of Cimino's resurrection had begun in 1996 at the Cannes Film Festival. Its president, Gilles Jacob, put *Sunchaser* in competition for the most prestigious prize, the Palme d'Or. Given that the movie was disastrously reviewed and a financial flop in the United States, it seemed a curious choice. The other directors nominated were a much more predictable selection of critical favorites—Bernardo Bertolucci, David Cronenberg, the Coen brothers, and Robert Altman. The fact that Cimino's movie did not win (the prize went to Mike Leigh's *Secrets and Lies*) was immaterial—just to be included in the competition was an extraordinary gesture of faith by the French film community in a director who had no champions whatsoever in his own country.

In Europe, and particularly France, critics had a very different attitude to cinema. They concentrated on the directors they considered auteurs—the ones with a specific, recognizable artistic vision. More often than not, they tended to be American, because influential critics (and later filmmakers themselves) like Jean-Luc Goddard and François Truffaut had an evangelical passion for American cinema. The dismissive reviews and poor box office of films by these directors were regarded as a source of pride in Europe—to be misunderstood in a country that film critics felt was philistine and money-obsessed brought with it a certain kind of kudos.

Careers that had died for lack of interest and finance in their home country were disinterred and made fashionable. Directors like Orson Welles and Nicholas Ray became heroes of European cinema in the 1960s and '70s. Welles's career after 1947—checkered though it was—was entirely financed out of Europe. In the US, his income tended to be from appearing on chat shows and as the front man in a series of commercials for Gallo wine, the kind of cheap wine that Welles, with his predilection for the finer things in life, would never have touched. He found those things in Europe, where he was mobbed in the street as the most auteur of auteurs.

Unlike their American counterparts, European critics were more interested in Cimino's oeuvre than in his appearance. In the years after the 1996 Cannes Film Festival, Cimino began to spend more time there: he was a guest of honor at film events and all the prestigious festivals. He was president of the jury at Taormina in 1997. He gave a master class in Bologna in 2003 and one in Paris in 2005. In the same year, there was a retrospective of his movies at the Portuguese Cinematheque under the title "The Last of the Mavericks." In 2015, he appeared at both the Venice Film Festival and the Institut Lumière in Lyon.

He also gained a new career in France as a writer. At the Deauville Festival in 2001, he had been awarded the Prix Littéraire, an honor that had previously been given to Gore Vidal and Norman Mailer, in recognition of his novel *Big Jane*, which was published in translation in 2001 by Gallimard, one of the most distinguished publishing houses in France (*Conversations en miroir*, Cimino's bleak memoir, was also published by them, in 2004.) He said that Carelli—"my girl"—had typed the book for him from the handwritten manuscript.

The novel tells the picaresque story of a road trip that six-foot-tall Big Jane takes with a disaffected teenager called Billy on his motorbike. Along the way, they become involved with Sioux tribespeople in North Dakota. Billy is killed in a road accident, and Jane heads to Hollywood, where she becomes involved with a sleazy director who wants to make her a star before enlisting in the navy as a nurse and then serving in the Korean War. When she returns, she realizes that her true skill lies in riding motorbikes. As she is competing in the world championship, she sees a vision of the dead Billy heading toward her on his bike.

Cimino took *Big Jane* as seriously as all his other work: "The women who went to Korea really did fight alongside the men. Herman Melville said the American theme was space, Jack Kerouac said it was speed, and Big Jane is both." He told an interviewer that, as a sideline, he was considering starting a women's blue jean line called "Big Jane": "I think they should go lower in the front and then higher in the back.'

The launch party was held in the grand salon of his publishers, Gallimard. Anouk Aimée was there with Jeanne Moreau. Isabelle Huppert came in sneakers and a raincoat and talked to Florence Malraux, the daughter of the author of *Man's Fate*. At the event, Cimino was given another award, the Chevalier des Arts et des Lettres, and the beribboned gold medal was pinned to the lapel of his jacket before he made a graceful and emotional speech: "I feel tonight I'm in the hand of God. The road has been long and hard, and France was always here in triumph and disaster. Blessed France—may she always love me as much as I love her."

Although the book received enthusiastic reviews (*Paris Match* said, "Literature has, without doubt, gained a real author"), it's a flawed piece of work. All of Cimino's passions are there—America, Native Americans, masculinity, Hollywood, and war—but none of them are really integrated, and it lacks the firm structure and precision of his movies. The book was never published in America. He told some interviewers that he was looking for a US publisher and others that he did not want it to come out there at all.

After the years out in the cold, Cimino took evident pleasure in the adulation he received in Europe. When he was onstage, elfin, sun-glassed, and cowboy-booted, his behavior seemed to have altered along with his appearance. Before, his persona—in public, at least—had been rather solemn and ungiving, with no hint of humor. Now, in Europe, he exhibited a great deal of charm, and even a beguiling eccentricity.

In 2007, he got the opportunity to make one last film. Thierry Frémaux, who had become director of the Cannes Festival as well as running the Institut Lumière in Lyon, asked Cimino and thirty-three other directors, including the Coen brothers, Roman Polanski, and Jane Campion, to each make a three-minute film, shown together as *Chacun son cinéma* (*To Each His Own Cinema*), to celebrate the sixtieth anniversary of the festival. "I was surprised that he accepted, but it was good to have him back behind the camera," Frémaux told me. His movie, *No Translation Needed*, was shot in a theater in Santa Monica and was a vignette of a bad-tempered French director filming a music video of a salsa band performing onstage. Carelli produced it, and Calantha Mansfield was credited as Associate Producer.

When Cimino came to Cannes for the showing, he met Thierry Frémaux for the first time, and they became close friends. Frémaux had no idea what he would be like and was surprised: "Directors tend to talk about themselves and their films. I was very flattered. He asked me about me, my life, my youth. He was curious about people, but he was quite a lonely guy." Frémaux was unconcerned about Cimino's changed appearance: "There were always rumors, and I didn't want to spread them more. I never asked questions—he had the right to be who he wanted. It was a sign of his strength."

Cimino, Isabelle Huppert, and Thierry Frémaux, Lyon, 2012 (Photograph courtesy Thierry Frémaux)

Whenever he went to festivals in Europe, he received standing ovations. Carelli told me that when he appeared at the Institut Lumière in Lyon in October 2012, she had not let him know how big the audience was going to be. When he came out from the wings and saw five thousand people cheering him, he was moved to tears. Frémaux told me, "Isabelle Huppert came up onstage. Cimino said, 'When we did *Heaven's Gate,* we were Les Enfants du Paradis, but we didn't know it.' [*La porte du paradis* was the French title of the movie.] There's a popular song 'C'est comme un oiseau,' and we sang it as 'C'est comme Cimino.' He loved that."

Carelli did not always accompany him to Europe, but when she did, she kept well in the background, as she always had, and was almost never photographed. The person who was constantly with him was her daughter, Calantha Mansfield. She appears in scores of photos with him, and, taken over a period of about fifteen years, there is a curious time-lapse quality to them. She grows up before your eyes as she changes from a teenager to an elegant and sophisticated young woman.

Cimino and Calantha Mansfield, Rome,
2008 (Alamy)

The two of them are unashamedly affectionate. Sometimes they hold hands; she raises an umbrella over his head in the rain; as he becomes older, she gently takes his arm as he climbs the steps to the stage.

In the last twenty years of his life, she was the person he was closest to, and they had a mutually loving relationship that was warm and unconditional. I asked Carelli if I could meet her daughter. She told me that Calantha was too protective of Michael to want to talk.

Cimino was just as protective of her. James B. Harris, Stanley Kubrick's first producer, remembered meeting Cimino, Carelli, and Calantha at the Lyon festival in 2013. Harris's girlfriend, Katy, closer in age than any of the others to Calantha, spent a lot of time with her and told me how considerate and loving Cimino was toward her. He asked Katy if she would take Calantha dancing but made sure that a limo was

Cimino in Lyon, 2013 (Photograph courtesy
Thierry Frémaux)

organized to take them and wait outside until they were ready to come
back to the hotel.

Both Carelli and Calantha accompanied Cimino to his last public
appearance, in Locarno, Switzerland, in 2015, the year before he died.
The film festival there takes place every year in August and tends to be
less commercial than some of the other ones. At Cannes, the Croisette
is lined with giant billboards advertising films that have just been made
as well as films that have not been made—and may never be. Beneath
the prestigious awards that are handed out lies a labyrinth of frenzied
dealmaking by both buyers and sellers.

There are no billboards at Locarno, and no deals done. The festival has always taken pride in celebrating the art of filmmaking
above everything else. Cimino came to the sixty-eighth festival to

be given the prestigious Pardo d'onore—the Leopard of Honor—a lifetime-achievement award that had been given to other American directors who were generally thought of as difficult and unfashionable mavericks in their own country. Samuel Fuller, one of the most unashamedly B-movie directors ever, was awarded one in 1993; Abel Ferrara, who directed such controversial movies as *Ms .45*, *The Driller Killer*, and *9 Lives of a Wet Pussy*, was awarded it in 2011.

The awards ceremony was held on the night of August 10 in the Piazza Grande, one of most beautiful squares in Europe, which can hold as many as eight thousand people. That evening it was crammed with people who had come to see not only *The Deer Hunter*, which was shown on a giant screen that took up most of one side of the square, but more importantly, Cimino being presented with the award.

When Cimino got out of the black limo that had driven through the crowds of people to the center of the square, he cut a frail figure. Dressed simply in a tan jacket and white shirt, he climbed carefully to the stage in the piazza. There was a frenzied reception: people were cheering and shouting his name. The president of the festival, Marco Solari, welcomed him warmly, and Cimino came to the center of the stage, bowing gracefully three times to different sides of the crowd, much as an actor would do at curtain call to make sure no part of the audience was immune from his appreciation. He blew a kiss and raised his hands triumphantly in the air like Sylvester Stallone in *Rocky*, a gesture that was rather touching since many years earlier, before his changed appearance, he had resembled Stallone.

His first words were, "I want to say to you, '*Ciao, bella gente!*'" The audience loved it. Other American directors who had won the Pardo d'onore in the past did not have the courtesy or the knowledge to speak in Italian. Then he added "*Facciamo la festa!*"—Let's make a party.

Marco Solari came forward, shook his hand, and presented him with the Golden Leopard. Cimino held it up, looked at it critically, and said, "I'm trying to convince the president to change the design." This could have been construed as an ungracious remark at an event that was in his honor, but the audience began to clap. Then he added, "This does not look like a leopard; it looks like a chicken!" The laughter was uproarious: Cimino could do no wrong.

The Deer Hunter began, and the bravura opening sequence of a Russian wedding in a Pennsylvania steel town that introduced the main characters of the film—Robert De Niro, Christopher Walken, and John Savage—lit up the piazza-wide screen. It was not a particularly warm night, and before long it started to rain. Undaunted, the audience raised umbrellas and then, in an extraordinary kindness-of-strangers gesture that would not have happened in Hollywood, a man came out of a restaurant on the edge of the piazza and passed through the crowd with a blanket to put around Cimino's shoulders.

The next day, the weather had cleared and the people in the Spazio Cinema outdoor forum, smaller than the piazza but just as crammed, were waiting for Cimino to appear again, this time for a much-anticipated interview and, the allotted hour permitting, a short Q&A session. An amateur cameraman filmed the whole event, and the first moments of it show a small gaggle of people following Cimino onto the stage. He was dressed entirely in black, with his trademark pair of cowboy boots and aviator shades. Hovering at the back were Carelli and Calantha, who were also wearing aviator shades, as if they were members of the same rock band.

He moved to the center of the stage, where there was a large table, two chairs, and two microphones. He was to be interviewed by Stéphane Gobbo, a distinguished journalist. Cimino was at his most mercurial and idiosyncratic: he ignored the table and his interviewer, took a microphone, and came down from the stage to stand in front of the audience. This was clearly not what had been planned, and as Cimino began to speak, Gobbo looked flustered, like the best man at a wedding discovering that his speech was being dispensed with.

Like the previous night, he opened with *"Ciao, bella gente."* As he spoke, Joann Carelli moved across the back of the stage and spoke in a whisper to Marco Solari. They kept glancing over to Cimino, and it looked as if she was not pleased, as if some detail of the arrangements for Cimino at this event were not entirely to her satisfaction. After all these years, she was as protective as she always had been.

He went on, "I can't sit behind a desk because I am not a teacher, so this is not a class. OK? I'm not a preacher. I'm a reacher. You know what it means to reach? I'm trying to do the same things you're trying to do, except we're at different stages in our reaching and our development, but we're all in the same boat together."

Cimino went on with his self-deprecating introduction: "I have nothing to teach. I have nothing to say. I have no speech. I made no preparations. I did nothing." Hardly pausing for breath, he looked at someone in the audience and said, "Hello, how are you? Good?" and then he walked into the crowd and shook the hand of a man in a wheelchair. He seemed to be working the audience like a revivalist preacher.

"Excuse my bad Italian, because my English is worse. I have to pretend I speak English." He gave a little laugh. "So what can I possibly say to you? You want me to sing?" And then he did exactly that, singing a verse of "Can't Take My Eyes Off of You."

Although it was rather charming, it was not quite as spontaneous as it seemed—Cimino had also performed it onstage at the Institut Lumière in Lyon. It obviously had some resonance for him, because Robert De Niro sings along to it when it's playing on a jukebox in *The Deer Hunter*. Crooning onstage was not what David Lean or Martin Scorsese would have done at a prestigious festival, but Cimino already had the audience in his hands, and there was a giant cheer.

A nervous-looking Calantha had a hurried word with the redundant interviewer. She looked as if she was worried that the session might be heading into uncharted territory. But somebody speaking up from the audience brought everything back onto a more conventional track: "Why did you go into movies, Mr. Cimino?"

"Please, call me Michael. Mr. Cimino scares me because that was my dad's name. I'm Junior. When I made this crazy suicidal turn off the road I was on, my longtime associate and producer, Joann Carelli—Giovanna is her real name, but she insists on Joann, which I don't like—said, 'Michael, you're going to have to write a screenplay.' I said, 'But I don't know how to write,' and Carelli said, 'You're going to have to learn very fast.' I'm talking too much, as usual. You have to ask the questions now, otherwise I'll go on talking for two hours or three days. Then it will rain on us, we all get sick—and my God, who knows what happens after that?"

Someone put their hand up. "What is your name?" Cimino asked.

"Bruno."

He rolled the word around his tongue: "*Brooono!*"

"I just wanted to know if you are still in touch with David Mansfield."

Cimino's reaction was lightning-fast and abrupt: "No."

"No? Not all?"

"No." After all these years, David Mansfield, Carelli's long-ago lover and Calantha's real father, was clearly a no-go area.

He swiftly turned away from the man and looked across the audience. "Somebody else?"

A man put his hand up, and once again Cimino asked his name. "Valerio? A beautiful name!"

"What kind of friends do you have?"

"My best friends are cowboys, I mean real cowboys—not Hollywood cowboys, who walk around with fake costume hats, tight leather trousers tucked into boots—cowboys who rodeo and compete. I'm inspired by people like that." It was a rather unconvincing statement from someone who was no stranger himself to fake costume hats and tight leather trousers tucked into boots.

Calantha came forward to whisper in his ear. "I'm trying," Cimino said testily. He turned to the audience: "She told me to keep things short. I talk too much—maybe we have to go past one hour."

The audience, cheering, had no problem with this, but the organizers onstage looked at one another nervously while Cimino plowed on, answering more questions at some length. He talked about a bewilderingly random series of subjects, about how the fattest actors make the best dancers, about how mountains talked to him, about how he doubted whether Pavarotti's singing would be improved if he read his reviews.

He got irritated when he couldn't hear the questions. "Where's that man's microphone? We need a red flag to wave like in motor racing. *Mamma mia!*" Someone in the audience displeased him: "Umberto, wake up, please! Pay attention!"

There was someone who restored his good mood. "Hello. My name is Ulrika Koch. You may remember many years ago at the Taormina Film Festival, you were the jury president and you gave me the Charybdis for my film. It was very, very moving for me."

"Ah!" he shouted. "I must come and give you a hug." He came through the audience and embraced her. "You did a wonderful, wonderful movie. I loved this movie!"

As soon as he got back in front of the audience, the interviewer jumped in assertively: "We just take time for two more questions."

"Why are we doing only two more questions?" Cimino asked. When told that they had run out of time, he waved his hand in the air. "No, no, no, no. If you have more questions, keep going. Speak, speak!"

A hand went up. "Before my question, I want to tell you that in France we feel you are a very French filmmaker."

"Why do you think that is?" Cimino said, then he added cheerfully, "People say I look Chinese. Do I look Chinese?" The audience clearly did not quite know how to respond to this question, because the truth was, with his smooth and pulled-back face, he did look rather Chinese.

The man's question was about whether war was different now, and for the first time, Cimino had an outburst of passion. "What has not changed, what is even more reinforced today, more pronounced today, is the tragedy of war. OK? War is madness! Young men pay the price. Always!" His voice began to break with emotion. "It's time to stop the madness. It's all created by old men with white hair." He gestured toward his own hair as if he had forgotten that it was not white but rather an unconvincing shade of brown.

The reaction of the audience was becoming a little muted now as Cimino's stories became more rambling. The exasperated interviewer tried to assert himself again: "We have just time, sorry, for one more question."

"Why are we being rushed? Do we have to go somewhere?"

"There is another Q-and-A for a film here."

"And what are they going to talk about? Are they going to have a more interesting time? Another question."

"Do you have new things you're working on? A new film? A new script?"

"Always, yes. I never stop. If you stop you die." He tapped the top of the microphone rhythmically: "My heartbeat."

"How do you deal with a competitive environment, a lot of aggression, a lot of ego? How do you find your place?"

"People are always aggressive. People are trying to kill you. There's only one thing to do—you have to be more aggressive, you have to fight harder. You have to be stronger, tougher, smarter, faster." It sounded like a heartfelt personal statement.

By now, Team Cimino was getting nervous. Calantha came over to him, and, reluctantly, he handed over the microphone. "They're throwing me out!"

"Yes," the interviewer said, "this time I think it is really the end."

Cimino came forward into the audience, and once again he went over to the man in the wheelchair he had spoken to at the beginning. He bent down and kissed the top of his head. "You're a beautiful person," he said. "And you're smart. When I call, you must come!" The man looked grateful, and for a moment, you could believe that the European film community might think that a great auteur was capable of curing the halt and the lame.

Then, Cimino came back onto the stage and sat behind the table that had been prepared for the conventional interview that had never happened, and he was suddenly dwarfed by a mob crying out for his autograph, a small man in aviator sunglasses wearing cowboy boots to increase his stature, profoundly moved by the adulation he found in a country that was not his own.

IN AMERICA, THE reevaluation took longer. Richard Brody of *The New Yorker* believed that it might have been a quicker process if the internet had existed at the time of the movie's release. The film Kenneth Lonergan made before *Manchester by the Sea*, 2011's *Margaret*, starring Anna Paquin, also had a troubled production, extensive recutting by the studio, and a brutal reception. A second wave of viewers dubbed themselves #teammargaret after seeing the director's own cut and began championing it on social media. If it had existed, #teamheavensgate might not have been enough to make Cimino's film a commercial success, but it might have at least turned it into a succès d'estime.

One of the reasons for the reappraisal was that critics began to look at the movie in a different way. In 1980, the reviews tended to focus on the inflated budget and Cimino's impossible behavior rather than on the film itself. Richard Brody believed that the criticisms belonged "less to the history of cinema than to the sociology of the mob. . . . Critics closed their eyes, minds, and hearts and instead reviewed the gossip. . . . Critics sought merely to outdo themselves in the art of stone-throwing, each one's hostile cruelty shielded by everyone else's."

As the years passed, the cost of *Heaven's Gate* became curiously irrelevant. Budgets began to rocket from the 1980s onward, and nobody seemed to question that *Terminator 2: Judgment Day* should cost $100 million in 1991 or the third *Pirates of the Caribbean* movie should boast an eye-watering price tag of $300 million in 2007. Forty million dollars for Cimino's movie seemed almost good value, a nostalgic throwback to a golden age of austerity.

So, too, was Cimino's impossible conduct, which had seemed unforgivable in 1980, reevaluated. As the press became more celebrity-obsessed and the internet fed on scurrilous rumors of excess and vanity in show business, bad behavior by directors and stars began to seem commonplace. Even the film's much-criticized length worried people less: The BBC's Nicholas Barber felt that "to viewers who binge-watch ten-hour HBO series' [*Game of Thrones* first aired in 2011], *Heaven's Gate* seems less problematic." For the first time, with the baggage removed, it was judged on its merits.

In 2007, Thierry Frémaux—always a fan of the movie—suggested to Cimino that *Heaven's Gate* should be restored. "He never answered me," he told me, "and then one day, I was having a drink at the Four Seasons in LA and suddenly—boom!—Michael was there. He said, 'Thierry, I don't want to restore the film. I don't want to go back to such bad memories.' Then later he contacted me and said, 'I'm going to do it!' "

Of course, it was Carelli who was instrumental in this. In 2011, she approached the most prestigious and passionate DVD company in the US and asked them if they would be interested in restoring and releasing *Heaven's Gate* at its original length of 219 minutes with her and Cimino's cooperation. The Criterion Collection's DVDs could not have been further removed from the mass-produced and cheap supermarket ones. The company pioneered the "Special Edition" concept, containing commentaries, documentaries, alternative endings, and deleted scenes—what they described as "a film school in a box." They had already restored such classics as *Citizen Kane, Les Enfants du Paradis,* and *Seven Samurai.*

It was not going to be a cheap project—the original negative of *Heaven's Gate* had been cut to make the short version of the movie, and existing prints were a mess and often incomplete. The restoration team had to scan each color-separation negative individually and combine them. Every scratched frame would have to be digitally restored, as would the muddy soundtrack. It took a year to complete the work. Joann Carelli told me that Cimino was initially reluctant to get involved—he did not want to revisit something so painful—and he had not watched the movie for more than thirty years. After he agreed, he told Curtis Tsui, who was in charge of the project at Criterion, that the main reason he was doing it was that he wanted the much-maligned Carelli to finally get the credit she deserved.

The work was done on the Sony lot in Culver City. Tsui told me that Cimino was nervous as it started, but his obsessive attention to detail did not take long to resurface. "There was an exacting quality to him. I had to provide exact data to him, nothing imprecise. Talking to him was not quite a minefield, but definitely a situation where I had to think about what I said," he said. Nonetheless, "there was a charm to him, a real raconteur who told great stories."

The most radical change Cimino made was to the look of the movie. When originally released, he and the cinematographer, Vilmos Zsigmond, had overlaid the images with a sepia tone, making the Old West look as if it was shrouded in cigar smoke. It was certainly atmospheric, but it was one of the many things critics hated: Roger Ebert said, "Why is 'Heaven's Gate' so painful and unpleasant to look at? . . . This is one of the ugliest films I have ever seen." Now Cimino removed the tint, and the results were astonishing—the snowy mountains of Montana had never looked so pristine, the lush landscape had never looked so green. It enabled people who had already seen the movie many years before to look at it freshly and judge it anew.

The boxed set included an interview with Cimino and Carelli (even though she hardly said a word), and separate ones with Kris Kristofferson and David Mansfield. To the astonishment of the Criterion staff,

Mansfield brought his violin to the office and played the Heaven's Gate waltz for them.

After the work was finished, Cimino phoned Curtis Tsui: "Michael told me how gratifying the entire experience of remastering the film had been. I couldn't have been more thrilled to hear his words, not only because we'd been able to match his standards, but also because he was finally, rightfully able to find joy in his film once more. So I stuttered out a reply. 'Wow, Michael, that really means a lot to me. I don't know what to say.' [Cimino said,] 'What about "Thank you," Curtis?' Sometimes "Thank you" is enough.'"

The Criterion restoration was premiered at the sixty-ninth Venice Film Festival in August 2012. The movie had been shown there in 1982 to booing and slow hand-claps. Now its reception was ecstatic. Cimino spoke briefly before the screening: "I've had enough rejection for thirty-three years. Being infamous is never fun." The journalist Harlan Kennedy—in an extraordinary indication of Cimino's revised status—noted, "Martyrdom never is. We remember another fellow who had a difficult life for thirty-three years before qualifying for the word 'crucified.'"

The first screening in the United States was in November at Lincoln Center—the tickets sold out in ten minutes. In Cimino's speech, he called New York, where the first brutal reviews of the movie had come out, "the scene of the crime," and spoke of his initial reluctance to get involved. "The thought of it was like revisiting Golgotha," but Carelli had persuaded him: "Joann has a way of making you say yes when you're saying no." Kris Kristofferson was at the screening and said, "It was a catastrophe for both our careers, but it was worth it." After the screening, there was a standing ovation.

The new version was glowingly reviewed everywhere and became a news story. *Mostly Film*: "It seems inconceivable that this bold and strikingly beautiful film could ever have been described in the press as 'an unqualified disaster.'" The London *Independent*: "*Heaven's Gate* is back in a new director's cut—and (whisper it) it may go down as a masterpiece." *The New Yorker*: "Distinctive, passionate, grand, intimate, devastating." *AV Club*: "It's a film of rare beauty and scope, a feast for the eyes and a harrowing, unflinching meditation on the cruelty of capitalism." *Financial Times*: "Greatness took time to arrive: it has taken, you could say, 32 years. . . . Centreless? Or multicentred? Does *War and Peace* have a centre?""

Some critics discovered a relevance to it that nobody had picked up on before. The BBC's Nicholas Barber said, "To hear the Stockgrowers denouncing these immigrants as 'thieves and anarchists' . . . is to imagine a screenwriter parodying some of Donald Trump's more divisive remarks. There hasn't been a more urgently topical film." Dana Stevens wrote in *Slate*, "[*Heaven's Gate's*] relentlessly unheroic vision is clearly in part intended as a commentary on the Vietnam War"—something of an achievement for a director who had had no intention of commenting on the Vietnam War in the movie he had actually made about it. Now, too, critics were noting directors they thought had been inspired by *Heaven's Gate*: Richard Brody wrote in *The New Yorker*, "Even Martin Scorsese's use of 3-D in *Hugo* [in 2011] is reminiscent of Cimino's detail-popping tableaux and vertiginous whirl of action."

With the release of the director's cut, something was possible that hadn't been possible before: you could actually see the full version of the movie. It had only been shown for less than a week in one movie theater in New York thirty-two years before. As well as the reviews, the release of the Criterion restoration received a great deal of publicity, and there was social media that allowed people to voice their opinion. And, of course, there was the excitement of discovering what seemed like buried movie treasure—almost as exciting as it would have been to uncover the sixty minutes of lost footage from Orson Welles's brutally butchered *The Magnificent Ambersons*.

It seemed that everyone now loved the movie. Curtis Tsui told me that after the New York screening he, Carelli, and Cimino went out for a dinner that extended into the early morning. All the while, waiting for him to finish eating, two teenage boys, born years after *Heaven's Gate* was first released, waited patiently outside the restaurant, both of them holding a poster of the movie that they wanted the great director to sign.

CHAPTER 18

JUNE 30, 2016

ALTHOUGH CIMINO'S STATURE as a director had been largely restored, Hollywood—not caring much about European and American critics' reevaluation of a flop movie from more than thirty years earlier—still had a residual hostility to him. Industry people treated him with little respect. In an act of extreme discourtesy by one director to another, Steven Soderbergh, the director of the *Ocean's 11* series, posted on his website a version of *Heaven's Gate* in 2014 that he called with some accuracy "The Butcher's Cut." He had deleted two hours from the movie. Brazenly he announced, "I acknowledge that what I have done with this film is both immoral and illegal." Soderbergh enjoyed this kind of thing: he had also recut *2001: A Space Odyssey* to 110 minutes and changed *Raiders of the Lost Ark* into a silent, black-and-white movie. Although Soderberg's cut was in some ways a travesty, it counterintuitively underlines the strength of Cimino's movie: it is a different experience cut down to 90 minutes, but it holds together remarkably well.

Few spoke warmly of Cimino in Hollywood. The actor Richard Dreyfuss, who had never met him, made an extraordinarily vicious attack on BBC radio: "I saw Steven Spielberg one night at a restaurant, and he was sitting with this guy, and after about two minutes I said to Steven,

'Would you come outside for a moment?' I say, 'Who is that guy you're sit-ting with?' and he says, 'It's Cimino.' I said, 'Well, I got this bath of nega-tive, horrible, disgusting vibes from him. He's a disgusting creature.'"

Whatever negative vibes Dreyfuss may have felt, Cimino had become rather a benign figure in the years before his death. In 2009, he helped Ali Mostafa, a young director from the United Arab Emir-ates, to realize his first low-budget feature film, *City of Life*. Mostafa was overwhelmed by his generosity: "A great filmmaker and great man. He guided me never to lose sight of what I believed as a filmmaker and, most importantly, as a man." His friends noticed a softening to him. His once spiky personality was overlaid with a warmth and vulnerability that they had not often seen before. The actress and director Irene Miracle told me that she felt closer to him as he began to change into a different Cimino. "He was warm and compassionate, rather demure. I loved him for his honesty and insight," she said.

He was also generous to people who had once been the target of his displeasure. His friend F. X. Feeney told me, "He took deliberate care to mend fences with as many people as he could, including me. He told me, 'I have to face up to the fact that there are too many people out there I've treated very shabbily.' You could feel that sort of private reckoning."

Katy Haber, whom he had treated unkindly when they worked together on *The Sicilian* in 1986 and had not seen him since then, ran into him at the Locarno festival in 2015. Haber told me that he said an apology for his behavior on the movie was long overdue. He hated the producer David Begelman, he told her, and had taken it out on her. He asked her to forgive him.

Penny Shaw, whom he had been so close to until he cut her off after *Heaven's Gate*, told me that she was astonished to receive a phone call from Joann Carelli in 2008. She had not spoken to either her or Cimino for nearly thirty years. Carelli told her that Michael wanted her to edit the short movie he was making for the sixtieth anniversary of the Cannes Film Festival. Shaw had left the industry long ago and said that she couldn't do it, but she was touched that they had asked her, even though she was a little hurt that Cimino had not made the call himself. In the years before his death, at festivals and in interviews, he often told the story of how people were crying in the lobby after the first screening of *The Deer Hunter* in 1978. He always mentioned Shaw by name as the person who had dragged him out of the screening to come and see them.

In 1979, he had sacked his lawyer, Eric Weissmann—who had negotiated his extraordinary contract with United Artists for *Heaven's Gate*—because he had been unable to reach him one weekend and was outraged to find he was at the Kentucky Derby. Weissmann told me that Cimino then wrote him a three-page, single-spaced letter listing his shortcomings as a lawyer. Now he apologized and asked him if he would take him back as a client. He became close to Weissmann and his analyst wife, Mary Lou, and was often at their house. Shortly before his death, they came home from a walk to find Cimino waiting for them alone in the sitting room. He had asked the housekeeper to let him in because he just felt like spending time with them.

Although he continued to see some friends, a great deal of his communication was on the telephone. He spent time in Europe and on the East Coast with Carelli and Calantha, but his life became more circumscribed in Los Angeles. He had lost touch with Cindy Lee Duck, whom he had been close to. Van Robinson, his driver from *Heaven's Gate*, told me, "I probably didn't see him for the last five years of his life. I'd call when I was in LA, but he never picked up anymore. He just shut me out. He was obviously pretty sick. He didn't look the same man at all, like he was chasing a ghost. It seemed to go against the way he looked at life. Maybe I didn't know him like I thought."

Cimino stayed mostly inside his home, where his life could be as different from the outside world as he wanted it to be. As usual, he showed different sides of himself to the people he saw. His friend Stefan Wenta told me, "Ten days before he died, we went out for dinner. He was so happy," but Irene Miracle said that she "could feel his loneliness and pain."

Valerie Driscoll, who knew one side of him better than anybody, guessed his life had become difficult. Cindy Lee Duck was emphatic that he never drank, but Driscoll told me that after ten dry years, Cimino started again: "He had trouble sleeping and started using pills as well. Sometimes I would be talking to him and he would fall asleep on the phone. I stayed on the line to hear his gentle snoring and read him bedtime stories. I knew he was depressed and drinking again and invited him to stay with me. He could have had his own room, and I said I would prepare meals if he didn't want to go out. He screamed at me, saying, 'You can't force me to do anything!' After we hung up, I'm like, 'I'll wait till he calls me back.' He never did. That was the last time we spoke."

"When I last had lunch with Michael, on June 19, he was full of energy and plans," his friend F. X. Feeney told me. "That last day he was more reflective than I'd ever known him to be about his early life—'My dad's on my mind.' He said he was a ruthless perfectionist. His hobby was tying flies for fishing, he would build fishing rope. 'Those beautiful rods . . . ,' Michael said."

A few weeks before his death, Cimino consulted a physician about a mild respiratory complaint, but otherwise suffered no signs of ill health. "Nevertheless," Feeney said, "because he was an intuitive man, I feel certain that he had an inkling his life was drawing to a close. He was flying east in a few days, and I said, 'Why don't we check in with each other before you go?' He smiled, sunglasses flashing, as he clapped a hand on my shoulder. 'No need.' I think he was telling me goodbye, but I didn't know it."

After June 28, Feeney said that Cimino stopped returning phone calls. Nobody could reach him. Carelli, in the Hamptons, got in touch with his lawyer, Eric Weissmann, and he alerted the police. They broke into the house on June 30 and found him dead. He was seventy-seven. Carelli told me that Calantha was in Greece, and she had to call her with the news. There was no formal press release about his death. The first person she got in touch with was Thierry Frémaux: "Joann sent me a message saying that Michael had passed away. It was a surprise. He was in good health, but he was so mysterious as a human being. I couldn't get in touch with Joann, but I thought it was official, so I posted a message on Twitter." The message was picked up by *People* magazine and read: "Michael Cimino died peacefully, surrounded by his family and the two women who loved him." Frémaux had presumed that was the case, but Cimino had not seen any members of his family for thirty years, and neither of "the two women who loved him" were in Los Angeles at the time of his death. This was just one of the pieces of misinformation that made Cimino's death as confusing as his life.

There were many obituaries, most of them respectful, even though all of them centered on the disaster of *Heaven's Gate*. The headline of one cruelly stated, "Cimino Is Gone, Although He 'Died' Decades Ago." One thing the obituaries had in common was that they all gave his date of death as July 2, even though he had died somewhere between June 28 and June 30. Even in death, it was impossible to pin Cimino down.

There were a few pro forma statements from industry figures—William Friedkin: "I wish I had paid tribute to Michael Cimino while he was alive"—but because so few people knew him, there were almost no personal tributes except one from F. X. Feeney: "A beautiful textbook tough guy. That was my friend, Michael. He was also profoundly sensitive—quick to anger, if he felt unjustly dealt with, or meanly slighted. (He could often be rude to others as a result. That this was a childlike defensive tactic was never much consolation to those he was rude to.) Yet his deepest instincts inclined toward kindness—and my most abiding memories of him will always be of his no-holds-barred generosity, of his diamond-like self-discipline, and his ability to suffer life's body blows with such stoic pride, courageously and without complaint."

The confusion about his death escalated. Even as other newspapers were running obituaries, *Rolling Stone* stated, "A representative for the director could neither 'confirm or deny' whether Cimino had died." The *Hollywood Reporter* listed his survivors as his nephew, T. Rafael Cimino; his grandniece, Stephanie; and five cousins called Capozzoli. However, *Variety* reported that there were "no survivors."

The *New York Times* ran its obituary on July 3. On July 22, a correction was printed: "An earlier version of this obituary included a reference to the screenwriter and producer T. Rafael Cimino as Mr. Cimino's nephew. That relationship was later questioned, and the reference has been removed because it could not be independently confirmed. T. Rafael Cimino did not respond to email requests for comment." The following day, there was a further correction: "An obituary . . . on July 3 . . . using information from a friend and former lawyer, referred incorrectly to the survivors. They include two brothers, Peter and Edward; it is not the case that he left no immediate survivors."

With the newspapers not being able to agree on something as simple as who survived an internationally known movie director, Cimino was as mysterious in his death as his life. Neither Joann Carelli or Calantha

Mansfield were mentioned in any of the obituaries. However, on the memorial website that Forest Lawn cemetery had set up, there was a moving message: "With great regret we announce the passing of Michael Cimino, beloved, extraordinary, exceptional and loving friend, husband and father. Michael passed away of natural causes, peacefully in his sleep. Our hearts are broken—Joann and Callie. We love you forever."

As Calantha was not his daughter, there was no particular reason to believe that Carelli was his wife. However, months later, I found a tiny piece on the website mynewsLA.com about Cimino's will: "*Deer Hunter* Oscar director's widow named to oversee estate." She was identified as "Joan [*sic*] Carelli." If they did wed, Carelli had had a second marriage as private as her first to David Mansfield.

One of the many other confusions about Cimino's death was what precisely he had died of. The Los Angeles County coroner's office deferred a cause of death, pending investigation. The results of that investigation were never released.

As there was no information about his death, it was inevitable that speculation would take its place, and—as always with Cimino—there was no consistency to it. One friend, who asked not be named, believed he had died by suicide. Another one, who had known and worked with Cimino for many years, told me, "Natural causes? I just tend to doubt that." Irene Miracle wondered if he was suffering from terminal cancer. Roanna Martin-Trigona had the most extreme theory: "It was not suicide. I think someone came in and killed him. The whole thing was hushed up. Knowing Michael, that would not be unlikely. He did like to rile people." F. X. Feeney simply said, "I don't know what he died of, and prefer to honor his privacy."

As most of his friends did not know one another, there was no opportunity for any kind of communal mourning. Nor was there a memorial or a funeral. For Hollywood, the uncertainties of Cimino's life segued seamlessly into the mystery of his death.

CHAPTER 19

WIZARD

CIMINO HAD ALWAYS been elusive, and his two other brothers proved to be equally so. All T. Rafael Cimino (Todd) had been able to tell me was that his father, Peter, had been dead for fifteen years. He knew nothing about the whereabouts of the other two brothers, Edward and Christopher, or even if they were alive. He had never met them. Todd had told me that all the brothers had left their hometown on Long Island as soon as they could, fleeing a toxic family and never going back. Michael's own stories bore this out, but strangely, I found the surviving members of the Cimino family where the story started—in the house they had grown up in in Westbury.

I found a telephone number for an Edward Cimino, and I called it. When a man answered, I told him who I was looking for. He said, "Edward's not here. This is his brother Peter." That was surprising—I believed that Peter had been dead for many years. Just as surprising was the fact that he said there was no younger brother called Christopher. In a very brief conversation, he told me that he and Edward never spoke about Michael. However, a few days later, I received an email: "I talked to my brother and he and I agree that I should meet with you to help clear up a lot of misinformation, some of it by Michael, that is out there about him."

Cimino with his parents, 1939 (Photograph
courtesy Lucy Cimino archive)

It turned out that the brothers had not fled the "toxic" family that Michael described. In fact, Peter had never left Westbury and had lived for years in the Cimino family home on Whitney Street. He had taken over his father's music publishing business after his death and later started a company called North Fork Wine Cellar Designs, building custom wine cellars for collectors. Edward lived in New York City and then moved to Florida fifteen years later, where he is a real estate broker. The brothers are still close. In 2019, they sold the family house, and Peter moved to Southold on the North Fork of Long Island, by coincidence an hour's drive from Carelli and Cimino's adjoining beach houses in East Hampton. We met in a private wine club called Roanoke Vineyards near his home.

When Peter got up to greet me, I saw the first of many contradictions in Michael's story: he had said, "My siblings were like him [their father], tall and thin. I was just a tiny kid." In fact, Peter was not particularly tall. If Michael had been a "tiny kid," so would his brother have been.

At the end of his email to me, Peter had made a curious statement: "Just to let you know, you should not believe anything said or given to you by T. Rafael Cimino." We spoke about him first, and Peter told me forcefully, "He is in no way related to Michael or our family." Clearly he was not the son of the Peter Cimino I was talking to now (who has no children). I told him what Todd had said to me about the confusing references to survivors in the various obituaries: "They wanted to know who Michael was survived by. I gave them the first list. Then it was changed. What happened was that they had sent three or four emails to me wanting to know about Edward. I had no communication with Edward, had no way to confirm, to deny. They're asking me to be the family spokesman for a family I hadn't even met."

Peter filled in the family's version of the story, and as he spoke, Todd's account, which had initially seemed so plausible, began to shimmer like a mirage. The family had been bothered by Todd's claims for many years. When Michael died, he and Edward had seen the reference to T. Rafael Cimino as a surviving nephew they had no knowledge of, with no mention of them—the surviving brothers—and they asked Edward's son-in-law, an attorney, to write a cease-and-desist letter to him. They never heard from him.

Cracks began to show in Todd's story—the only Christopher Cimino was Edward's son, not his brother. There was also the fact that Todd's "father," Peter, seemed to be both dead and alive at the same time. Todd told me that he had been represented by Michael's lawyer, Eric Weissmann, but when I checked with him, Weissman emailed me to say, "I don't remember any of the things T. Rafael told you as being true." When I asked Todd if he knew Carelli, there was a long pause and he said, "Um, that's a good question. That's a blank, a complete blank."

Peter reiterated that he and the rest of the family had no idea who Todd was. He said there were few remaining Ciminos, and he knew all of them, but it was just about possible that Todd could be a very distant cousin. It seemed fitting that Michael, a man who was continually rebooting his past, should have a shadow figure following behind him with an equally confusing story about Michael's past and his own. When I emailed Todd to ask if he could help me with some of the contradictions, he did not answer.

The Cimino brothers (Photograph courtesy
Lucy Cimino archive)

When we began talking about Michael, Peter said, "I hope you
can tell me something about him. I hadn't seen him for thirty years."
Cimino once defined his relationship with his brothers as "nothing,
nothing, nothing," and would not even say what they were called—"no
one's goddamned business." Peter said that the "nothing" was only true
for those last thirty years, and it had been entirely Michael's doing. The
family had never wanted to lose touch with him and were very hurt by
his conscious denial of the relationship.

It was true that the brothers had not spent that much time with
Michael as children. Peter was four years younger than him, Edward eight
years younger—and they had gone to different schools. Originally, the single public high school was in Old Westbury, which Michael attended—his
only connection, despite his fanciful statement that his father was "like
a Vanderbilt or a Whitney," to the more privileged Gold Coast side of the

tracks. His younger brothers went to a newly built school on the other side of the divide, in Carle Place. Michael may not have been particularly involved in their lives because of the age difference, but they looked up to him: F. X. Feeney told me that his uncle had grown up in Westbury and had gone to school with Cimino's brothers. "They were always talking about him. He was a legend to them—their genius brother."

Peter told me that he had no idea why Michael had written himself out of his family's story. He felt that everything had changed after the disaster of *Heaven's Gate* in 1980, but in fact, the stories about his terrible childhood had begun some years before, even though he was still in touch with the family at that point. Peter had had a relatively warm relationship with Michael up till then, although they did not meet often. He saw him sometimes in New York in the 1960s, when Michael was working there, and remembered a business trip he had made to Los Angeles for the family music publishing company in 1974. Michael was working on *The Rose* screenplay at the time, and he welcomed Peter in his swanky Rolls-Royce convertible. He had taken him around the studio and showed him his house—the only time Peter ever saw it. "I felt comfortable with him," he told me. Edward's son, Christopher, remembers his father telling him that he used to stay with Michael in New York and took him to wild parties and bought him a Jaguar.

Michael had invited Peter, his wife, and their mother to attend the premiere of *Heaven's Gate* with him in 1980, and he often came to family events. He was at their mother's sixtieth birthday party, but Peter felt he only came because he happened to be in New York at the time. He was at her second wedding in October 1983 to Michael Zadis (their father had died in 1975), and he walked her down the aisle. Peter believes that that was the last time Michael saw their mother, who lived for another twenty-seven years.

He told Valerie Driscoll that one of the problems he had with his family was that he did not like his new stepfather. However, Peter pointed out that he met him only once—at the wedding. Pat, Michael's girlfriend when he lived in New York, was close to the family and remained so after she and Michael parted, but Carelli had no relationship with them at all.

The most glaring divergence in the brothers' stories was around Michael's relationship with his parents. Peter said the Ciminos were

Michael and his mother at her
wedding (Photograph courtesy Peter
Cimino)

a warm and loving family with an extended clan of grandparents and
cousins. However, Michael's only warm recollection of his family was
his grandmother taking him to the movies "three times a week" (his
grandparents had stayed in Brooklyn when the rest of the family moved
to Westbury when he was ten). Michael implied that their mother was
cold and their father was macho and domineering, that he had had to
take up wrestling to please him and to keep up with his "tall" brothers.
Peter told me that their father was not particularly athletic and not much
of a disciplinarian.

Michael painted a picture of parents who "ignored" their son, which
is not how Peter remembers it. Michael said they were totally dismissive of
his career and himself. He was angry that his father, also called Michael,
did not speak to him for a year because of it. However, Peter told me
that when their father died, Michael insisted on paying for the funeral
expenses and went back to Westbury to be part of it. About his mother,

Cimino with his parents and brothers at his graduation, 1956 (Photographs courtesy Lucy Cimino archive)

he said, "We have very bad relations. Don't go there." According to him, she mentioned his success only when his name was a clue in the *New York Times* crossword after he became famous with *The Deer Hunter*. In fact, Peter told me, his mother always saved any newspaper clipping that mentioned Michael and was simply joking when she said that she finally knew he was successful when she saw the crossword—she had always known it.

Peter said, they were delighted by Michael's success and Oscar triumph. They had never been in any doubt that whatever he chose to do, he would have had an extraordinary career: "He could have been an incredible artist if he hadn't been a director. We watched the Oscar ceremony when he won and we were all so excited." According to Peter, not only were their parents always immensely proud of Michael, but his mother idolized him. Interviewed by the local paper, she was described as being "overwhelmed by her son's success."

Peter felt that she was the one who found it the most difficult when Michael vanished from their lives in the mid 1980s. "She was a very strong woman. She never said it was painful. She never verbalized it, not once, but she held very close to her the yearly Christmas cards he sent until she died in 2010." What upset Peter was that Westbury was just off the Long Island Expressway that went to East Hampton, where Michael and Carelli spent a great deal of time. "Who can't make a fifteen-minute detour to see their mother?" he said angrily. His mother, he told me, always believed that one day Michael would return home for a visit, but he never did. Peter's wife, Lori, made an album of photographs of Michael for his mother, who added little notes to the pictures. "You are so beautiful," she wrote alongside a baby picture. Next to another photo, she wrote, "Handsome—wish I could see you."

Around 1986, Peter spent some time in the Hamptons with Michael and Carelli. He had a business agreement with his brother and was remodeling several houses that Carelli had bought there. They were cordial to him but not particularly friendly. Peter said, "I didn't really hang out with them. We never had a meal together." When I told Carelli I had met Peter, she made no comment and moved on to a different subject. A couple of years later, Peter ran into him by chance in the Hamptons. Then Michael was warmer, and he opened up to him about his sadness over his friend David Nagata's suicide. From time to time after, Peter tried to call Michael, but the number was always out of service.

When Lucy Cimino died in August 2010, the funeral notice described her as "Loving mother of Michael, Peter and Edward" and listed her three grandchildren, Edward, Christopher, and Michelle. Peter did not know how to contact Michael but told me, "We had some numbers for Joann and we left a message about my mother's passing." Michael did not call back, but Carelli got back to Peter to say that Michael wanted to know if his mother had the rosary beads he had once sent her from Rome. Peter said that she did, but Michael did not come to the funeral or speak to Peter. Afterward, Peter had to send him some legal papers that needed to be endorsed, and they were signed and returned with no note. When Michael died, according to his nephew, there was a specific provision in his will that stated that he left absolutely nothing to his two brothers or their children.

I asked Peter if Michael's attitude had been painful for him or if he had just accepted it. "A bit of both," he said. "We didn't talk much about him. It only came up when someone would ask if we were related." He added sadly, "Sometimes we said we weren't."

Lucy Cimino's photo album (Photograph
courtesy Lucy Cimino archive)

Peter put me in touch with his nephew, Edward's son, Christopher,
who lives with his wife and three German Shepherds in Upstate New
York, where he owns an outdoor clothing and equipment store. By the
time Michael vanished from the family in 1983, Chris was only two years
old and never met him, but has always been fascinated by his mysterious, unknown uncle. "When I was young, I would always ask questions:
'Where is he? Who is he?'" Although his father and Peter seldom talked
about him, "my grandmother would say only wonderful things about
him. She would sometimes call me Michael as a senior slip." Once,
Christopher tried to reach out to Michael. He found someone who said
he was a friend of his on Facebook, but—like Todd Cimino—it seemed
to be not entirely true, and the trail led nowhere.

Christopher told me something rather surprising: his sister,
Michelle, had actually been in touch with Calantha about twelve years
ago. "She met with her in the city, outside, in a park. Michelle told me

that Calantha just sort of stared at her, kind of taken aback—she had never seen anyone related to Michael. At one point she reached out and touched Michelle's arm and said how much she looked like Michael. Calantha asked if she could go meet Lucy, but Lucy was suffering from Alzheimer's in a care home and Michelle thought it was not a good idea."

Christopher told me he had spotted something extraordinary: "I knew that Michael had had a lot of plastic surgery, and in the last few pictures I saw of him, he was wearing sunglasses. If you put a pair of sunglasses on Lucy, you could hardly tell them apart."

THERE IS NOTHING more like *Rashomon* than siblings' memories of their childhood, and Peter acknowledged this. "Maybe Michael thought it was terrible—I don't know—but as far as my brother and I are concerned, what he says about his past is just not true." Even if Peter's past is actually less rosy than he remembers (Cimino's school friend Arthur French recalled that "Michael's parents were difficult. If you went over to the house, they wouldn't talk to you"), the divergences between the brothers' recollections are not ones of nuance or degree—they are descriptions of two utterly different pasts.

Cimino is certainly not the only person to feel different from their family and wish they had been born into another one—when he first went to New York, Bob Dylan said he was an orphan who had run away from the circus. However, in order to create the Michael Cimino he wanted to be, his family became collateral damage. Their "rejection" of him was an integral part of his story, implying that his triumph was to make it on his own with no support, love, or approval from them. Maybe he had the shame of the ordinary—there was nothing distinctive about his family that he could relish. They were a solid and honest middle-class Italian family. They were not aspiring to be creative or intellectual in any way, and their parameters were different from the ones he had set himself.

Just as he had sometimes denied screenwriters' contributions to ensure that his movies were seen as his sole creation, he seemed to sacrifice his family so it would seem as if his life was equally his creation, that despite them there was nothing ordinary about him. The irony is that there had never been anything ordinary about him in the first place. He was an astonishing talent who had come out of nowhere and reinvented himself. I think it's the "nowhere" that was so difficult for him—both literally and metaphorically. It was not an interesting enough backstory. That exciting tabloid mix of wealth and abuse, pain and striving, and then—against all the odds—success–was.

The hard thing to know is how much Cimino believed his own stories, or whether they were inventions that became true with repetition. What was curious is that there was no definitive version of his life, no final draft, no perfect circle drawn around it. Parts were added and subtracted, like a jazz musician's riffing or an actor's improvisation. What was true, and what was not? Maybe he was born in 1939 or 1951. Maybe he had fought in Vietnam. Maybe he created *The Deer Hunter* single-handedly. Maybe he had no facial surgery. Maybe he hung with the working-class bad boys even though he came from a privileged family and was educated at private schools. Whatever the variations, the central part of his story never changed. His family—whether old-money Wasp or middle-class Italian—was defined by conflict and pain, a childhood "like a Eugene O'Neill play," *Long Day's Journey into Night* played out in a Long Island suburb.

Even though he had created his kaleidoscopic persona himself, he found it hard to integrate the various Michael Cimino's into a single one. He told F. X. Feeney, "I googled myself one time. I don't know most of the people I've been." The many versions of himself that he showed to the world created a confusion that helped to hide one of his personae, the one that he had shared with Valerie Driscoll in Torrance, which possibly meant the most to him.

In *The Wizard of Oz*, the wizard presents himself to people in various forms: a giant head, a beautiful fairy, a ball of fire, a monster. When Dorothy and the others finally meet him, he is revealed as a small man hiding behind a giant curtain—a con man from Omaha who has used magic tricks to make himself seem "great and powerful." Cimino, too, presented himself in various forms—certainly as a ball of fire or a monster while making movies—but they were not a bluff to hide a minor talent. His skills as a director and his formidable intellect were always great and powerful. The figure behind the curtain was not a diminished version of him; it was simply a different one that he did not want to show, the one that came closest to the final draft that he could never quite pull together.

His tag line for *Heaven's Gate*—"The things one loves about life are the things that fade"—had been wrong. In fact, the things one loves about life are the things that do not fade. His reputation and the greatness of his first three movies certainly faded, but by the end of his life, and afterward, they came back into sharp focus. Which particular Michael Cimino he was, or wanted to be, has nothing much to do with it.

EPILOGUE

JOANN CARELLI SAID the reason she had left the house in the Hollywood Hills untouched after Cimino's death in 2016 was that clearing
it out was such a gargantuan task. She and Calantha have now started,
she told me. I never did get into that mysterious house. I suggested I
could help, an offer that Carelli passed over with no discernible reaction. At another dinner, she asked me where I thought his scripts
and papers should go, and I suggested the Harry Ransom Center at
the University of Texas (where Robert De Niro's archive is stored) or
the Academy's extensive collection of papers at the Margaret Herrick
Library in Los Angeles. Later, when I asked her what she had decided,
she was noncommittal.

Cimino had lived in the house for nearly forty-five years. In the
last twenty years of his life, Carelli did not go to Los Angeles often, but
Calantha spent time there with him—the only person who did. Only
they know what is in the house. Cimino worked constantly, so there will
be mountains of scripts, maybe still in the locked room that he could not
bear to go into. He was a compulsive reader, so there might be forty-five
years of books there, as well as contracts, files, and correspondence from
his long career. He never stopped painting, he said, although nobody I
talked to had ever seen any of them. "I'm starting to flirt with anorexia
again," he said in his memoir, so his fridge might have been as empty as

it was when the visitor found the sandwich with a bite taken out of it and the half bottle of champagne in it. I never asked Carelli about Cimino's transformation in his later years, but Valerie Driscoll told me that he stored his wardrobe of women's clothes there.

The house will eventually be sold, as their two neighboring apartments in the United Nations Plaza in New York already have been. Carelli has bought an apartment close by, she told me. She is keeping the two adjacent houses on the beach in East Hampton. Calantha lives in New York. She worked for a small French movie distribution company but now has a career in fine art. When she was young, Cimino was proud that she was a "champion jumper" on her horse, Lord Byron, and she still rides. She and Carelli are very involved in the affairs of East Hampton. Along with her mother and other local residents like Steven Spielberg and Deepak Chopra, she sponsors a scholarship at the prestigious Ross School, providing tuition for students from southern African countries. Carelli is still the keeper of the Cimino flame. She

Cimino, Calantha Mansfield, and Joann Carelli, Lyon, 2014 (Alamy)

spends time in Europe, looking for funding for movies based on some of his unproduced scripts.

Calantha spent the grim Covid summer of 2020 at Cimino's house. Joann stayed in New York. One afternoon in June, she called me from there, and when I asked her how she was coping with the problems of living with the pandemic and the demonstrations and the riots, she laughed and said, "After *Heaven's Gate?*"

ACKNOWLEDGMENTS

There are many people to thank for their help. Firstly, John Preston, himself a distinguished biographer, who suggested writing a book about Michael Cimino when I had run out of ideas for novels and had never even considered nonfiction. He pushed me to do it and then helped all the way through.

This book would have been hard to write without the extraordinary support of F. X. Feeney, who died on February 5, 2020. We always met at Coogie's in Santa Monica, where he ate with Cimino often, and over many talks, he shared the story of their long friendship. He suggested people to see and let me read his unpublished autobiography, as well as a moving memoir he wrote about Cimino. His expertise and knowledge about movies and directors were unparalleled, and his death leaves a huge gap in film scholarship.

Penny Shaw Sylvester was enormously generous with her time, and we had many meetings in Agoura Hills, where she lives. She revealed a warm and needy side to Cimino that he did not often show, and she was by his side during the two years he took to make, edit, and reedit *Heaven's Gate*. She suggested a variety of people for me to see and took a great deal of trouble to organize meetings with them. She also let me use her photographs taken in Montana during shooting.

Katy Haber, the doyenne of the British filmpack in Los Angeles who worked with Cimino on *The Deer Hunter* and *The Sicilian*, gave me a pile of production files and memos written by Cimino during the making of the latter—normally the first things that are thrown away after a production has finished. They were extraordinarily revealing about the way Cimino operated as a director on the movies he made after *Heaven's Gate*.

Meeting Peter Cimino, and his decision to talk about his brother for the first time, unlocked the key to many aspects of Cimino and the past he hid behind a smoke screen. Some of these were painful areas for Peter, and I'm grateful for his kind cooperation.

Christopher Cimino, Michael's nephew, gave me a fascinating perspective on how his uncle's strange legacy affected the second generation of Ciminos. He was kind enough to let me use photographs from his grandmother's album.

Cimino's school friend Mike Strasberg went out of his way to help me piece together what life was like in Westbury in the 1950s. He tracked down three other school friends I would never have been able to find otherwise. Sharp and witty, he acted as a kind of private detective. "I'm eighty," he told me. "I live in Arizona, I've been married to the same woman for forty years, and I've run out of box sets to watch. This is fun."

In Yucca Valley, Valerie Driscoll told me an extraordinary story about the most hidden aspect of Cimino's life. She did not particularly want to be found or to talk about what was a very private relationship, but her warmth and love for him shone through everything she told me.

I owe an unusual kind of debt to Joann Carelli, even though she did not contribute to, or collaborate with, this book in any conventional sense of those words. Her approval was neither asked for nor given. She has never sought any kind of biography of Cimino, and she has no interest in setting the record straight about either Cimino or herself. When the restored *Heaven's Gate* was shown in Venice in 2012, she said, "I don't want to revisit old, erroneous stories and try to correct them," and she didn't do that with me. She offered me no guidance. She did not give me access to any papers or his unproduced scripts like *Man's Fate* or *The Fountainhead*, which I found by other routes. She did not suggest people I might talk to, and she rarely asked about the book or who I was meeting. However, in her own unique way, she was enormously helpful, and our dinners were some of the high points of working on this book.

Our meetings and phone calls were wide-ranging conversations during which we talked about Cimino as well as other things. They were always fascinating because of her sharp intelligence and uncompromising belief in Cimino as a great artist. She was often abrasive, but at other times she could be quite warm and funny. The drawbridge would go up and down, but the areas she would talk about and those she evaded were revealing in themselves. She never wavered in her belief that most of the things written about Cimino are lies, although she acknowledged that the things he said about himself were not necessarily true either.

Once she said to me, "You'll figure it out," and I hope I have gone some way to doing that.

I interviewed more than eighty people either by telephone or in person. Some people who talked to me did not want to be identified. Others were happy to be quoted by name but asked me not to attribute some of the things they told me.

I want to thank the following:

In the United States: Rutanya Alda, Bill Brame, Melissa Bretherton, Bryan Buchanan, Sal Butta, Joann Carelli, Christopher Cimino, Peter Cimino, T. Rafael Cimino, Valerie Driscoll, Joe D'Augustine, John Dellaverson, Cindy Lee Duck, Pamela Dylina, Carol Eads, F. X. Feeney, David Field, David Freeman, Arthur French, Richard Gazda, Francis Grumman, Michael Gruskoff, Katy Haber, Patty Nelson Haglund, James B. Harris, Mady Kaplan, Charles Kauffmann, Larry Konner, Shanda Lear-Baylor, Charles Leavitt, Kona Luke, Freya Manfred, David Mansfield, Roanna Martin-Trigona, Bruce McNall, Irene Miracle, Thom Mount, George Parker, Michael Peretzian, Dean Pitchford, Thomas Pope, Quinn Redeker, Van Robinson, Samantha Roland, Marion Rosenberg, Mark Rosenthal, Al Ruddy, John Savage, Robert Shapiro, Barry Spikings, Michael Strasberg, Penny Shaw Sylvester, Curtis Tsui, Lucy Walker, Deric Washburn, Eric Weissmann, Mary-Lou Weissmann, Stefan Wenta, Irwin Winkler, Brian Wood, Cary Woods, and Garry Wunderwald.

In Europe: Jane Bonham Carter, Eleanor Fazan, Thierry Frémaux, Tess Gallagher, Lizi Gelber, Eoghan Harris, Charles Hubbard, Rupert Perry, Michael Stevenson, Alexandra Shulman, and Nicholas Woodeson.

There were others who were helpful in many different ways: Peter Biskind, John Brown, Julia Brown, Jane Charteris, Tim Corrie, Dan Edelman, Abraham Elton, Lotte Elton, Sue Freathy, Natasha Fairweather, Isaac Fitzsimons, Misha Glenny, Mike Hazard, Zoë Heller, William Humble, Andrew Jarvis, Steve Kenis, Margy Kinmonth, Kirsty Lang, Robert McCrum, John Penrose, Jonathan Powell, Minnie Scott-Russell, Christopher Silvester, Miriam Segal, Sarah Spankie, Rochelle Stevens, Heather Stewart, Nicholas Underhill, Rupert Walters, and Nick Ward.

My agents, Felicity Rubinstein at Lutyens Rubinstein in London and David Forrer at Inkwell Management in New York, were supportive of this from the beginning and offered much help and guidance all the way through.

Jamison Stoltz, editorial director of Abrams Press, took a chance on an English guy who had never written a biography writing one on an entirely American subject and then edited the manuscript brilliantly, with an enormous knowledge of movies.

Neil Jaworski was the best of movie friends. He was a screenwriter with an unbelievable knowledge of the most obscure British movies of the 1960s and '70s and the work of Saul Bass. He was as sharp and witty as the great Hollywood screenwriters and directors he loved, from Ernst Lubitsch to I. A. L. Diamond to Billy Wilder. He died ridiculously young in June 2019 at the age of forty-three. This would be a better book if he had been able to help me through its final stages.

NOTES AND SOURCES

All interviews by the author unless stated otherwise

PROLOGUE

2 **a character in a crazy French novel:** Yannick Haenel, *Tiens ferme ta couronne* (Paris: Éditions Gallimard, 2019).

4 **"I am not who I am":** Steve Garbarino, "Michael Cimino's Final Cut," *Vanity Fair*, March 2002.

5 **One day they were working at the house:** Eleanor Fazan interview, April 19, 2018.

CHAPTER 1: THE TARNISHED COAST

Michael Strasberg interview, August 5, 2019; Arthur French interview, November 13, 2019; Charles Kauffman interview, November 9, 2019; Richard Gazda interview, October 25, 2019

T. Rafael Cimino material from interview, February 18, 2019.

11 **"he was very quiet, very somber":** Barbara Grywin interview with Lucy Walker in her documentary short *Whatever Happened to Michael Cimino*, 2003.

13 **"Let's put an end to all this":** Steve Garbarino, "Michael Cimino's Final Cut," *Vanity Fair*, March 2002.

14 **"One doesn't need to know":** Jean-Baptiste Thoret, *Michael Cimino, Les voix perdues de l'Amérique* (Paris: Flammarion, 2014), 34. English version by Lucas Carvallo-Phillips.

14 **"Nothing, nothing, nothing.":** Nancy Griffin, "Last Typhoon Cimino Is Back," *New York Observer*, February 11, 2002.

14 **she was amazed to take a phone call:** Patty Nelson interview, April 26, 2019.

14 **he had not lost his resentment:** Garbarino, "Michael Cimino's Final Cut."

14 **"We have very bad relations.":** Griffin, "Last Typhoon."

15 **"Mr. Cimino grew up in Old Westbury":** Griffin, "Last Typhoon."

15 **His father, he said:** Garbarino, "Michael Cimino's Final Cut."

15 **"I was always hanging out":** Jean Vallely, "Michael Cimino's Battle to Make a Great Movie," *Esquire*, January 2, 1979.

15 **"Michael is an aristocrat":** Thoret, *Michael Cimino*, 184.

16 **"I was a child prodigy.":** Garbarino, "Michael Cimino's Final Cut."

16 **He told a story of walking:** David Field interview, September 26, 2019, an anecdote quoted to him by Joann Carelli, Kalispell, 1979.

CHAPTER 2: COFFEE MOMENT IN MALIBU

Yesterdays material from Lincoln Diamant, ed., *The Anatomy of a Television Commercial: The Story of Eastman Kodak's "Yesterdays"* (New York: Hastings House, 1970).

20 **He never saw him chasing women:** David Freeman interview, June 19, 2018.

20 **"I used to walk by the drama school":** Jean Vallely, "Michael Cimino's Battle to Make a Great Movie," *Esquire*, January 2, 1979.

21 **"They taught me how to use":** Leticia Kent, "Ready for Vietnam? A Talk with Michael Cimino," *New York Times*, December 10, 1978.

21 **"I met some people":** Nancy Griffin, "Last Typhoon Cimino Is Back," *New York Observer*, February 11, 2002.

21 **had heard a less glamorous:** Francis Grumman interview, July 10, 2018.

22 **"That dynamic period":** George Lois, "TV 'Mad Men' Real? I Don't Think So," interview, CNN, March 27, 2012.

23 **"Pablo's apartment was a beehive":** Julian Barry, *My Night with Orson* (Self-published, CreateSpace Independent Publishing, 2011), 91.

23 **an intriguing picture of Cimino's desire:** Sal Butta interview, October 2, 2019.

24 **Alan Pakula, later to direct:** Harry Ufland to Alan Pakula, December 27, 1963, in Alan J. Pakula papers, Margaret Herrick Library, Academy of Motion Picture Arts and Sciences.

24 **Francis Grumman, a cameraman there, told me:** Grumman interview.

25 **"Do you remember":** Griffin, "Last Typhoon."

25 **"He lived well and partied":** Grumman interview.

25 **George Parker was an English:** George Parker interview, May 29, 2018.

25 **he remembered Cimino asking him:** Michael Strasberg interview, August 5, 2019.

26 **"Most directors were doing it":** Grumman interview.

28 **"Michael would just bulldoze":** Grumman interview.

28 **worked with Cimino for two years:** Parker interview.

28 **"Mike decided that it would be a nice":** George Parker, *Confessions of a Mad Man* (Boise: Parker Communications, 2014).

CHAPTER 3: THE SECRET WORLD

31 **Patty Nelson, Cimino's longtime secretary:** Patty Nelson interview, April 26, 2019.

31 **"[Cimino] sat down and ceremoniously":** Nancy Griffin, "Last Typhoon Cimino Is Back," *New York Observer*, February 11, 2002.

32 **"A talented person chooses":** Dale Pollock, "Women and Power: The New Hollywood," *Los Angeles Times*, 1980.

32 **she said rather aggressively:** Joann Carelli dinner conversation, June 6, 2018.

32 **"My girl. . . .":** Olivier Nicklaus, "Michael Cimino—American Psycho," *Les Inrockuptibles*, September 25, 2001.

32 **"She's simply the person I trust":** Jean-Baptiste Thoret, *Michael Cimino, Les voix perdues de l'Amérique* (Paris: Flammarion, 2014), 12. English version by Lucas Carvallo-Phillips.

32 **"She was indispensable. . . .":** Thoret, *Michael Cimino*, 36.

32 **"We were deeply":** Steve Garbarino, "Michael Cimino's Final Cut," *Vanity Fair*, March 2002.

32 **"Giovanna is her real name":** Transcript of amateur film footage, Locarno Film Festival, 2015.

32 **When I asked her about it:** Joann Carelli dinner conversation, March 25, 2019.

32 **"I've had a lot of experience":** Garbarino, "Michael Cimino's Final Cut."

33 **"Cimino sat silently eating":** Email from Eoghan Harris, February 6, 2019.

33 **Carelli told me that she believed:** Joann Carelli dinner conversation, January 16, 2020.

33 **he had heard a story that:** Nicholas Woodeson interview, June 20, 2018.

34 **unlike many people who worked with Carelli:** Eleanor Fazan interview, April 19, 2018.

34 **When we met, she told me contemptuously:** Joann Carelli dinner conversation, January 6, 2018.

35 **"Carelli was his handler"**: George Parker interview, May 29, 2018.
36 **"She tried to protect him "**: Francis Grumman interview, July 10, 2018.
36 **She simply told me that she had no ego**: Carelli conversation, June 6, 2018.
36 **"They existed in a secret"**: Mady Kaplan interview, September 27, 2019.

CHAPTER 4: THUNDERBOLT IN HOLLYWOOD

37 **"Joann Carelli . . . actually talked me"**: Mark Patrick Carducci, "Stalking *The Deer Hunter*: An Interview with Michael Cimino," *Millimeter*, March 1978.
37 **"He took me to lunch"**: Deric Washburn interview, June 12, 2018.
38 **Gruskoff, now in his eighties**: Michael Gruskoff interview, June 11, 2018.
38 **"What a director does"**: Peter Brown, "Behind the 'Heaven's Gate' Disaster," *Washington Post*, November 30, 1980.
40 **"the thirteen years between Bonnie and Clyde"**: Peter Biskind, *Easy Riders, Raging Bulls* (New York: Simon & Schuster, 1988), 17.
42 **"Producer Mike Gruskoff is"**: A. H.Weiler, "A-Jive in Denmark," *New York Times*, February 22, 1970.
42 **"I used to know Mike Cimino quite well"**: "Thomas McGrath—A Conversation," *Another Chicago Magazine* 23, 1991.
42 **McGrath's archive**: McGrath papers, Chester Fritz Library, University of North Dakota.
43 **"I distinctly remember he came in the door"**: Freya Manfred interview, 1/2/21.
43 **"He had got to Universal"**: "Thomas McGrath—A Conversation."
44 **"I wanted to make a SF movie"**: Trumbull commentary, *Silent Running* DVD.
44 **"I don't find it interesting"**: Jorge Mourinha, "'I Never Knew How to Make a Film—Michael Cimino in 2005," *Filmmaker*, July 5, 2016.
45 **"It's just a job"**: Carducci, "Stalking *The Deer Hunter*."
45 **Cimino being overstretched**: Gruskoff interview.
45 **"My recollection is that we didn't"**: Washburn interview.
45 **"I have my own particular passions"**: Mark Kermode, *Silent Running*, British Film Institute, London, 2014.
47 **Gene Hackman to play the lead**: Gruskoff interview.
48 **"I had been going to California"**: Transcript of amateur film footage, Locarno Film Festival, 2015.
49 **Frank Yablans, then president**: Jean Vallely, "The Opening and Closing of Heaven's Gate," *Rolling Stone*, February 5, 1981.
49 **"I didn't go to film school"**: Mourinha, "'I Never Knew."
50 **She told me that when he didn't want to do it**: Joann Carelli dinner conversation, January 16, 2020.
50 **Milius, of course, did not like**: Alfio Leotta, *The Cinema of John Milius* (Lanham, MD: Lexicon Books, 2018), 42.
52 **"Mike looked at me and said"**: Michael Nordine, "Jeff Bridges Remembers Michael Cimino," *Indiewire*, July 5, 2016.
52 **"I knew that the only way"**: Nancy Griffin, "Last Typhoon Cimino Is Back," *New York Observer*, February 11, 2002.
53 **"I would go to Clint"**: Seth Abramovich, "Michael Cimino—the Full Uncensored *Hollywood Reporter* Interview," March 2, 2015.
53 **called it a proto-bromance**: Richard Brody, "Clint Eastwood and Jeff Bridges's Modern Western," *The New Yorker*, July 3, 2017
53 **"Tightass and Cocksucker"**: Peter Biskind, *Gods and Monsters* (New York: Nation Books, 2004).

53 **"This put my ego":** Carducci, "Stalking *The Deer Hunter*."

54 **"It was four years after":** Jean Vallely, "Michael Cimino's Battle to Make a Great Movie," *Esquire*, January 2, 1979.

54 **"In architecture, you're not looking":** Mourinha, "'I Never Knew.'"

55 **Steven Bach . . . noted with some relief:** Steven Bach, *Final Cut* revised edition (New York: Newmarket Press, 1999), 98.

55 **Statements that Cimino made:** Jean Vallely, "Michael Cimino's Battle."

CHAPTER 5: STALKING THE DEER HUNTER

59 **"People were just driving up":** Seth Abramovich, "Michael Cimino—the Full Uncensored *Hollywood Reporter* Interview," March 2, 2015.

62 **"I intended to stay the course":** Michael Deeley, *Blade Runners, Deer Hunters and Blowing the Blood Doors Off* (London: Faber & Faber, 2010), 131.

63 **In Cimino's later account of the meeting:** Jean Vallely, "Michael Cimino's Battle to Make a Great Movie," *Esquire*, January 2, 1979.

64 **"They said, 'OK. Do it.' ":** Vallely, "Michael Cimino's Battle."

64 **it was not a totally accurate account:** Marion Rosenberg interview, June 11, 2019.

64 **"all the frustrations of the previous":** Vallely, "Michael Cimino's Battle."

65 **she would bet on her life:** Marion Rosenberg interview, June 11, 2018.

66 **It was a good way of working:** Deric Washburn interview, June 12, 2018.

66 **"although it masquerades more easily":** Mark Patrick Carducci, "Stalking *The Deer Hunter*. An Interview with Michael Cimino," *Millimeter*, March 1978.

66 **"I don't know what provoked":** Abramovich, "Uncensored *Hollywood Reporter* Interview."

66 **"Most of the things in":** Vallely, "Michael Cimino's Battle."

67 **"The deer hunter concept came":** Washburn interview.

67 **Deeley, however, remembered that Cimino:** Deeley, 164.

68 **"I called him [Washburn] every single night":** Peter Biskind, "Peter Biskind on Michael Cimino's Tortured, Twisted Legacy," *Hollywood Reporter*, July 13, 2016.

68 **"At the end of every day":** Washburn interview.

69 **"He was a sweet little":** Geoffrey McNab, "*The Deer Hunter*: A Quietly British Film," London *Independent*, July 15, 2014.

69 **he should go into a meeting:** Joann Carelli dinner conversation, June 6, 2018.

69 **Rosenberg told me that she sensed trouble early on:** Rosenberg interview, June 11, 2018.

70 **Cimino was being "difficult":** Thom Mount interview, September 17, 2018.

70 **"Well, Deric, it's fuck-off":** Peter Biskind, "The Vietnam Oscars," *Vanity Fair*, February 19, 2008.

71 **"I could not believe what I read":** Biskind, "Vietnam Oscars."

71 **James Toback had written a script:** John Henry Gallagher, *Film Directors on Directing* (Westport, CT: Praeger, 1989).

72 **"Mike, looking back on the thing":** Washburn interview.

74 **Carelli told me that she did a lot:** Carelli conversation, June 6, 2018.

75 **Thom Mount called her:** Mount interview.

75 **"The first person we approached":** Vallely, "Michael Cimino's Battle."

75 **"I liked the story and dialogue":** Jay Glennie, "An Oral History of How Robert De Niro Was Cast in *The Deer Hunter*," *GQ*, December 19, 2019.

75 **Thom Mount told me that another actor:** Mount interview.

75 **Scheider was gone:** Diane C. Kachmar, *Roy Scheider—A Film Biography* (Jefferson, NC: McFarland & Company, 2002), 73.

76 **"If you're fool enough to ask":** Deeley, 170.

76 **"vague, stock girlfriend"**: Katrina Longworth, *Meryl Streep: Anatomy of an Actor* (New York: Phaidon Press, 2013), 19.

77 **Savage told me he could sense their bond**: John Savage interview, September 30, 2019.

77 **"I walked in and he [Cimino] asked me"**: Janet Maslin, "Movies 'Discover' Christopher Walken, *New York Times*, December 26, 1978.

77 **She told me that she wrote**: Joann Carelli phone conversation, May 27, 2018.

78 **"The good news was"**: Mount interview.

78 **in some ways took a sunnier view**: Barry Spikings interview, June 11, 2018.

78 **she never understands why people think**: Carelli conversation, June 6, 2018.

78 **"For a man of Bob's"**: Deeley, 171.

79 **Deeley described him as**: Deeley, 172.

79 **why he could not live at home**: Rosenberg interview, June 11, 2018.

79 **cast at the last moment**: Rutanya Alda interview, July 7, 2018.

80 **"It was a lot of fun"**: Savage interview.

80 **"He was a real pleasure"**: Alda interview.

80 **"Being in that movie with the spirit"**: Savage interview.

81 **There was another problem**: Vallely, "Michael Cimino's Battle."

82 **"a documentary with actors"**: Cimino commentary, *The Deer Hunter* DVD.

82 **why he had presumed she would be able**: Alda interview.

83 **"if I was Coppola"**: Alda interview.

84 **"This plan was to be advanced"**: Deeley, 173.

84 **he had a technique**: Penny Shaw interview, June 10, 2018.

84 **the actors were told that**: Alda interview.

84 **he had taken Cimino aside**: Spikings interview.

84 **Deeley believed that his fellow**: Deeley, 176.

84 **"It was such a beautiful wedding"**: Cimino commentary, *The Deer Hunter* DVD.

85 **"The mist is a gift from"**: Cimino commentary, *The Deer Hunter* DVD.

85 **"These little deer arrive"**: Vallely, "Michael Cimino's Battle."

86 **As soon as they arrived in Bangkok**: Vallely, "Michael Cimino's Battle."

87 **Spikings remembered that the general**: Spikings interview.

87 **"What would David Lean"**: Cimino commentary, *The Deer Hunter* DVD.

88 **"When you see the first shot"**: Vilmos Zsigmond, "Behind the Scenes of *The Deer Hunter*," *American Cinematographer*, October 1978.

88 **He told me he applied to be a runner on the movie**: Charles Hubbard interview, September 11, 2019.

89 **According to Carelli, John Peverall**: Joann Carelli dinner conversation, January 16, 2020.

89 **"Cimino ate him"**: Spikings interview.

89 **"We knew we were making something"**: Biskind, "Vietnam Oscars."

89 **They proposed that a small**: Vallely, "Michael Cimino's Battle."

90 **he was alarmed having to improvise**: Savage interview.

91 **"I was trying to make all this work"**: Vallely, "Michael Cimino's Battle."

91 **"had nothing to do with excess"**: Vallely, "Michael Cimino's Battle."

91 **Charles Hubbard remained in Thailand**: Hubbard interview.

92 **Spikings told me that he felt**: Spikings interview.

CHAPTER 6: THE BODY COUNT

93 **When Spikings and Deeley saw**: Michael Deeley, *Blade Runners, Deer Hunters and Blowing the Blood Doors Off* (London: Faber & Faber, 2010), 179.

94 **"was a continuing nightmare":** Thom Mount interview, September 7, 2018.
94 **brought him to LA to see:** Deric Washburn interview, June 12, 2018.
94 **"The first places people attack":** Jean Vallely, "Michael Cimino's Battle to Make a Great Movie," *Esquire,* January 2, 1979.
95 **"a cinematic event unto":** Mount interview.
95 **"Verna was no slouch":** Peter Biskind, "The Vietnam Oscars," *Vanity Fair,* February 19, 2008.
95 **"The thought that I would be":** Vallely, "Michael Cimino's Battle."
96 **he told me how moved he had been:** Irwin Winkler interview, October 2, 2019.
97 **Carelli told me that she had met:** Joann Carelli phone conversation, May 27, 2018.
98 **"In their Nazi wisdom":** Leticia Kent, "Ready for Vietnam? A Talk with Michael Cimino,'" *New York Times,* December 10, 1978.
98 **"I was informed that the credit":** Letter from Stephen Scharf to Leonard Chassman, executive director of the Writers Guild, July 3, 1978, Margaret Herrick Library, Los Angeles.
99 **More than that, Deeley was furious:** Deeley, 193.
99 **"I loved Michael":** Barry Spikings interview, June 11, 2018.
99 **"The one flaw I find":** Deeley, 5.
99 **"I came away with no respect":** Peter Biskind, "Peter Biskind on Michael Cimino's Tortured, Twisted Legacy," *Hollywood Reporter,* July 13, 2016.
100 **"It had been a war":** Vallely, "Michael Cimino's Battle."
100 **"the long Detroit screening":** Mount interview.
100 **He had bribed:** Cimino commentary, *The Deer Hunter* DVD.
100 **He thought that shortening:** Robert Hofler, *Party Animals: A Hollywood Tale of Sex, Drugs and Rock 'n' Roll Starring the Fabulous Allan Carr* (Boston: Da Capo Press, 2010).
100 **if the short version was released:** Mount interview.
101 **When Spikings and Mount talked:** Hofler, *Party Animals.*
101 **Universal agreed to pay him:** Mount interview.
102 **"Everybody would be asking if you saw it":** "How *The Deer Hunter* Stalked the Wild Oscar," *Los Angeles Times,* April 8, 1979.
103 **"a suffering courageous people":** John Pilger, "The Gook-Squad," *New York Times,* April 26, 1979.
103 **"could just as well":** Cimino commentary, *The Deer Hunter* DVD.
104 **"If it is about anything":** Peter Biskind, *Gods and Monsters* (New York: Nation Books, 2004), 91.
104 **Thirty years later:** Pat H. Broeske, "Michael Cimino Is Back with Desperate Hours," *Los Angeles Times,* October 7, 1990.
105 **"That happened there":** Biskind, "Tortured, Twisted Legacy."
105 **Still justifying himself:** Cimino commentary, *The Deer Hunter* DVD.
105 **"anyone who was there":** Kent, "Ready for Vietnam?"
105 **"Try not to look for symbolism":** Michael O'Connor, "Battling the Past—an Encounter with Michael Cimino," *Three Monkeys Online* website, February 2003.
106 **"Michael Cimino, 35, a self-described":** Kent, "Ready for Vietnam?"
107 **"People often abandon uncongenial identities":** Tom Buckley, "Hollywood's War" *Harper's,* April 1979.
108 **"It's hard to tell with Michael":** Biskind, "Vietnam Oscars."
108 **"I can't shake off *The Deer Hunter*":** John Pilger, "It's the Other Oscars—and Yet Again the Winner Slips Away," *New Statesman,* January 20, 2014.
108 **"I know this guy":** Biskind, "Vietnam Oscars."

108 **Wasserman called in a favor:** Mount interview.
109 **"I was measuring somebody's outfit":** Seth Abramovich, "Michael Cimino—the Full Uncensored *Hollywood Reporter* Interview," March 2, 2015.
109 **Cimino then found himself sharing:** Biskind, "Vietnam Oscars."
109 **"she wouldn't even look":** Abramovich, "Uncensored *Hollywood Reporter* Interview."
109 **He told me that Cimino and Carelli:** Washburn interview.
109 **"We had our differences":** Peter Zinner obituary, *New York Times*, July 11, 2019.
109 **"Zinner was a moron":** Nancy Griffin, "Last Typhoon Cimino Is Back," *New York Observer*, February 11, 2002.
111 **"My brother Timmy had been":** Jean Vallely, "The Opening and Closing of Heaven's Gate," *Rolling Stone*, February 5, 1981.
111 **Cimino got a phone call:** Cimino commentary, *The Deer Hunter* DVD.

CHAPTER 7: OPENING THE GATE

115 **Cimino said that he came across the story:** Scott Foundas, "Michael Cimino Revisits His Notorious Flop *Heaven's Gate*, Which Maybe Was a Masterpiece All Along," *Village Voice*, March 20, 2013.
116 **Jere Henshaw, the head of production:** Rex McGee, "Michael Cimino's Way West," *American Film*, October 1980.
120 **"Mike has a lot of ideas":** Steven Bach, *Final Cut* revised edition (New York: Newmarket Press, 1999), 101.
121 **Bach made a very perceptive:** Bach, 119.
121 **Stan Kamen, Cimino's agent at:** Frank Rose, *The Agency* (New York: Harper Collins, 1995), 367.
122 **Steve Bussard, felt that there were:** Bach, 122.
123 **Bach remembered that Field and he:** Bach, 137.
123 **"I don't have to ask your permission":** Bach, 105.
123 **Field was a quiet, reflective:** Bach, 105.
124 **He told me something that Bach":** David Field interview, September 26, 2019.
124 **"I was prepared to take the gamble":** Bach, 161.
124 **one of the problems he had with it was the lack:** Field interview.
126 **Carelli said that when Cimino doing the casting:** Joann Carelli dinner conversation, March 25, 2019.
126 **Cimino's version was that:** Sandy Gillet, "Michael Cimino—Paris Master Class," *EcranLarge* website, July 20, 2005.
126 **Bach also felt that not only did she have:** Bach, 186.
126 **Cimino had already talked to:** Robert Shapiro interview, September 20, 2018.
127 **he gave the director forty-eight hours:** Field interview.
130 **he thought United Artists:** Irwin Winkler interview, October 2, 2019.
130 **Bach says that on Field's:** Bach, 212.

CHAPTER 8: THE CIRCUS COMES TO TOWN

132 **"I had a call from Michael":** Garry Wunderwald interview, April 9, 2020.
134 **"I was a grad student":** Bryan Buchanan interview, October 5, 2019.
134 **"I responded to an ad":** Kona Luke interview, October 5, 2019.
134 **heard about a casting call:** Brian Wood interview, October 5, 2019.
134 **"We found some of them tough":** *Kalispell Weekly News*, undated, 1979.
135 **"We called ourselves 'The Bohunk Cavalry'":** Pamela Dylina interview, October 6, 2019.

135 **She loved the outdoors life:** Carol Eads interview, October 6, 2019.
135 **a member of the powerful Teamsters' union:** Van Robinson interview, November 22, 2019.
136 **Joseph Stanley, one of the location:** "Time Turned Back for Movie at Wallace," *Sanders County Ledger*, June 28, 1979.

CHAPTER 9: KURTZ IN KALISPELL

139 **as being "made with a crystal ball":** Steven Bach, *Final Cut* revised edition (New York: Newmarket Press, 1999), 218.
140 **"We seem to be in the ironic":** Bach, 220.
140 **"I had a lot of respect":** David Field interview, September 26, 2019.
141 **Bach imagined what Carelli:** Bach, 228.
142 **"Carelli was worried":** Bach, 228.
142 **"Originally Cimino was only going to shoot":** Bryan Buchanan interview, October 5, 2019.
143 **he went to Kalispelll only "a few times":** Steve Garbarino, "Michael Cimino's Final Cut," *Vanity Fair*, March 2002.
144 **"You will have equal authority":** Bach, 135.
144 **"Feelings of unrest, if not dissension":** Bach, 230.
144 **"a West Coast project and David would be in charge":** Bach, 220.
144 **"We were not Darryl":** Field interview.
145 **"He told Joann he doesn't want to talk":** Bach, 234.
146 **"If he did all of those":** Jean Vallely, "The Opening and Closing of Heaven's Gate," *Rolling Stone*, February 5, 1981.
147 **he asked the desk clerk for Cimino's room number:** Field interview.
147 **"I had consented readily":** Bach, 252.
148 **There was an occasional satirical newsletter:** *Heaven's Dirt* newsletter, May 22, 1979.
148 **"Chris Walken told me that he would trust":** Michael Bonner, "Michael Cimino Remembered," Uncut, July 4, 2016.
148 **"It's very hard to refuse":** Sandy Gillet, "Michael Cimino—Paris Master Class," *EcranLarge* website, July 20, 2005.
151 **"The Ayatollah":** "Michael Cimino's *Heaven's Gate* Teaches Us That Great Art Ultimately Triumphs No Matter the Circumstances," *Cinephilia & Beyond* website, undated.
151 **"He was not overfriendly":** Mady Kaplan interview, September 27, 2019.
151 **"The extras got a mud puddle":** Bryan Buchanan interview, October 5, 2019.
152 **"I was in a lighting setup, and someone told me a joke":** "Willem Dafoe Breaks Down His Career, from 'The Boondock Saints' to 'Spider-Man,'" *Vanity Fair* YouTube, November 5, 2019.
152 **"I was warned that Michael comes on":** Van Robinson interview, November 22, 2019.
153 **She saw a posting from a "Writer-Director":** Patty Nelson interview, April 26, 2019.
154 **"Michael got along with women very well":** Penny Shaw interview, April 26, 2019.
154 **"We had such a good time with Michael":** Nelson interview.
155 **"Crew people tend not to listen to a woman":** Dale Pollock, "Women and Power: The New Hollywood," *Los Angeles Times*, undated 1980.
156 **Carelli denied to me that she had had an unpleasant time:** Joann Carelli dinner conversation, June 6, 2018.
156 **"Joann was on the set in spurts":** Robinson interview.
157 **"My friend was the manager of the Outlaw":** Gary Wunderwald interview, April 9, 2020.

157 **Bach, however, considered her to be overly enabling:** Bach, 255.
157 **"I mean, you gotta take my *calls*":** Bach, 254.
157 **"We should have said, 'No, Michael, no' ":** Vallely, "Opening and Closing of Heaven's Gate."
157 **Bryan Buchanan told me about an evening in the bar:** Buchanan interview.
158 **the story of the Donner Pass:** Robinson interview.
158 **they had been wrong about Isabelle:** Bach, 255.
158 **"I know what you think of me":** David Field interview in *Final Cut* documentary, 2004.
159 **they had offered him a reasonable deal:** Barry Spikings interview, June 11, 2018.
160 **he and Bach had a cryptic conversation:** Bach, 348.
161 **"I packed no revolver":** Bach, 269.
162 **"He's going to agree":** Bach, 276.

CHAPTER 10: THE RETREAT FROM MOSCOW

165 **"He called me at one in the morning":** Garry Wunderwald interview, April 9, 2020.
165 **"The problem was an accumulation":** Brian Kennedy, "Iverson Didn't Foresee Movie Difficulty," *Daily Inter Lake*, June 3, 1979.
166 **"Iverson is exhibiting":** Larry Stem, "Cimino Levels Blast," *Daily Inter Lake*, June 11, 1979.
166 **"I was appalled at the thousands":** Wilbur P. Werner, *Daily Inter Lake*, undated, 1979.
166 **"between 75 and 80 percent of the":** "Park Recovers from Filming," *Pioneer Press*, June 13, 1979.
168 **He revealed pretty accurately how far the movie:** Les Gapay, "Shoot-Out at *Heaven's Gate*," *Washington Post*, September 2, 1979.
170 **"It has an epic sweep":** Herb A. Lightman, "On Location with Heaven's Gate," *American Cinematographer*, November 1980.
171 **"What Napoleon's retreat from Moscow":** Nicholas Woodison interview, June 20, 2018.
171 **"I didn't know what to give Michael":** Wunderwald interview.
171 **at the party "when everyone was hugging":** Bryan Buchanan interview, October 5, 2019.
172 **He demanded that United Artist censure:** Steven Bach, *Final Cut* revised edition (New York: Newmarket Press, 1999), 298.
172 **"I didn't get fired, I got whipped":** Bach, 299.
172 **"The longer you stay in a place":** Rex McGee, "Michael Cimino's Way West," *American Film*, October 1980.

CHAPTER 11: THE VIOLINIST ON ROLLER SKATES

175 **the poet Allen Ginsberg described as having:** Larry "Ratso" Sloman, *On the Road with Bob Dylan* (London: Helter Skelter, 2005), 60.
175 **"I didn't tend to fall":** David Mansfield interview, July 6, 2018.
177 **Penny Shaw, who had the room next to him:** Penny Shaw interview, April 26, 2019.
178 **"I don't think anyone saw them together":** Bryan Buchanan interview, October 5, 2019.
178 **"David and Joann—it kind of flared up":** Van Robinson interview, November 22, 2019.
178 **David Field wondered if they were having:** Steven Bach, *Final Cut* revised edition (New York: Newmarket Press, 1999), 194.
180 **"Somebody's got to tell him":** Shaw interview.

CHAPTER 12: THE GATES OF HELL

181 "We had bars put on the cutting room": Penny Shaw interview in *Final Cut* documentary, 2004.

183 "Everyone thought it was because": David Field interview, September 26, 2019.

183 "I have one regret in my life": David Field interview in *Final Cut* documentary, 2004.

184 As there was no tree there: *American Cinematographer*, December 1980.

184 "Michael was fascinated by class": Eleanor Fazan interview, April 19, 2018.

184 "Michael wanted real aristocrats": Michael Stevenson interview, April 1, 2019.

185 "I really liked him": Fazan interview.

186 "I find it incredibly sad, Michael": Steven Bach, *Final Cut* revised edition (New York: Newmarket Press, 1999), 276.

186 "It makes me want to dance again": Fazan interview.

187 She told Cimino that the size of the phone bill: Penny Shaw interview, April 26, 2019.

187 "In every friendship": Leticia Kent, "Ready for Vietnam? A Talk with Michael Cimino,'" *New York Times*, December 10, 1978.

188 "The battle, the pandemonium, the chaos": Bach, 338.

188 how that long version differed from the final version: Shaw interview, April 26, 2019.

189 "She politely (or not)": Bach, 331.

189 Carelli told me that he was extraordinarily rude: Joann Carelli phone conversation, May 27, 2018.

190 "I started making some recordings": David Mansfield interview, July 6, 2018.

190 When Steven Bach asked Carelli who was doing the music: Bach, 342.

191 On later versions, the credit was only for Mansfield: Mansfield interview.

191 She told me that Cimino was brilliant: Carelli phone conversation May 27, 2018.

193 Don Winslow was hired to be an usher: Don Winslow, "Marquee Values & My Night at Heaven's Gate", *Deadline*, April 7, 2020.

193 Jeff Bridges remembered: Nancy Griffin, "Last Typhoon Cimino Is Back," *New York Observer*, February 11, 2002.

193 "when a well-known New York": Patrick Goldstein, "The Dubious Anniversary of *Heaven's Gate*," *Los Angeles Times*, December 12, 2000.

195 "I can't even describe what happened": Patty Nelson interview, April 26, 2019.

196 Columbia held a sneak preview: David Cobb, "Close Encounters of the Absurd Kind," *Maclean's*, December 26, 1977.

197 "Michael was just not talking about it": Nelson interview.

198 However, the reaction was marginally better: Bach, 383.

199 he talked to Gene Shalit on NBC: Peter Brown, "Behind the *Heaven's Gate* Disaster," *New York Times*, November 30, 1980.

199 "Michael was a little crazy": Jean Vallely, "The Opening and Closing of Heaven's Gate," *Rolling Stone*, February 5, 1981.

199 "I would respond to *Heaven's Gate*": Serge Kaganski, "Michael Cimino—The American Night," *Les Inrockuptibles*, February 7, 1991.

199 "At least in the old days": Vallely, "Opening and Closing of Heaven's Gate."

200 Carelli told me that the only constant for Cimino: Joann Carelli dinner conversation, March 25, 2019.

202 There was really no downside for them: Bach, 410.

203 Field asked him why Bach was not calling himself: Field interview, September 26, 2019.

203 **"It should be classified as fiction":** Nancy Griffin, "Last Typhoon Cimino Is Back," *New York Observer,* February 11, 2002.
203 **After it was published, he called Field:** Field interview, September 26, 2019.
204 **"It would be like wishing ill":** Steve Garbarino, "Michael Cimino's Final Cut," *Vanity Fair,* March 2002.
204 **at the screening, he saw Joann Carelli watching it:** Field interview, September 26, 2019.

CHAPTER 13: FOOTLOOSE IN HOLLYWOOD

Tess Gallagher quotes from interview, April 18, 2019.
Dean Pitchford quotes from interview, April 24, 2019.
207 **"He was poison":** Cary Woods interview, May 24, 2018.
207 **"This is all nonsense":** Patty Nelson interview, April 26, 2019.
207 **Carelli told me that she did not find it painful herself:** Joann Carelli phone conversation, May 27, 2018.
208 **"The telephone is the sharpest":** Michael Cimino, *Conversations en miroir* (Paris: Gallimard, 2004), 16. English version by Lucas Carvallo-Phillips.
208 **"*Heaven's Gate* undercut us all":** Peter Biskind, *Easy Riders, Raging Bulls* (New York: Simon & Schuster, 1988), 402.
208 **"If you look at the cost overruns and films out of control":** Peter Biskind, "Peter Biskind on Michael Cimino's Tortured, Twisted Legacy," *Hollywood Reporter,* July 13, 2016.
208 **"There was a kind of coup d'etat":** Biskind, *Easy Riders,* 402.
208 **"One time he asked me":** Van Robinson interview, November 22, 2019.
209 **"At the beginning of the decade you had a group":** Biskind, *Easy Riders,* 406.
210 **"The pictures that they [the studios] have to make":** Biskind, *Easy Riders,* 402.
215 **"*The eye keeps going to that juggler*":** Raymond Carver, "The Juggler at Heaven's Gate—for Michael Cimino," *All of Us—The Collected Poems* (New York: Vintage, 1996).
215 **"ponderous, boring and inconsistent":** Carol Sklenicka, *Raymond Carver—A Writer's Life* (New York: Scribner, 2009), 393.
215 **"Is there a storyline here?":** Raymond Carver and Tess Gallagher, *Introduction to Dostoevsky: A Screenplay,* New England Review and Bread Loaf Quarterly, vol 6, no 3, Spring 1984, 355–393.
219 **"I really love music":** Sandy Gillet, "Michael Cimino—Paris Master Class," *Ecran-Large* website, July 20, 2005.
219 **"It's fair to say he has difficulty":** Pat H. Broeske, "Michael Cimino Is Back with Desperate Hours," *Los Angeles Times,* October 7, 1990.
219 **"Cimino was anxious to prove":** "In a Surprising Career Move, Filmmaker Michael Cimino Casts Himself as Odd Man Out," *People,* March 7, 1983.
219 **"Dan's attitude was":** Dean Pitchford interview, April 24, 2019.
220 **"I get along with gangsters":** Cimino commentary, *Year of the Dragon* DVD.
220 **"It might have been a good":** Broeske, "Michael Cimino Is Back."
220 **"Michael was very proud of Joann":** Nelson interview.
221 **"I felt people were thinking":** David Mansfield interview, March 20, 2019.
221 **"Mansfield never took Joann away":** Francis Grumman interview, July 10, 2018.
221 **"After the critical bombs":** David Mansfield interview, July 6, 2018.
221 **"Joann Carelli became the mother of a daughter":** Steven Bach, *Final Cut* revised edition (New York: Newmarket Press, 1999), 418.
221 **"As we worked over the years":** Mansfield interview, July 6, 2018.

CHAPTER 14: CHASING THE SUN

Lizi Gelber quotes from interview, June 12, 2019. '

223 **"We had to keep our relationship secret":** Olivier Nicklaus, "Michael Cimino—American Psycho," *Les Inrockuptibles,* September 25, 2001.

223 **a project that is instructive:** *The Pope of Greenwich Village*—American Film Institute catalogue.

224 **Freddie Fields, the president of MGM, told him:** Peter Bart, *Fade Out: The Calamitous Final Days of MGM* (New York: William Morrow, 1991), 118–121.

225 **He employed an Italian couple:** Mark Rosenthal interview, September 16, 2018.

225 **"Michael, let's be absolutely clear":** Tullio Kezich, *Dino: The Life and Films of Dino De Laurentiis* (New York: Miramax Books, 2004), 288.

226 **Cimino loved *Platoon* and asked:** Matt Zoller Seitz, *The Oliver Stone Experience* (New York: Abrams, 2016).

226 **Stone got on very well:** Nancy Griffin, "Last Typhoon Cimino Is Back," *New York Observer,* February 11, 2002.

226 **"the most Napoleonic director I ever worked with":** "Michael Cimino's 'Year of the Dragon' is one of the most significant action movies of the period," *Cinephilia & Beyond* website, undated.

226 **"one of the greatest writing talents":** Cimino commentary, *Year of the Dragon* DVD.

226 **'They're the most wonderful people":** Cimino commentary, *Year of the Dragon* DVD.

226 **"People think that cities":** Cimino commentary, *Year of the Dragon* DVD.

227 **"He was the Michael I knew":** Francis Grumman interview, July 10, 2018.

227 **"When I did *Thunderbolt,* they said I was homophobic":** Cimino commentary, *Year of the Dragon* DVD.

229 **he talked to me about the ups and downs of his colorful career:** Bruce McNall interview, September 12, 2018.

229 **"I could tell right away he had his own agenda":** Pat H. Broeske, "Michael Cimino Is Back with Desperate Hours," *Los Angeles Times,* October 7, 1990.

230 **Cimino sent him the Shagan script:** F. X. Feeney interview, June 12, 2018.

230 **"Michael wanted me to go and help Gore":** Katy Haber interview, September 17, 2018.

230 **"Michael was very convincing":** McNall interview.

231 **"I never met a hit man":** Cimino commentary, *Year of the Dragon* DVD.

231 **"Michael had letters":** Michael Stevenson interview, April 1, 2019.

231 **Bill Krohn, the LA correspondent:** Bill Krohn, "The Making of The Sicilian," unpublished article.

232 **"I was told that Sicily":** Memo from Cimino to David Begelman, undated.

232 **"I cut 12,500 extra":** Memo from Cimino to David Begelman, June 10, 1986.

232 **he wrote these detailed memos:** Katy Haber interview, September 17, 2018.

232 **"Please try to use your considerable":** Telex from David Begelman to Cimino, August 22, 1986.

233 **"I am greatly annoyed and disappointed":** Memo from Cimino to Bruce McNall, August 21, 1986.

234 **he considered it to be:** Donald E. Biederman et al., *Law and Business of the Entertainment Industries* (Westport, CT: Prager Publishing, 2006), 427.

235 **Cimino had been "emotional":** John Dellaverson interview, September 13, 2018.

235 **"[Cimino's] inattention is a far cry":** Biederman et al., 428.

235 **"I didn't recognize much of":** Broeske, "Michael Cimino Is Back."

235 **"We could never get the short version":** McNall interview.

237 **"Any film had to be sensitive":** Eoghan Harris email February 6, 2019.

237 **"Michael Cimino made a quaint":** Sarah Miles, *Bolt from the Blue* (London: Phoenix, 1997).

237 **"One day, the Columbia production team"**: Jean-Baptiste Thoret, *Michael Cimino, les voix perdues de l'Amérique* (Paris: Flammarion, 2014), 282. English version by Lucas Carvallo-Phillips.

238 **an unnamed Nelson representative gave the usual**: Claudia Eller, *Hollywood Reporter*, August 18, 1987.

238 **"a tight-lipped rep in Cimino's office"**: Leonard Klady, "Checking on Cimino," *Los Angeles Times*, October 4, 1987.

238 **the cancellation occurred**: Michael Cieply, "Firm Cancels New Cimino Film Project," *Los Angeles Times*, January 26, 1988.

239 **"We're told Chris Cain is fired"**: Mark Rosenthal interview, September 16, 2018.

240 **Carelli had no doubt that *Desperate Hours***: Joann Carelli dinner conversation, June 6, 2018.

240 **Richard Brooks, the director**: Feeney interview.

242 **"When I was very young"**: Thoret, *Michael Cimino*, 121.

242 **he took the logical next step in how he dealt**: Charles Leavitt interview, October 1, 2019.

242 **"It was kind of eerie"**: Steve Garbarino, "Michael Cimino's Final Cut," *Vanity Fair*, March 2002.

243 **"The guy was crazy"**: Joe d'Augustine interview, October 23, 2019.

246 **"I made a huge casting mistake"**: Vincent Maraval, "Michael Cimino—The Myth," *Sofilm*, December 17, 2014.

246 **"The worst thing was that he [Mickey Rourke] was the one"**: Thoret, *Michael Cimino*, 183.

CHAPTER 15: SHADOW CONVERSATIONS

249 **"The entrance gates, a few centimeters thick"**: Michael Cimino, *Conversations en miroir* (Paris: Gallimard, 2004), 9. English version by Lucas Carvallo-Phillips.

249 **"Not even once!"**: Steve Garbarino, "Michael Cimino's Final Cut," *Vanity Fair*, March 2002.

249 **"He lives in Beverly Hills"**: Patrick Goldstein, "The Dubious Anniversary of *Heaven's Gate*," *Los Angeles Times*, December 12, 2000.

250 **His agent, Mike Wise**: Garbarino, "Michael Cimino's Final Cut."

250 **"I don't need a publicist"**: Garbarino, "Michael Cimino's Final Cut."

250 **"He needed people, but at the same time"**: F. X. Feeney interview, June 12, 2018.

250 **told me that he had no idea**: Stefan Wenta interview, April 25, 2019.

252 **he told me that Cimino had said to him**: Feeney interview.

252 **"For a couple of years"**: F. X. Feeney, *Cimino: An Introduction*, unpublished memoir.

253 **Feeney adored Cimino**: Irene Miracle interview, September 25, 2018.

253 **Feeney had helped edit his novel**: Feeney interview.

254 **She is a multitasker of the kind that thrives**: Cindy Lee Duck interview, June 11, 2018.

254 **"My personal life is work, sex, and cars"**: Garbarino, "Michael Cimino's Final Cut."

255 **Cimino suggested that Duck take her for her first visit**: Duck interview.

255 **"She's brilliant"**: Garbarino, "Michael Cimino's Final Cut."

255 **Mansfield told me that they seemed**: David Mansfield interview, March 20, 2019.

256 **"We had an instant chemistry"**: Roanna Martin-Trigona interview, April 18, 2019.

256 **she had gone to her hairdresser**: Shanda Lear-Baylor interview, May 14, 2019.

257 **"I think Cimino is sitting behind me"**: Jim Hemphill, "My Dinner with Michael," *Talkhouse*, July 7, 2016.

257 **"He was simmering in his bitterness"**: Wenta interview.

257 **Francis Ford Coppola was**: Nancy Griffin, "Last Typhoon Cimino Is Back," *New York Observer*, February 11, 2002.

257 "He should be writing poetry": Jorge Mourinha, "'I Never Knew How to Make a Film—Michael Cimino in 2005," *Filmmaker*, July 5, 2016.

258 "Mr. Cimino rants that the nouveau Hamptoners": Griffin, "Last Typhoon."

258 Carelli told me that they had discussed a project: Joann Carelli dinner conversation, January 16, 2020.

258 F. X. Feeney helped him with a script: Feeney interview.

258 He wanted Taylor Swift: Vincent Maraval, "Michael Cimino in 5 Dream Movies," *Sofilm*, September 22, 2016.

259 "If you edit it down, it could be a very tight": Griffin, "Last Typhoon."

259 "The screenplay, I think": Garbarino, "Michael Cimino's Final Cut."

260 "it takes ten years, and it can be impossible": Vincent Maraval, "Michael Cimino—The Myth," *Sofilm*, December 17, 2014.

261 "I am a myth. I seldom smile these days": Michael Cimino, *Conversations en Miroir*.

262 He often said he was allergic to alcohol: Garbarino, "Michael Cimino's Final Cut."

263 "He had had some run-ins with alcohol": Van Robinson interview, November 22, 2019.

CHAPTER 16: THE WOMAN FROM TORRANCE

Valerie Driscoll material from interview, April 24, 2019, and emails, April 19–September 20, 2019.

265 "Michael Cimino . . . is small, has dark curly hair": Jean Vallely, "Michael Cimino's Battle to Make a Great Movie," *Esquire*, January 2, 1979.

265 "Mr. Cimino is dressed in": Leticia Kent, "Ready for Vietnam? A Talk with Michael Cimino,'" *New York Times*, December 10, 1978.

266 "Your problem, Michael, is that no one knows": Michael Cimino, *Conversations en miroir*. Paris: Gallimard, 2004. English version by Lucas Carvallo-Phillips.

266 The writer reported that he felt he had: Steve Garbarino, "Michael Cimino's Final Cut," *Vanity Fair*, March 2002.

266 "many false things [have been] written about me": Seth Abramovich, "Michael Cimino—the Full Uncensored *Hollywood Reporter* Interview," March 2, 2015.

266 "late-stage Bette Davis": "*Talkhouse* Film Contributors Remember Michael Cimino," *Talkhouse*, May 7, 2016.

266 "Even in Los Angeles, where nip-and-tuck surgery": Garbarino, "Michael Cimino's Final Cut."

266 "looks like a cross between": Nancy Griffin, "Last Typhoon Cimino Is Back," *New York Observer*, February 11, 2002.

268 Army Archerd, the legendary *Variety* gossip columnist: Eric Weissmann interview, June 13, 2018.

268 Sometimes he had a sense of humor: F. X. Feeney interview, June 13, 2018.

268 "Can you imagine cutting": Garbarino, "Michael Cimino's Final Cut."

268 "If you can't stop somebody": Abramovich, "Uncensored *Hollywood Reporter* Interview."

268 Kris Kristofferson was asked about the rumors: Griffin, "Last Typhoon."

269 F. X. Feeney said: Griffin, "Last Typhoon."

269 he was definitely not transitioning: Cindy Lee Duck interview, June 11, 2018.

CHAPTER 17: PHOENIX

277 "The women who went to Korea": Geoffrey Macnab, "Michael Cimino: War Stories," London *Guardian*, December 6, 2001.

277 **he was considering starting a women's blue jean line:** Steve Garbarino, "Michael Cimino's Final Cut," *Vanity Fair*, March 2002.

277 **The launch party was held in the grand salon:** Nancy Griffin, "Last Typhoon Cimino Is Back," *New York Observer*, February 11, 2002.

278 **He told some interviewers that he was looking:** Garbarino, "Michael Cimino's Final Cut."

278 **and others that he did not:** Seth Abramovich, "Michael Cimino—the Full Uncensored *Hollywood Reporter* Interview," March 2, 2015.

278 **"Directors tend to talk about themselves":** Thierry Frémaux interview, January 14, 2021.

279 **Carelli told me that when he appeared:** Joann Carelli dinner conversation, June 16, 2018.

280 **I asked Carelli if I could meet her daughter:** Joann Carelli dinner conversation, September 4, 2018.

280 **Harris's girlfriend, Katy, closer in age:** James B. Harris interview, September 17, 2018.

282 **His first words were, "I want to say to you":** Transcript of amateur film footage, Locarno Film Festival, 2015.

287 **it might have been quicker process:** Richard Brody, "Would the Internet Have Rescued *Heaven's Gate?*" *The New Yorker*, November 4, 2012.

288 **"to viewers who binge-watch":** Nicholas Barber, "*Heaven's Gate*: From Hollywood Disaster to Masterpiece," BBC Culture website, December 4, 2015.

288 **"He never answered me":** Thierry Frémaux interview, January 14, 2021.

289 **Joann Carelli told me that Cimino was initially:** Carelli conversation, June 16, 2018.

289 **After he agreed, he told Curtis Tsui:** Curtis Tsui interview, September 7, 2018.

289 **"Michael told me how gratifying":** Curtis Tsui, "A Tribute to Michael Cimino," *Production Notes—The Criterion Collection*, July 9, 2016.

290 **in an extraordinary indication of Cimino's:** Harlan Kennedy, "A Lion's Tale," *American Cinema Papers*, print archive, 2012.

290 **"It seems inconceivable that this bold":** Phil Concannon, "Reopening Heaven's Gate," *Mostly Film*, July 5, 2011.

290 **"*Heaven's Gate* is back in a new ":** Geoffrey McNab, "Can the Worst Film Ever Get a Happy Ending?" *Independent*, August 3, 2012.

290 **"Distinctive, passionate, grand":** Richard Brody, "Heaven's Gate," *The New Yorker*, November 25, 2015.

290 **"It's a film of rare beauty and scope":** Nathan Rabin, "My Year of Flops Case File No. 81—*Heaven's Gate*," AVClub website, November 1, 2007.

290 **"Greatness took time to arrive":** Nigel Andrews, "*Heaven's Gate* the Restored Cut," *Financial Times*, August 2, 2013.

290 **"To hear the stockgrowers denouncing":** Nicholas Barber, "*Heaven's Gate:* From Hollywood Disaster to Masterpiece," BBC Culture website, December 4, 2015.

291 **"[*Heaven's Gate*'s] relentlessly unheroic vision":** Dana Stevens, *Slate* website, March 29, 2013.

291 **after the New York screening, he, Carelli and Cimino:** Tsui interview.

CHAPTER 18: JUNE 30, 2016

293 **The actor Richard Dreyfuss:** *Kermode & Mayo's Film Review*, BBC Radio 5 Live, April 17, 2020.

294 **"A great filmmaker and great man":** Ali Mostafa, Twitter, July 2016.

294 **she felt closer to him as he began to change:** Irene Miracle interview, September 25, 2018.

294 **"He took deliberate care to mend fences":** F. X. Feeney interview, June 13, 2018.

294 **Katy Haber, whom he had treated unkindly:** Katy Haber interview, September 17, 2018.

294 **Penny Shaw, whom he had been so close to:** Penny Shaw interview, June 10, 2018.

295 **In 1979, he had sacked his lawyer:** Eric Weissmann interview, June 13, 2018.

295 **"I probably didn't see him for the last five years":** Van Robinson interview, November 22, 2019.

295 **"Ten days before he died":** Stefan Wenta interview, April 25, 2019.

295 **"could feel his loneliness and pain":** Miracle interview.

295 **"He had trouble sleeping and started using pills":** Valerie Driscoll interview, April 24, 2019.

296 **"When I last had lunch with Michael":** Feeney interview.

296 **"Nevertheless," Feeney said:** F. X. Feeney, "Irish Lament for a Friend," *Elsewhere* website, July 2016.

296 **They broke into the house on June 30:** Weissmann interview.

296 **"Joann sent me a message":** Thierry Frémaux interview, January 14, 2021.

297 **"Cimino Is Gone":** Obituary, *Elsewhere* website, July 2016.

297 **"I wish I had paid tribute":** Obituary, *Celebrity News*, July 2016.

297 **"A beautiful textbook":** Feeney, "Irish Lament."

298 **Irene Miracle wondered if he was suffering from:** Miracle interview.

298 **"It was not suicide":** Roanna Martin-Trigona interview, April 18, 2019.

298 **"I don't know what he died of":** Feeney, "Irish Lament."

CHAPTER 19: WIZARD

Peter Cimino material from interview, January 15, 2020.

Christopher Cimino material from interview, May 25, 2021.

301 **"They wanted to know who Michael was survived by":** T. Rafael Cimino interview, February 18, 2019.

301 **"I don't remember any of the things":** Eric Weissmann email, January 4, 2020.

303 **F. X. Feeney told me that his uncle had grown up in:** F. X. Feeney interview, June 13, 2018.

309 **"I googled myself one time":** Quoted by F. X. Feeney in interview, June 12, 2018.

BIBLIOGRAPHY

Abramowitz, Rachel. *Is That a Gun in Your Pocket?: Women's Experience of Power in Hollywood*. New York: Random House, 2000.

Alda, Rutanya. *The Mommie Dearest Diary: Carol Ann Tells All*. Privately published. New York, 2015.

Bach, Steven. Final Cut: *Art, Money, and Ego in the Making of* Heaven's Gate, *the Film that Sank United Artists*. Revised ed. New York: Newmarket Press, 1991.

Balio, Tinio. *United Artists, Volume 2, 1951–1978*. Madison: University of Wisconsin Press, 1987.

Barry, Julian. *My Night with Orson*. Self-published, CreateSpace Independent Publishing, 2011.

Bart, Peter. *BOFFO!: How I Learned to Love the Blockbuster and Fear the Bomb*. New York: Hyperion, 2006.

———. *Fade Out: The Calamitous Final Days of MGM*. New York: William Morrow, 1991.

———. *The Gross: The Hits, the Flops—The Summer That Ate Hollywood*. New York: St. Martin's Press, 2000.

———. *Infamous Players: A Tale of Movies, the Mob (and Sex)*. New York: Weinstein Books, 2011.

———, and Peter Guber. *Shoot Out: Surviving Fame and (Mis)Fortune in Hollywood*. New York: G. P. Putnam's Sons, 2002.

Baxter, John. *Stanley Kubrick*. New York: Carroll & Graf, 1997.

Biskind, Peter. *Down and Dirty Pictures: Miramax, Sundance, and the Rise of Independent Film*. London: Bloomsbury, 2004.

———. *Easy Riders, Raging Bulls: How the Sex, Drugs, and Rock 'n' Roll Generation Saved Hollywood*. New York: Simon & Schuster, 1998.

———. *Gods and Monsters: Thirty Years of Writing on Film and Culture*. New York: Nation Books, 2004.

Bliss, Michael. *Martin Scorsese and Michael Cimino*, Metuchen, NJ: Scarecrow Press, 1985.

Bochco, Steven. *Truth Is a Total Defence: My Fifty Years in Television*. Self-published, CreateSpace Independent Publishing, 2016.

Bogdanovich, Peter. *Who the Devil Made It?: Conversations with Legendary Film Directors*. New York: Ballantine Books, 1997.

Brown, Jared. *Alan Pakula: His Life and His Films*. New York: Back Stage Books, 2005.

Bullough, Vern L., and Bonnie Bullough. *Cross Dressing, Sex and Gender*. Philadelphia: University of Pennsylvania Press, 1993.

Carver, Raymond. *All of Us: The Collected Poems*. London: Vintage, 1996.

———, and Michael Cimino. *Purple Lake*. Screenplay based on a story by Joann Carelli, November 23, 1984.

———, and Tess Gallagher. *Dostoevsky: A Screenplay*. Santa Barbara, CA: Capra Press, 1985.

Cimino, Michael. *Big Jane*. Paris: Gallimard, 2001.

———. *Conquering Horse*. Screenplay, based on the novel by Frederick Manfred, undated.

———. *Conversations en miroir*. Paris: Gallimard, 2004.

———. *The Deer Hunter*. Original screenplay, March 1, 1977.

———. *The Deer Hunter*. Final draft screenplay, June 7, 1977.

————. *Desperate Hours*. Final draft screenplay, based on the screenplay by Lawrence Konner and Mark Rosenthal and the novel and Broadway play by Joseph Hayes, October 1, 1989.
————. *The Fountainhead*. Screenplay, based on the novel by Ayn Rand, 1976.
————. *Head of the Dragon*. Screenplay, 1976.
————. *Heaven's Gate*. Screenplay, January 26, 1979.
————. *Magnum Force*. Screenplay, March 5, 1973.
————, and Bo Goldman. *The Rose*. Screenplay, April 18, 1976.
————, and Deric Washburn. *The Deer Hunter*. Screenplay, January 28, 1977.
Coppola, Eleanor. Notes: *The Making of Apocalypse Now*. New York: Simon & Schuster, 1979.
Corder, J. M. *The Deer Hunter*. New York: Penguin, 1979.
Crist, Judith. Take 22: *Moviemakers on Moviemaking*. New York: Continuum, 1991.
D'Ambrosio, Brian D. *Shot in Montana: A History of Big Sky Cinema*. Helena, MT: Riverbend Publishing, 2016.
Daley, Robert. *Year of the Dragon*. New York: Simon & Schuster, 1981.
Dardis, Tom. *Some Time in the Sun: The Hollywood Years of F. Scott Fitzgerald, William Faulkner, Nathanael West, Aldous Huxley, and James Agee*. London: Andre Deutsch, 1976.
Dawson, Nick. *Being Hal Ashby: Life of Hollywood Rebel*. Lexington: University Press of Kentucky, 2009.
Deeley, Michael. *Blade Runners, Deer Hunters and Blowing the Bloody Doors Off*. London: Faber & Faber, 2008.
Diamant, Lincoln, edited by. *The Anatomy of a Television Commercial: The Story of Eastman Kodak's "Yesterdays."* New York: Hastings House, 1970.
Doron, Meir, and Joseph Gelman. *Confidential: The Life of Secret Agent Turned Hollywood Tycoon Arnon Milchan*. Jerusalem: Gefen Books, 2011.
Dunne, John Gregory. *Monster: Living Off the Big Screen*. New York: Random House, 1997.
————. *The Studio*. New York: Limelight Editions, 1985.
Eisner, Michael, with Tony Schwartz. *Work in Progress: Risking Failure, Surviving Success*. New York: Random House, 1998.
Engel, Joel. *Oscar-Winning Screenwriters on Screenwriting*. New York: Hyperion, 2002.
Evans, Robert. *The Kid Stays in the Picture: A Notorious Life*. New York: Hyperion, 1994.
Farber, Stephen, and Marc Green. *Outrageous Conduct: Art, Ego and the Twilight Zone Case*. New York: Arbor House, 1998.
Fleischer, Leonore. *The Rose*. London: Futura, 1979.
Fleming, Charles. *High Concept: Don Simpson and the Hollywood Culture of Excess*. New York: Doubleday, 1998.
Fox, Stephen. *The Mirror Makers: A History of American Advertising & Its Creators*. New York: William Morrow, 1984.
Freeman, David. *A Hollywood Education: Tales of Movie Dreams and Easy Money*. New York: G. P. Putnam's Sons, 1986.
Friedkin, William. *The Friedkin Connection: A Memoir*. New York: HarperCollins, 2013.
Fritz, Ben. *The Big Picture: The Fight for the Future of Movies*. New York: Houghton Mifflin Harcourt, 2018.
Gallagher, Tess. *At the Owl Woman Saloon: Stories*. New York: Scribner, 1999.
Garfinkle, Louis, and Quinn Redeker. *The Man Who Came to Play*. Screenplay, 1975.
Glennie, Jay. *One Shot: The Making of The Deer Hunter*. Self-published, Coattail Publications, 2019.
Grade, Lew. *Still Dancing*. London: Collins, 1987.

Griffin, Nancy, and Kim Master. *Hit & Run: How Jon Peters and Peter Guber Took Sony for a Ride in Hollywood*. New York: Simon & Schuster, 1997.

Hamsher, Jane. *Killer Instinct: How Two Young Producers Took on Hollywood and Made the Most Controversial Film of the Decade*. London: Orion Books, 1997.

Hanson, Peter, and Paul Robert Herman, eds. *Tales from the Script: 50 Hollywood Screenwriters Share Their Stories*. New York: HarperCollins, 2010.

Harris, Mark. *Pictures at a Revolution: Five Movies and the Birth of the New Hollywood*. New York: Penguin Press, 2009.

Hayes, Joseph. *The Desperate Hours*. New York: Random House, 1954.

Heard, Christopher. *Mickey Rourke: High and Low*. London: Plexus, 2006.

Hickenlooper, George. *Reel Conversations: Candid Interviews with Film's Foremost Directors and Critics*. New York: Citadel Press, 1991.

Hofler, Robert. *Party Animals: A Hollywood Tale of Sex, Drugs, and Rock 'N' Roll Starring the Fabulous Allan Carr*. Cambridge, MA: Da Capo Press, 2010.

Horton, Andrew. *The Films of George Roy Hill*. New York: Columbia University Press, 1984.

Itzkoff, Dave. *Mad as Hell: The Making of* Network *and the Fateful Vision of the Angriest Man in Movies*. New York: Henry Holt & Co., 2014.

Jackson, Carlton. *Picking Up the Tab: The Life and Movies of Martin Ritt*. Madison, WI: Bowling Green State University Popular Press, 1994.

Jones, Brian Jay. *George Lucas: A Life*. London: Headline, 2016.

Jewison, Norman. *This Terrible Business Has Been Good to Me*. New York: St. Martin's Press, 2005.

Jordan, Neil. *Michael Collins*. London: Vintage, 1996.

Kachmar, Diane C. *Roy Scheider: A Film Biography*. Jefferson, NC: McFarland & Company, 2002.

Keesey, Douglas. *Brian De Palma's Split-Screen: A Life in Film*. Jackson: University of Mississippi Press, 2015.

Kezich, Tullio, and Alessandra Levantesi. *Dino: The Life and Films of Dino De Laurentiis*. New York: Hyperion, 2004.

King, Emily. *Robert Brownjohn: Sex and Typography*. New York: Princeton Architectural Press, 2005.

Kramer, Stanley, with Thomas M. Coffey. *A Mad, Mad, Mad, Mad World: A Life in Hollywood*. London: Aurum Press, 1998.

Krampner, Jon. *The Man in the Shadows: Fred Coe and the Golden Age of Television*. New Brunswick, NJ. Rutger's Unversity Press, 1997.

LaPorte, Nicole. *The Men Who Would Be King: An Almost Epic Tale of Moguls, Movies, and a Company Called DreamWorks*. Boston: Houghton Mifflin, 2010.

Laurents, Arthur. *Original Story By: A Memoir of Broadway and Hollywood*. New York: Alfred A. Knopf, 2000.

Leavitt, Charles. *The Sunchaser*. Screenplay, September 1992.

Linson, Art. *What Just Happened?: Bitter Hollywood Tales from the Front Line*. New York: Bloomsbury, 2002.

Levy, Shawn. *De Niro: A Life*. New York: Crown, 2014.

Lois, George. *On Creating the Big Idea*. New York: Assouline Publishing, 2008.

Lumet, Sidney. *Making Movies*. London: Bloomsbury, 1995.

Macor, Alison. *Rewrite Man: The Life and Career of Screenwriter Warren Skaaren*. Austin: University of Texas Press, 2017.

Mankiewicz, Tom, and Robert Crane. *My Life as a Mankiewicz: An Insider's Journey Through Hollywood*. Lexington: University Press of Kentucky, 2012.

McBride, Joseph. *Steven Spielberg: A Biography*. New York: Faber & Faber, 2012.

McClintock, David. *Indecent Exposure: A True Story of Hollywood and Wall Street*. New York: Warner Books, 1994.

McGilligan, Patrick. *Clint: The Life and Legend*. New York: St. Martin's Press, 2002.

———. *Robert Altman: Jumping Off the Cliff*. New York: St. Martin's Press, 1989.

McNall, Bruce, with Michael D'Antonio. *Fun While It Lasted: My Rise and Fall in the Land of Fame and Fortune*. New York: Hachette, 2003.

Medavoy, Mike, with Josh Young. *You're Only as Good as Your Next One: 100 Great Films, 100 Good Films, and 100 for Which I Should Be Shot*. New York: Simon & Schuster, 2002.

Miles, Sarah. *Bolt from the Blue*. London: Phoenix, 1997.

Millard, Joe. *Thunderbolt and Lightfoot*. New York: Award Books, 1974.

Mosley, Leonard. *Zanuck: The Rise and Fall of Hollywood's Last Tycoon*. London: Granada, 1984.

Mottram, James. *The Sundance Kids: How the Mavericks Took Back Hollywood*. London: Faber & Faber, 2006.

Myles, Lynda, and Michael Pye. *Movie Brats: How the Film Generation Took Over Hollywood*. London: Faber & Faber,1979.

Norman, Marc. *What Happens Next: A History of American Screenwriting*. New York: Harmony Books, 2007.

Obst, Lynda. *Sleepless in Hollywood: Tales from the New Abnormal in the Movie Business*. New York: Simon & Schuster, 2013.

Ovitz, Michael. *Who Is Michael Ovitz*. London: W. H. Allen, 2018.

Parish, James Robert. *Fiasco: A History of Hollywood's Iconic Flops*. Hoboken, NJ: John Wiley & Sons, 2006.

Picker, David. *Musts, Maybes, and Nevers: A Book About the Movies*. Self-published, CreateSpace Independent Publishing Platform, 2013.

Puzo, Mario. *The Sicilian*. New York: Random House, 1984.

Relyea, Robert E., with Craig Relyea. *Not So Quiet on the Set: My Life in Movies During Hollywood's Macho Era*. New York: iUniverse Inc., 2008.

Rensin, David. *The Mailroom: Hollywood History from the Bottom Up*. New York: Ballantine Books, 2003.

Rose, Frank. *The Agency: William Morris and the Hidden History of Show Business*. New York: HarperCollins, 1995.

Ross, Lillian. *Picture*. London: Gollancz, 1952.

Salamon, Julie. *The Devil's Candy: The Anatomy of a Hollywood Fiasco*. Boston: Houghton Mifflin, 1991.

Schickel, Richard. *Clint Eastwood: A Biography*. New York: Alfred A. Knopf, 1996.

Schulman, Michael. *Her Again: Becoming Meryl Streep*. New York: Harper, 2016.

Schumacher, Michael: *Francis Ford Coppola: A Filmmaker's Life*. New York: Three Rivers Press, 1999.

Segaloff, Nat. *Arthur Penn: American Director*. Lexington: University Press of Kentucky, 2011.

Shagan, Steve. *The Sicilian*. Screenplay, revisions by Michael Cimino and Gore Vidal, July 4, 1986.

Sharp, Kathleen. *Mr. & Mrs. Hollywood: Edie and Lew Wasserman and Their Entertainment Empire*. New York: Carroll & Graf, 2003.

Silverman, Stephen M. *Dancing on the Ceiling: Stanley Donen and His Movies*. New York: Alfred A. Knopf, 1996.

Singular, Stephen. *Power to Burn: Michael Ovitz and the New Business of Show Business*. Secaucus, NJ: Birch Lane Press, 1996.

Sinyard, Neil. *The Films of Richard Lester.* London: Croom Helm, 1985.

Sloman, Larry "Ratso." *On the Road with Bob Dylan.* London: Helter Skelter, 2005.

Spiegel, Maura. *Sidney Lumet: A Life.* New York: St. Martin's Press, 2019.

Squire, Jason E., ed. *The Movie Business Book.* New York: Simon & Schuster, 1992.

Stone, Oliver. *Chasing the Light: Writing, Directing, and Surviving* Platoon, Midnight Express, Scarface, Salvador, *and the Movie Game.* New York: Houghton Mifflin Harcourt, 2020.

———, and Michael Cimino. *Year of the Dragon.* Screenplay, based on novel by Robert Daley, September 4, 1984.

Thompson, David, ed. *Altman on Altman.* London: Faber & Faber, 2006.

———. *Levinson on Levinson.* London: Faber & Faber, 1992.

Thompson, Harlan. *Silent Running.* New York: Scholastic Press, 1972.

Thoret, Jean-Baptiste. *Michael Cimino: Les voix perdues de l'Amerique.* Paris: Flammarion, 2013.

Turner, Adrian. *Robert Bolt: Scenes from Two Lives.* London: Hutchinson, 1998.

Washburn, Deric, and Michael Cimino. *Silent Running.* Screenplay, December 6, 1970.

Wasson, Sam. *The Big Goodbye:* Chinatown *and the Last Years of Hollywood.* New York: Flatiron Books, 2020.

Waxman, Sharon. *Rebels on the Backlot: Six Maverick Directors and How They Conquered the Hollywood Studio System.* New York, HarperCollins, 2005.

Winkler, Irwin. *A Life in Movies: Stories from 50 Years in Hollywood.* New York: Abrams Press, 2019.

INDEX

INDEX

INDEX

INDEX